A Banker Tells You How to Borrow All the Money You'll Ever Need

BEN B. BOOTHE

CB
CONTEMPORARY
BOOKS
CHICAGO

Library of Congress Cataloging-in-Publication Data

Boothe, Ben B.
    A banker tells you how to borrow all the money you'll ever
need / Ben B. Boothe.
        p.   cm.
    ISBN 0-8092-3920-5 (cloth)
    1. Commercial loans—United States.   2. Commercial
credit—United States.   I. Title.
HG1642.U5B66   1992
332.7′43—dc20   92-11227
                                          CIP

Published by Contemporary Books, Inc.
180 North Michigan Avenue, Chicago, Illinois 60601
Manufactured in the United States of America
International Standard Book Number: 0-8092-3920-5

Contents

Introduction

One of the enduring economic necessities for success and mastery of financial goals is credit. It is equally crucial for businesses and individuals. But in America alone, an estimated forty thousand loan applications are turned down every day. In about half of those cases, the loan could have been made but for the applicant's lack of knowledge and skill. This book is intended to help you master the credit system to your advantage.

In the past a traditional means of developing credit often went something like this. At an appropriate age, a father would introduce his young son or daughter to the local banker. The message and implication to the banker were clear. It was time to teach the youngster how to master credit. Usually the young person was encouraged by the father to borrow small amounts while also learning the lessons of discipline, hard work, and savings. The banker was a partner in this process of personal banking education. At some point, after the young person had repaid several loans, his or her credit was established.

That was the day of the personal banker, the locally owned community bank, and an environment often unlike that of today. It was a wonderful way to learn the nuances of borrowing money. But the modern world of banking, in a global business environment, often strains traditions. It calls for more sophistication, more preparation. In this day you might be dealing with a branch of a foreign bank or with a bank owned by stockholders throughout the nation. The banker-manager might well be from far away, working in the local community for only a few years until he or she climbs up the corporate ladder to a bigger bank in a different city. The mentality is often different. The modern banker is often a different animal, with an MBA degree, a stack of policy manuals, and a personal computer on his or her desk.

The traditional approach to establishing credit had a central goal: to build credibility with bankers. The approach may have changed with the times, but the goal is more important now than ever. I was taught credit by my father and his "personal" banker in the traditional way. But I have since learned that the most powerful and successful individuals and corporations in the world strive for the mastery of credit. Access to credit can open doors you never dreamed would open . . . most important, *vault doors*.

It is amazing to think that a majority of people who go to the bank to borrow money do so with little forethought or preparation. Often their requests are for loans to buy something that is critical to their lifestyle or business success. Yet they do not seem to realize that a person or business without a banking relationship should not just decide to borrow one day, bop into the bank, and obtain a loan. It rarely happens that way.

As economic cycles boom and bust, bankers tend to change with the times. But the rapid changes in the economy of this age have tended to make bankers more and more cautious and detail-oriented. That trend will continue for many years. This has made it more important than ever that the borrower—whether an individual or a business—be prepared with the proper tools, skills, knowledge, insight, and documentation to make a case.

This book provides powerful tools that give you the best chance of getting your loan approved and bringing your dreams within reach. The book does not show you how to hide facts that hurt your case, but demonstrates how to make your best points effectively. It outlines how to present your story with integrity and candor. It shows how you can achieve respect and strengthen your case. Individuals or businesses that have had bad luck in the past are sometimes able to get loans because of an impressive and credible presentation and the impression of integrity and excellence they give the banker. This book does not show how to borrow more than you should or more than you need, but it does demonstrate how to get loans approved in a fashion that will be good for you and your banker. One of my basic premises is that good business, based upon integrity and excellence, is good for all parties involved. When you follow the steps and principles of this book, you will be doing a favor to yourself, your business, your banker, your employees, your community, your family, and the economy.

The style of this book is to generate questions and thinking. That is a part of the process of learning to get your loan approved. When you ask yourself more questions than your banker does, then you have mastered the art of borrowing money. You need to have pondered every question, every detail *before* you see your banker. Bankers are professional "balloon busters." They make a living asking questions to find weaknesses in your proposal. This book will pose many of those questions so that you can prepare, and it will stimulate you to consider the answers in advance.

By reading this, you have already begun to learn and consider your next loan application as a strategic presentation—one well prepared, positively presented, with realistic expectations of success. Now I will make a bold statement. If you will follow every item, every step in this book, and if you qualify your loan as set forth in this book, I guarantee that you can have a successful loan experience.

1

If Only My Business Had the Money, We Could . . .

It was a cold day in March when my secretary received a call from a young couple, John and Lori Jones. They wanted an appointment to see the "bank president." Although I didn't know them, we went ahead and scheduled an appointment. As they came in I noticed that they seemed nervous. John was wearing work jeans and Lori a homely dress. When we shook hands I felt the callouses on his hands. After the greetings I asked, "What can I do for you?"

John looked down at the floor and then mumbled, "Uh . . . we were wanting to borrow some money. The busy season is coming, and we need some money to work with."

"I see," I said. "And just what business are you in?"

"We build fences and do remodel jobs."

"Tell me about your business."

He looked a little uncomfortable as he replied, "Well . . . I told you . . . we build fences and do remodeling."

5

I just sat there in silence with the "banker's stare." The banker's stare is famous in the industry. It is a pause really. Some might say a pregnant pause. A pause when the banker is waiting for some information . . . but is also studying the customer. It is an important moment in the loan interview process. Some bankers simply stare the customer down (which can be very uncomfortable for the subject). Some bankers use an object, such as a pipe or a cigar, and simply fiddle with it silently until the customer opens up.

John was dying as he squirmed in his chair. Then Lori spoke up. The instant she spoke, I knew that she was an important part of this team. "Mr. Boothe, we build fences, patio decks, and do small remodeling jobs. In our bidding, we have found that the customer prefers that we buy the materials and do the jobs turnkey. Since our capital is limited, it has kept us from bidding on several large jobs. We believe we could increase our income a great deal if we could bid on these jobs."

I softened my expression a little bit. Now we were getting somewhere. "Just how many jobs, in dollars, do you do?" I asked her.

"We will do in peak season eight stockade fences a month, and three or four redwood patio decks. I don't know the exact dollars, but we seem to be doing all right."

By now it was obvious that this couple had never borrowed money. They didn't seem very knowledgeable about their business. I was tempted to turn them down and go on to other things. It was a busy day, and there were *good* customers to deal with. But, to give them the benefit of the doubt, I asked, "May I see your books?"

John looked up at me and said, "We don't have anything but our checkbook, and Lori takes care of that."

"Yes, I understand," I grinned. "My wife and kids have a way of taking care of mine, too."

At that they both smiled, and she handed me their company checkbook. When I looked at the numbers, I could hardly believe my eyes. They had over $18,000 in their commercial account. I spun my chair around to the terminal on my credenza and ran a quick check on the bank computer. It blinked up an average balance of $18,000, no overdrafts, no checks drawn against an account with inadequate funds, average deposits of $3,000 per week, and average checks of $1,000 per week. Yes, they had a good little business. Now they had my attention.

"Mr. and Mrs. Jones, you have a good account record here at the bank. If you need to expand your business, we will help you. But first you need to master the art of obtaining and using credit."

"What does that mean?" John asked.

Lori spoke up. "It means we need to learn how to borrow money, right?"

I nodded.

"We nearly blew it, didn't we?"

I nodded again.

She was quick. Both of them were pleasant and likable people. They just needed some help.

"I'll invest some time in you two. You have built a fine little business, and you keep a good account with the bank. With good management and some capital, you have a lot more potential."

By this time John and Lori had relaxed somewhat, and their nervousness was being replaced with enthusiasm.

"Tell me more about your business and your life." And with this they opened up. They told the story of how they had met and gotten married right after he left the armed services. He had tried working for several companies but just didn't like working for someone else. Then one Saturday while John was helping a neighbor build a wooden stockade fence, someone saw the workmanship, stopped, and asked John what he would charge to build another one like it. "From there, we were in business," John said, and the business grew. John worked at giving his customers a quality product in a timely manner, and people appreciated his attention to little things. Lori took the telephone calls, paid bills, and made the deposits. By now they had gained a reputation that was providing opportunities to do larger jobs—jobs that required several work crews and more money than they had on hand.

I mentally ran the numbers. With a quick calculation and with the information about potential jobs on which John was working, it was easy to see that they could increase their annual net profit substantially. This, provided they had bank financing to purchase materials in advance and pay additional work crews while the jobs were in process. They would also find purchasing in larger quantities good for the business with bulk discounts.

Projecting further, John could see that he could purchase the new truck he had wanted. They could look forward to moving out of the cramped apartment in which they now lived and on to a nicer home. Finally, they could begin to build the financial security and lifestyle they had wanted for years but had feared that they would not have the opportunity to achieve. Lori was the most enthusiastic when she said, "Now maybe we can plan to send our son to college."

"Son?!" John said. "I didn't know we had a son."

"We don't. But if we can get our finances in order, then we can start on another project." She winked and smiled.

John and Lori were seeing the advantages of mastering the art of borrowing money for their business. They were learning that the promises of the society in which we live can be achieved when people do away with the self-imposed perception that they cannot borrow money. They had made the first smart move when they worked up the courage to try, the initiative simply to go to the banker and ask. No doubt, their request would have been more effective had they prepared, but at least they took that critical first step.

There are several basic steps that every businessperson and every individual must take in order to reach the point to which this young couple had come:

1. Review your business or life, and find out if you have financial barriers to your success.
2. Identify specifically what those barriers are.
3. Determine and review the alternative solutions.
4. Take the initiative, decide to act on your need, and ask for help.
5. Seek out a banker who will help you.
6. Educate the banker; let him or her know who you are.
7. Be prepared.
8. Be persistent.

These steps will start you on the path toward mastering the art of credit and borrowing.

Step 1: Review Your Business or Life

Bob Collier is one of the best pharmacists I have ever known. Yet he operates a drugstore in Post, Texas, a town with a population of perhaps 3,000. The man who created the town, C. W. Post (of Post Cereals), had a dream and already had mastered the financial barriers to his success . . . all but one. He would create a completely preplanned city. To that end, Post, who had great sums of capital at his

disposal, hired the best architects in the nation to formulate the plans for "his town." They drew a city for him. It
was designed to be the flagship city of west Texas. The
streets were designed extra wide. In fact, the Main Street
of Post, Texas, is wider than Fifth Avenue in New York City.
Although C. W. Post had no financial barriers to his success, unfortunately he died before his dream city could
grow up. Fate had not allowed time for enough people to
"catch" his dream to create the momentum and the organization to carry it beyond his death.

But some people did grasp the dream of Post. One of
them was Bob Collier's father. He opened Collier Drug
Store, right on the wide Main Street in Post. There he built
a thriving business, which was taken over by Bob's older
brother. When his brother died, Bob took over the business. Now Bob is known all over the world. He has been
the president of the Texas Pharmaceutical Association and
is a sought-after speaker. But he still lives in Post, Texas,
and still runs a little drugstore.

I once asked him why he didn't expand to other areas
or why he didn't have more stores. His answer was revealing: "Ben, I learned how to run a good business, and I
figured out that if I could just borrow enough money, I
could operate a chain of stores using that same knowledge. I had a great banker back then, who understood my
business potential, and we started expanding. But then as
we were expanding to other fields, my banker moved. I
never found another banker like him, and other things
started distracting me, so I have been happy to run my
business here in Post." The definitive phrase is "if I could
just borrow enough money."

Few people make their fortunes from the money they
earn in their day-to-day job. Most businesses, industries,
and corporations are founded on the basis of someone
else's money. If you are established, the stock market

offers a way for you to bring in new capital without having to go to the debt markets. But few people have the ability or the credentials to tap the equity markets. Often partners are a source of financing, but even more often partnerships also create problems. So the vast multitude of individuals and businesses must resort to borrowing money to achieve those special dreams. Sam Walton borrowed money to get his first stores going. H. Ross Perot had to borrow money to get his computer business off the ground. Trammell Crow would never have become the greatest real estate developer in the nation had he not had access to borrowing money. Rockefeller, Carnegie, Du Pont, the Rothchilds, all of the greatest masters of wealth were successful because they first learned the secrets of how to borrow money, how to unlock the vault doors of the banks for their projects, and how to use that knowledge with great effect.

Clint Murcheson had attained several hundred million dollars when he was asked by a reporter, "If you had to start all over today, could you again become wealthy?"

His reply was instructive: "If I had but a thousand dollars and a good banker who would loan me money, I could become a millionaire in a year . . . *but only if I could borrow money.*" He recognized that the absence of credit could stop his ability to achieve financial dreams.

This has powerful implications not only for individuals planning their personal financial future, but for businesses and nations as well. For example, on a national level, powerful politicians know that if the government restricts the flow of funds and constricts lending in the banking industry, then the economy will suffer, and with it businesses and individuals. Therefore, no politician will dare to urge the Federal Reserve Board to shrink the money supply in an election year. It would be political suicide.

Once when I turned down a job to run a bank, the

chairman of the board asked, "Is the problem financial? If it is, that is the least of our problems. We can always solve financial-related problems."

Is the attainment of your goals blocked because of a financial problem? If it is, by careful work and study, you can learn how to solve financial problems. One of the keys is to master credit.

Step 2: Identify Barriers to Success

Next, get specific about what barriers are standing between you and financial success. How much do you need? What do you need? When do you need it?

Prepare a detailed study of your goals. What exactly do you wish to accomplish? As a child of fifteen, John Goddard, who now lives in California, observed that his father had a most boring life. So he set forth a series of 127 challenging lifetime goals. One of them was to travel around the world. Another was to lead the first expedition to explore the length of the world's largest river, the 4,180-mile Nile. When he achieved that goal in 1950, the *Los Angeles Times* called it "the most amazing adventure of this generation." One of his goals was to read the entire set of the *Encyclopaedia Britannica*. Another was to fly a jet airplane, and he set a speed record then of 1,500 miles per hour in the F-111 fighter-bomber. That man is now well past what some people call their prime, and he is still working on the list he wrote as a fifteen-year-old. To date he has accomplished 107 of these ambitious dreams, establishing an impressive list of records in the process. He told me, "In setting goals one creates power to achieve," and, "In setting and visualizing goals, one also specifies the obstacles."

In detailing financial barriers, you can systematically determine how to overcome them. For example, do you wish to start a new restaurant? You might create a list of barriers and ways to overcome them:

Barriers	Potential Solutions
Zoning	Request zoning board to grant variance; public petition; lobby neighbors; meet city council members
Equipment costs	Consider leasing; buy used
Initial operating funds (need $5,000 per month for about 6 months to break even)	Commercial bank loan; mortgage other real estate; sell other assets; seek silent partner to cosign or invest
Money to purchase ($450,000)	Place business up for collateral on bank loan; ask prior owner to carry paper; consider Small Business Administration loan
Parking	Identify and meet all adjacent owners; check lease arrangement; investigate city variance; pave additional space

Step 3: Determine and Review Solutions

The process of determining and reviewing solutions is just a continuation of the preceding step. Robert Schuller, the great minister, has said, "When faced with a mountain, I will either find a way to go over it, go around it, go under, tunnel through, or just create a gold mine at its base . . . I will not quit."

Alternative solutions can be many and can often make the difference between a success and a failure. David Harmon, senior vice president of the Lubbock National Bank, told me of an incident involving real estate developer Trammell Crow. The financing had fallen through on a property Crow had purchased. Foreclosure was imminent, and Crow knew that he was about to lose the property, which represented a great potential value. Near the foreclosure deadline, one of Crow's attorneys found an obscure law that said that if a property was in the name of a legislator while Congress was in session, state law required all legal proceedings to stop until the legislative session was over. Trammell Crow had the property transferred to a legislator's name. All foreclosure proceedings ceased. With the help of the time delay, Crow was able to obtain the needed financing. The project was saved! A few years later, he sold the same property for millions of dollars' profit. In the same manner, sometimes creative solutions can save your loan proposal.

Step 4: Ask for Help

When you need help, you must take the initiative. Decide to act on your need, and ask for help. Sometimes this is the hardest part, because it requires several emotional and logical decisions as well as commitments on your part. After you have considered your project, its merits, obstacles, the alternatives, and the possible rewards, then you are ready for the commitment. You must really believe in your loan if you hope to get a banker to believe in it with you. You must want to achieve your goal badly enough that you will work hard to achieve it. You must be willing to sacrifice to achieve it. If you aren't willing, why should anyone else be willing to back you financially? When you have completed these mental processes, then you must make the decision to go and (heaven forbid) ask someone else for money.

The word *ask* is so distasteful and threatening that it

alone has kept many a project from getting off the ground. But you don't have the money. You need it. The bank has it. The banker can lend it to you. And that is going to require some very skilled communication. For psychological reasons, you should take the word *ask* out of the vocabulary, then use the words *communicate an opportunity* instead. For a bank to survive and prosper, the banker must lend money. But if you want to be among the borrowers, you must be willing to communicate an opportunity.

A crusty old car dealer had made and lost several fortunes. He had accumulated a nice estate and kept several hundred thousand dollars in the bank. But he was very independent and proud. One day he learned of a unique investment opportunity that he really wanted. But to swing the deal without paying withdrawal penalties on his certificates of deposit, he was going to need a substantial loan. He got in his car, drove to the bank, walked into the lobby, stood for a moment, and then turned and walked out. He could not bear the thought of having to ask anyone for a loan. He lost the opportunity to another investor. When the banker found out about it, he called the customer and said, "We would gladly have made the loan." The customer said he was simply too proud to "beg for a loan." His perceptions of the process penalized him dearly.

Step 5: Find a Banker Who Will Help You

In this world of changes, with banks merging, closing, selling, bankers moving up or out and moving on, finding the right banker is another challenge. As the cyclical economy changes, so does the face of banking in various sections of the country. Vast mergers and buyouts also cause a great deal of job turnover. When a bank sells, often the new ownership group wants to staff the institution with their own employees. The phrase *Velcro banks* has been coined to describe banks that are changing names so often they put Velcro on the back of the signs so the institutions can change names more easily. Unfortunately, the bankers are changing as well.

This makes it harder than ever to find a banker who is suited to, or educated for, your particular banking need. You wouldn't consider going to a Ford dealer to buy a Chevrolet, nor would you consider going to a dentist for a kidney transplant. It is critically important that you find a bank and a banker who is willing and able to help you with your loan. In Figure 1, David Harmon, one of the leading bankers of west Texas, offers advice on the kind of banker to look for.

Many bankers don't want to make business loans for a commercial business. One banker I interviewed in New York told me that they handled only business for wealthy individuals; they did not want commercial loans. Some banks prefer lending only to giant companies in amounts of $1 million or more. Some banks won't consider loans to a new business or a small business. And still more bankers don't want to make business loans, but they don't want the public to know it. In these cases an initial telephone inquiry to the bank might lead you to believe that they do make all types of loans, when in actual practice they do not.

All of this is further complicated when two banks of different philosophy merge. For example, financial headlines recently announced the merger of two of the largest banks in the nation. One of the groups is considered very traditional and conservative in its philosophy, the other very aggressive and progressive. Analysts are already commenting on the many challenges and senior officer resignations that are occurring as a result of the problems

Figure 1
ADVICE ON FINDING A BANKER

**LUBBOCK
NATIONAL
BANK**

August 12, 1991

DAVID M. HARMON
Senior Vice President

Mr. Ben Boothe
Boothe & Associates
Western National Building
8851 Highway 80 West
Fort Worth, Texas 76116-6040

Dear Ben:

Here are some suggestions for someone trying to find a banker.

1) Choose a lender who understands your business. One who does not stare into space when you are talking.

2) It is important to choose a lender who will stay on the job. In this age of closed banks and S & L's, some bankers seems to work in a different place every week. There are still bankers who have been in one place ten to twenty years.

3) Find a banker that is not afraid to take risks. A good banker won't forget your name the first time you are facing a problem.

4) A good banker will do business with you, buy your product, and stop in your place of business.

5) Find a banker that will listen to you no matter how bad the news may be.

I hope you will find these suggestions helpful.

Sincerely,

David M. Harmon
Senior Vice President

DMH/nf

806 792-1000
P.O. Box 6100
4811 50th St
Lubbock, TX 79493

FAX # 806 792-0976

associated with combining these different philosophies. Paralysis or delays in loan decisions will occur during the transition phase, which could last for years. These events have important implications for the individual or business seeking credit. Is your bank managed with a philosophy that is consistent with and friendly to your type of loan application?

Step 6: Educate the Banker

John and Lori Jones, the young couple in the example that opened this chapter, made one of the classic mistakes. They did not give the banker an opportunity to know who they were and what they were about before presenting their needs. They just made an appointment cold and forged ahead. Among the first questions any good banker will ask are "Who are these people?" and "What is their background?"

Bankers are by nature conservative. They like to feel that they are in control, on top of the situation. After all, it is the combined assets of hundreds, perhaps thousands of savers and investors the banker is working to invest. One of the banker's sources of power is information. The banker likes to have a "file" on you containing key information to make loan decisions from, and if necessary to present your loan to a committee for their combined scrutiny. He or she needs to know a little about your business, your family background, your reputation, the location of your business, where you live, what kind of car you drive, if you pay your bills, your past successes and failures. The banker wants to know all about you for one simple reason. He or she is charged with loaning out someone else's money to you. This is a serious responsibility for a conscientious banker. He or she wants to be sure that the money the bank lends your business will be paid back and will provide a good rate of return to the bank.

It is not only a sense of responsibility that runs the banker, it is simple security. If the banker is a major stockholder or director in the bank, financial security may be what motivates his or her loan judgments. If the banker is an officer or a vice president, his or her success in lending will determine the banker's future, including salary, bonus, and perhaps even job security. The banker wants to know as much as possible about you in order to achieve a comfort level. If there is any hint that you are flaky, unreliable, or dishonest or that you deal in a questionable way or with questionable people, you can kiss your loan chances good-bye.

How do you give the banker this information? There are a number of ways. This book will detail them as it proceeds.

Step 7: Be Prepared

Remember the old Boy Scout motto: be prepared. It is also the watchword for the successful businessperson who wants to borrow money. John and Lori were not prepared. They just walked into the banker's office and asked for a loan. At least they got that far. But 99 percent of the time, that by itself will lead to denial of the loan.

Any profession requires preparation. Someone writing a book does not normally just call an agent or a publisher and say, "Hey, I've got an idea for a book. What about this?" Rarely is a book approved on such a slim idea, unless of course the person with the proposal happens to be a celebrity, a president, or a VIP. Normally what occurs is that the author is told to provide a detailed written proposal, complete with an outline, sample chapters, and a conceptual summary, as well as résumé and projections of the market.

A loan is obtained in much the same way. If you want to get your loan approved, you must prepare. Chapter 4 provides a detailed outline of what should go into the loan application, but the point here is that before you walk into a busy bank executive's office, you must be ready with the facts. The banker will deal with probably twelve personal interviews during an average day and handle perhaps another fifteen or more by telephone. He or she is busy, pressured, and likely stressed. When a banker gives you time, it is a valuable resource.

You should consider your preparation as like a bar exam for a lawyer. Know your facts. Have them memorized. Be ready for every question. Rehearse mentally what you want to communicate and how you will deal with objections. Visualize your meeting with the banker. Know your weak points, and prepare to defend them. Many times the banker will ask financial questions about a business, not totally because he or she wants to hear the financial numbers. The banker is also probing to see what you, the borrower, know, how sharp you are. If you haven't prepared well for the loan interview, how will you prepare for a business negotiation after the banker has made the loan to you?

Now, understand, not every customer who walks into the bank to borrow money prepares this well, and many loans are approved anyway. But many more get denied! This book is written to show you how to get your loan *approved.* It takes effort, time, and detail.

Again, consider the consequences. The lawyer studies long and hard for the bar exam. Why? Because it can affect the rest of his or her life. Diligent preparation will affect what kind of job, income, and house the lawyer can expect, as well as his or her entire lifestyle. The lawyer's professional and financial future hangs in the balance. In a comparable way, the banker holds the key to helping you make your dreams come true. The banker can finance your new business, your new home, your expansion. All of these can affect the rest of your financial life.

Consider again the author. He or she wants to present the best book proposal possible. Why? Because it influences the author's income, reputation, fame, and fortune. Like the author or the lawyer, the businessperson must prepare in detail before going to the banker. It is said that the loan officer in a community bank spends as much as 50 percent of his or her time educating customers. Most of this education is teaching customers how to provide all the necessary information in a format that will enable the banker to help them get their loan approved. The customer who walks in already prepared is well ahead not only in time savings but also in making that critical first impression. Both advantages will greatly enhance your chances of being approved. *That* is what this book is all about!

Step 8: Be Persistent

You may not get your loan approved the first jump out of the box. The first time you try, you are going through a learning process. First you are learning about the banker, what his or her needs and desires are. Second the banker is learning about you, your project, your style, and your integrity.

It is not unusual to be turned down the first time you apply for a loan. Often the banker needs more time to research your background or to gain a comfort level with you. If this occurs, it is very important for you to be professional; don't be hurt, mad, or otherwise emotional. On a professional level, ask the banker to give you detailed reasons for the denial. If you can, get the reasons in writing. And look for indirect reasons. For example, if the banker turns your loan down with a vague statement like "We just aren't doing loans like this now," you know there is a red flag. If the bank wasn't doing loans like this, why did the banker take the application, study it, require documentation from you, and take it to the loan committee? There must be some other reason. Perhaps the bank doesn't have the funds on hand to lend. Perhaps the loan is above the officer's limit. Perhaps there has been a change of loan policy. Perhaps the banker heard something bad about you or your industry.

The banker owes you specific reasons, and when you get them, you can proceed to deal with the objections in your revised loan application. If there is a personality problem with the banker, don't waste your time or the banker's. Find another banker. He or she may be in the same bank, or you may have to broaden your search. But there is a banker who will lend you the money for your project. This promise I can almost set in stone. If your reputation is good and you follow all the guidelines in this book, there is a banker and a loan for you. It may take you time to locate that person and to establish a rapport with him or her, but that banker does exist.

Bill Knox was a remarkably nice person, a young dentist in Ft. Worth who had a dream. If you knew "Knox," then you knew his dream, for he told it to anyone he could find who was willing to sit and listen. His dream was to build a multistory dental/medical building in southwest Ft. Worth. Dr. Knox was a great dentist, but he wasn't rich. He wanted to break out of the single focus of his practice and have an investment that would give him some appreciation and some tax advantages. He didn't want to be "just" a dentist, he wanted to be a dentist with a real estate investment that would not only benefit his practice, but would be a compliment to the community and a good retirement nest egg for him and his partners some day.

He came to my office on numerous occasions. Our

bank did not make construction loans at the time, so I couldn't approve his request, which was for several million dollars. But he would not give up. He wrote out proposals. He wrote out projections. One by one he whittled away at all of the objections bankers threw at him.

The last time I saw him, he had even built a scale model of the building. It was in little miniature modules. He carried it into the bank and set it down right in the middle of my desk. I had to give him my undivided attention, because everything else was buried somewhere under his scale model. He went through his project step by step, building his little scale model as he talked. I was squirming and hoping he would hurry up and finish, but he had me captive. Even my telephone was buried under some of his building blocks! (Later on I wondered if he had planned it all that way.) Then at the conclusion of his loan request, he set the last block on top. It was an impressive presentation, but I had little encouragement for him. High-risk loans for commercial office buildings were hard to get. His was a lost cause with our bank, because our policy simply ruled out that type of loan. I tried to let him down gently.

I later left that bank to become the president of a bank in another town. About eighteen months later, as I drove down Hulen Street in Ft. Worth, I looked over and could hardly believe my eyes. There on the lot (which had been vacant) was the scale model—except it was a life-size beautiful medical office building, just like Dr. Knox had dreamed of. The wheels of my car fairly squealed as I turned in, and then I walked through the front door and entered the atrium he had so meticulously described months before. A great sense of joy swept over me as I thought of this triumph of a man's idea and persistence over all objections. Yes, there is a banker for you somewhere.

2

How to Establish Credit
When You Have None

If you already have good credit, your sophistication allows you to skip on to the next chapter. But a book on borrowing money would be incomplete without a section on establishing credit. It is a foundation of all borrowing and is the first thing your banker will review. Understanding the credit system and knowing how to use the system to your advantage will have a substantial impact on your financial future.

Although I established credit at an early age in my hometown, my college years in a faraway town brought a new experience. I was but one of thousands of lowly college students in Arkansas. I wanted to purchase some property there. My income from a part-time job was $45 per week. Every cent of it was used for living expenses. Although I had good credit in Ft. Worth, the banker in Arkansas did not know me. He turned the loan request down. Why? I had no credit. I objected, "But you have me!" He smiled and shook his head: "That's just not enough at this bank." It was a disappointing but educational day.

The Credit Reporting System

Each major metropolitan area has a credit reporting bureau. Some have more than one. In some cases they share information, and in others they do not. There have been several attempts to merge all credit information into one national master credit file, but in the practical world, this has not been totally effective. There have been cases, for example, in which a customer borrowed money in Arizona, defaulted on those loans, then moved to Minnesota, starting out with a clean slate. Some con artists have filed bankruptcy in numerous states and still manage to subvert the system.

In a standard situation, banks report to the credit bureau, either automatically by computer or manually, the payment history of each loan and often a record of your checking accounts. The reports include information such as the number of payments made, how many days payments were past due, and whether or not you have had a default or a repossession. The credit bureau is also given information about your past record such as how many times you have been overdrawn or if the bank suffered a loss as a result of your failure to make deposits to cover all checks. This information is updated in the computer regularly. Some retail stores, especially the major chains, also report to credit bureaus.

A word of warning here: The big department store chains are often not very difficult to work with to get a mistake corrected. A few companies are notorious for taking years, if ever, to clear up incorrect credit reports. My wife and I had a personal experience with this while I was the president of a bank. We had two credit card accounts with the same department store chain. They applied the payment to the wrong account and then reported that we were in default on our credit account. We did not know of this "bad" credit for over two years, until my wife was turned down for credit at another business. We then wrote the company and asked them to clear up the mistake. After some twelve telephone calls, four letters, and a letter from our attorney, they finally corrected the problem . . . nearly a year later.

Several points can be made with that example alone:

- When you have credit, be very careful how you use it.
- Don't ever let incorrect reporting go uncorrected, no matter how much effort it takes.
- Realize that bad credit can hurt you for years, without your knowledge or long after you have forgotten the event that brought it on.
- Substantial credit reporting laws have evolved over the years, laws that give you some recourse if you or your business is unfairly harmed by inaccurate credit reporting.

Establishing Credit

The ways an individual or a business establishes credit are almost identical. Basically, you start with a loan arrangement that's easy to get, then work your way gradually up to credit with more stringent criteria. An example will show how this works.

Jerry Matheson was a college graduate with a business degree, and his wife, Patty, was a secretary. They had decided to start a business programming and selling computers. They had little income except Patty's salary of $1,500 per month. That was just enough to cover their living expenses. Jerry was proving to be successful at inducing companies to hire him to program their computers, although nearly every cent he made went back into computer equipment. They both knew that they would eventually need a loan to start up their business. They calculated that it would take at least $50,000 to get started, and probably much more.

Jerry tried to make arrangements to order the initial inventory on credit, but the suppliers consistently told him he had no credit record and their policy was impossible to break. He would have to pay cash or build a credit rating before they could deal with him. Without family wealth or connections, Jerry and Patty would have to do it all themselves. They went to their local bank, where they had banked throughout college, and set up an appointment to talk to the banker.

"Mr. Wright," said Patty when they met, "we have no credit, and we have to get started sometime. Can you help us?"

The banker smiled, for this was one of the favorite parts of his job. "Yes, we can help you get started. But one thing you must know: it is going to take some time, some discipline, and some thought on your part."

"What do we do?"

"First of all, you need to be established on the computer files of the credit bureaus as people who not only keep sums of money at the bank, but also borrow money regularly and pay it back as agreed."

"But we don't have any money except our little checking account," Patty said.

"Well, we are going to have to correct that," said banker Wright.

"How?" they asked almost in unison.

"We will loan you the money."

"But we don't have any collateral," Jerry said.

"We will take care of that too," said the banker.

"How?"

"We will loan it to you."

"But how will we ever pay it back?" Patty asked.

"With the money I loan you. Let me explain the process. This is a way to use the system to your advantage. You need a banker willing to take the time to help you get started, and you must be willing to make an investment in time and effort to establish credit. We already have those two elements. Now here is the strategy. The key is to get you in the system. I already know you are good people and feel you will be successful in your business venture. But the system is standing in your way. Well, with my help and your persistence we are going to establish your credit. It will take about a year, but when that year is over, you will have as good a credit rating as anyone in town."

"What do we do?" asked Patty.

"First the bank is going to lend you $2,000. You will deposit the $2,000 in a certificate of deposit that has a maturity of sixty days, the same maturity as the loan. In sixty days you will take the money out of the certificate of deposit, plus what it earns, and apply the full amount to your loan. You will not get the use of the $2,000. It will be assigned as collateral. In fact, you will never see the $2,000 proceeds of the loan. *But here is the secret: the computer will show that you not only had a $2,000 loan at this bank, but you had a $2,000 deposit as well, and you paid the loan off as agreed.*"

Jerry and Patty both smiled. "That's all we do?"

"Well, not totally. You will need to complete a loan application and start providing information to build your in-house bank credit file. Then, after the first loan has been paid back, we will do the same thing again, but a little differently the second time. The second time we will make a ninety-day note for $3,000, and you will put it in a ninety-day certificate of deposit, but this time we want you to make payments."

"Payments?" Patty said. "We only have about $50 per month extra as it is."

"Then that is how much your payments will be. You see, when you make regular monthly payments, a new report goes to the credit bureau every month. It shows that you have the discipline and skill to save a little every month and that you are a responsible, creditworthy individual—at least that is the theory."

"What happens at the end of ninety days?" Jerry asked.

"You pay off the balance of your loan . . . with one important difference from the first time."

"What is that?" Patty asked.

"The difference is that since you have been paying $50 per month, your balance is lower, and when you cash in your CD to pay off the loan, you will have money left over . . . like a forced savings plan."

The couple continued this procedure until they had a good credit report, just as the banker had promised.

The story I have just related is a true story, one I have as a banker played out many times to help young couples, divorcées, college graduates, and even older people to establish their credit. It works. It is risk-free for the banker and the customer, and when repeatedly practiced over a period of a year, creates a good credit file which will pass muster with any creditor. There is a real need for bankers who are willing to take the time to work with people to get them established.

In specific situations, this process takes on even greater importance. Consider what happens when a woman who has always let her husband take care of business finds herself a widow. She has no credit and is lost if she ever needs to purchase a car, furniture, or an appliance. I recommend that every spouse create a credit history in his or her own name, using the method outlined in the example. This method will work for young people getting started and people wanting to open a new business. Figure 2 summarizes the steps involved.

If you can't find a banker willing to take the time to work with you to get your credit history started, there is another avenue. Go to the local hardware store and open a credit account. Open an account or charge account at every business or oil company that will issue a credit card to you. Charge on each of those accounts *one* time, even for a minor item. Then tear up the card, destroy it, never use that charge account again. Pay for the purchase when you get the bill. When you use the credit card, and when you pay the bill, the transaction will be reported to the credit bureau. Even though your purchase is small, if you get enough of these reports, the volume of positive credit

Figure 2
ESTABLISHING CREDIT THROUGH A BANK

Borrow $2,000.
↓
Put the loan proceeds in a 60-day CD for collateral.
↓
Pay the loan off at maturity with the CD funds.
↓
Borrow $3,000.
↓
Place the loan proceeds in a CD for 90 days.
↓
Pay $50 per month.
↓
Pay the loan off at maturity (funds will be left over).
↓
Repeat the process with ever larger amounts.

Figure 3
ESTABLISHING CREDIT WITH CHARGE ACCOUNTS

Open a charge account at the local hardware store.

↓

Buy a small item on credit, destroy the credit card, and pay
the bill on time.

↓

Open a credit card account at a local department store.

↓

Buy a small item on credit, then destroy the credit card.

↓

Apply for a major general-purpose credit card.

↓

Buy a small item on credit, then destroy the credit card.

↓

At the end of one year, go to the local credit bureau and pay
$3 for a copy of your credit report. You should find an
excellent credit record.

builds up and looks very impressive. Figure 3 summarizes
this procedure.

There is an important thing to remember. Credit can
make you, individually or in business. It can destroy you
as well. Never, never charge for things you don't absolutely
know you can pay for on time by the due date. Never be
late on any payment, and if possible always pay a few days
early. With this approach you can build your business and
your individual credit within a year.

Establishing Credit for a Business

The only difference for a business is that you follow the
procedures in Figures 2 and 3 in your business name.
Also, send credit information and company background

Figure 4
BANKER'S LETTER TO HELP A BUSINESS ESTABLISH CREDIT

Dear Sir or Madam:

This is to verify that Jerry and Patty Matheson are the owners
of Spock Computer Company. They and the company have
banked with this bank for many years. Spock Computer has
kept accounts at our bank in a satisfactory manner, with an
average low four balance. The company as well as the owners
have borrowed money here on several occasions, and have
always paid as agreed. We offer our highest credit
recommendation and ask you to record the following loan
information on your credit records in their behalf.

Loan	Date	Payment Record	Deposits
$2,000	1-1-91	Paid off 3-1-91 as agreed	Low four
$3,000	3-2-91	Paid off 6-2-91 as agreed	Medium four

(Note: The 3-2-91 loan paid monthly and regularly, no
past dues.)

$4,000	6-3-91	Paid off early	Medium four

(Note: Customer paid monthly and regularly, no past
dues.)

$10,000	8-1-91	Paid off early	Low five

Respectfully,

Cameron Wright
President
Anytown National Bank

information to agencies such as Dun and Bradstreet and the Better Business Bureau. The credit will be reported differently, but there will be a rating and a record reflecting your credit with the bank and Dun and Bradstreet. It may be necessary for you to contact the bank and ask them to manually send in a credit update on you or your business, or have the banker write a letter like the one in Figure 4.

A letter like this can be invaluable in getting your credit started. You can send copies of it to trade creditors and establish immediate credit terms with them. (Also send copies to credit reporting agencies and sister businesses.) But the letter is only possible after months', usually a year's, effort. It will also be the beginning of a good credit relationship with the local banker, who by now will know you and understand who you are and what you are about.

You may be pleasantly surprised when you go to the banker with a real loan request after this period of building credit. If you have favorably impressed him or her— and you will have if you have followed the plan in this chapter—you will find that you also have a good credit line established with the bank.

This method for establishing credit worked for them. It has worked for me, and it will work for you!

3

Assembling Your Checklist and Documentation

You and your partners, associates, or spouse have thought it over. You have decided you are going to apply for bank credit. You have made a firm commitment, and now you need some practical guidance. You know you shouldn't just barge into the banker's office the way John and Lori did, and you know you need preparation, but where do you start? The following story illustrates the importance of using a checklist.

When I was a college student, I made a rush takeoff to fly a small Cherokee 140 airplane to northwestern Arkansas, where I was to make a speech. The takeoff run seemed to take much longer than normal; with full throttle, the end of the runway was rushing toward me at a disconcerting pace, and the plane still did not want to fly. The stripes marking the end of the runway rushed toward me, then in a blur were under the airplane wings. At the last possible instant, I pulled the nose wheel up. The plane flew, but not as well as it normally did, yet all instruments read normal.

Finally, after zigzagging around the countryside for two hours (looking for the right highways), I entered into the landing pattern for the destination airport. I radioed the airport, "This is Cherokee 4462 Tango for a landing."

"You may enter downwind for runway 18, number two in the pattern."

"Roger, downwind 18," I said, as I fought the controls.

As I entered the landing pattern and flew by the downwind stretch, the tower called back. "Cherokee 4462 Tango, we have a visual on you. You are dragging an object from your tail. Looks like a block with branches on it. Do you need assistance?"

It hit me like a brick. It was a brick. The tie-down block! In my rush to take off, I had forgotten to remove the tie-down block, the concrete block used to hold the plane steady on the ground. Embarrassed, I replied, "This is Cherokee 4462 Tango. No assistance required. I will be landing hot [faster than usual]."

After a bumpy landing, I jumped out of the plane to look, partly out of curiosity and partly out of embarrassment. I wanted to remove that block before every pilot on the field saw it and had a laugh at my expense. Sure enough, there on the end of a four-foot chain was a large concrete block with a small tree limb hanging on. Pilots gathered around and started laughing. One old pilot lingered just long enough to say, "Young man, the time spent on a checklist is less than 120 seconds. Those 120 seconds are very important to a good pilot."

He was right! In my rush, I had ignored one of the basic rules of flying: *always use a checklist*. The mistake could have been fatal.

Figure 5 is your checklist of things to prepare before going to your bank. It is a checklist only. As you go through the process of reviewing or accumulating the listed items, it should be obvious why they are necessary.

Figure 5
BORROWER'S CHECKLIST

☐   Are you philosophically committed to this endeavor?

☐   Have you researched the economy?

☐   Have you located the right bank?

☐   Do a background study of the bank, its condition, philosophy, expertise, and quality of personnel.

☐   Have you located the right loan officer?

☐   Do a background study of the loan officer: attitude, lending authority, ability, expertise in your field.

☐   Have you taken steps to see that the banker knows you and to establish a rapport with him or her?

Have you prepared financial data?

☐   a. Balance sheet

☐   b. Profit and loss statement for past 3 years

☐   c. Projected balance sheet

☐   d. Projected profit and loss statement for next 3 years

☐   e. Complete listing of inventory, tools, equipment, accounts receivable (with aging) detailing how long accounts have been owed, furniture, or any assets that can be used for reserve or capital.

☐   Collect tax returns for the past 3 years.

☐   Collect news items, articles, brochures, recognition about you or your business.

☐   Have you positioned yourself in proper civic clubs and charity events as a positive member of the community?

☐   Have you created a detailed budget for your business?

☐ Have you generated an operating plan?

☐ Collect comparative research about your operation versus others in the same business.

☐ Obtain written copies of credit reports on you and/or the business.

☐ Collect written letters of recommendation.

☐ Document and prepare 2 sources of repayment.

☐ Have you written a cash flow study showing the uses and sources of funds in a detailed report?

☐ Prepare a report showing 2 levels of collateral or backup reserve in the event something goes wrong.

☐ Have you reviewed all sources of capital and reserves for ultimate cash flow or capital backup?

☐ Prepare your location, office, or business for an on-site inspection by the lender.

☐ Have you acquired adequate life insurance to repay all of your debts in the event of your death?

☐ Have you created a contingency plan in the event of your illness?

☐ Have you allowed for depreciation and replacement of tools and equipment?

☐ Have you written a detailed contingency plan for expansion and a contingency plan for contraction?

☐ Have you reviewed standard average industry ratios (such as the acid test, debt coverage ratio, loan-to-equity ratio, cash/current liabilities ratio) and compared them to figures for your business?

☐ Have you prepared similar ratios for your business in a comparative report with conclusions?

☐ Have you collected confirmation about what your business or profession is worth on the current market for resale?

☐ Collect all deeds, titles, insurance policies, and legal documents relating to you and your business for easy access.

☐ Make photographs of the business location and staff at work, or make copies or exhibits of your completed product or service.

☐ Have you created a leaflet, advertisement, or brochure about you or your business or profession to demonstrate marketing?

☐ Have you written a detailed marketing plan?

☐ Have you selected, defined, and adopted a personal and corporate image you wish to project?

☐ Have you opened an account with the bank you hope to borrow from?

☐ Include all of these data in an organized, attractive, written loan proposal.

A checklist isn't meant to explain the items, only to remind you of their importance. The mere act of going through the checklist should stimulate your thought patterns, helping you formulate other items that are important to your specific loan application.

Use this checklist carefully. Don't try to rush, and don't try to skip or skimp. Some items will appear obvious, and some may appear to be overkill. But remember, if you just "fly off" without careful preparation, you are in for a possibly disappointing journey, one that could be fatal to your loan request and your dreams.

You may say, "Now wait a minute . . . all of that?" Understand, this list will assure that you are prepared to "take off" and that you will have the best possible chance of approval. This is your checklist before you even set up an appointment to talk about your loan. Of the people who go in and ask for a loan, 90 percent are inadequately prepared. That takes power away from them and gives more reasons for the banker to chip away and criticize their project, loan, or application. The easiest thing a banker can do is turn a loan down.

Consider this. Bankers are on a salary. They are not paid a commission for the loans they approve. But if a banker approves a loan that makes him or her look bad or that costs the bank money, the banker can be greatly injured personally. If a banker makes a loan, he or she has the added responsibility to service that loan, meaning more work. But while the easiest thing bankers can do is turn a loan down, they are hired, trained, and motivated to make good loans. Indeed, one of the things a good banker enjoys doing is making good loans. Loans are the main source of income for a bank, and without good loans, a bank is destined to have earnings pressures.

In the published call reports (which by law must appear in your local newspaper quarterly), you can observe which banks are aggressive lenders. A bank that has a loan-to-deposit ratio of 30, 40, or 50 percent is considered to have a conservative philosophy. "Tightfisted" you might say. These banks have established a pattern of lending less money to customers and investing more in lower-risk Federal Funds, municipal bonds, or government bonds. In most cases your chances of being approved at a bank with a 30 percent loan ratio are less than if you select a bank with a loan ratio of 55, 65, or 70 percent. The higher loan ratio may be an indication that the banker is more aggressive, or it may mean that the bank is "loaned up." Generally speaking, though, a higher loan ratio usually means a better chance that the loan officers at that bank are willing to take greater risks. They are willing to approve more loans to more people and more businesses.

Bankers must make loans to survive. I once visited with Marvin Carlile, a leading banker in west Texas who had been named "banker of the year" by one of the state banking associations. He made this statement: "A banker's job is to motivate people to ask the banker to do what he wants to do anyway and then make them grateful to him for doing so."

Consider this. People place their deposits with a bank. The bank has use of those funds to make loans and investments that will make the bank a profit. Then the same depositors are of the perception that they must go to the banker and "request" a loan. Some people may have more of their money on deposit at the bank than they want the bank to lend. The banker can then lend those funds back to the public at a higher rate than the bank pays and increase the bank's profits. Customers are pleading for loans, while the banker ultimately has some strong motivations to make the loans all along.

A key to the approach of using a checklist is that you are approaching the banker from a position of strength. You are prepared with facts, and you want to make it easy for the banker to do what he or she was hired to do: make a profitable loan.

There is another facet to consider. While turning down a loan makes a banker's life easier, the denial of the loan (that is, the actual confrontation with the applicants, where the banker has to look them in the eye and say, "I'm sorry, I will not make your loan") is stressful for the banker. Through the use of the checklist, *you want to make loan denial as difficult as possible* . . . because you want to take away all of the banker's objections. Indeed, rather than putting the banker through the stress of a denial, you want to win his or her enthusiasm for making your loan.

The banker will be impressed with your preparation. You are doing a lot of the paperwork that bankers normally have to do, or have to teach customers how to do. So you have a good chance at winning over the banker and making him or her an enthusiastic supporter. If you get the loan and pay it off promptly, the road will be paved for you to borrow again and again.

My father, Melvin E. Boothe, was one of those who mastered the art of credit at an early age. After his first loan, he never had a problem borrowing money again. He was eleven years old, the son of a poor farming family, during the depths of the Great Depression. He wanted a trumpet, but his father told him there was no way he could give him that much money. Melvin asked his father, "Dad, where *can* I get the money?" His father, who couldn't borrow a dime, said in jest, "Son, when I need money like you are talking about, I go to the bank!"

So Melvin, not realizing that it was a joke, went to the bank and applied for a $200 loan. The banker knew the young Boothe boy was honest and hardworking, because after school Melvin had a job delivering Special Delivery letters in town for the post office. The banker went to the back room and conferred with his president. Then he reappeared and approved the loan. He thought it was humorous that a child so young would apply for a loan.

That night, when Noel Boothe came home, Melvin said, "Dad, I got the money!" Noel was so surprised he hardly knew what to say. He was working sixteen hours a day, trying to make a few dollars a week. In disbelief, he said, "You did! Where?"

"I did like you said . . . and the bank loaned it to me."

Grandfather Noel's disbelief turned to amazement, a flash of anger, then he saw the humor in it.

Many years later, recounting that experience, my

father proudly said, "You know, in my entire life I never had difficulty borrowing money. And in my entire life I always paid my loans off early."

His generation didn't need a checklist. But this age does. As my father put it, "Nowadays there are too many worms in the woodwork, so the good man has a much harder time proving himself." Perhaps your checklist will separate you from the "worms in the woodwork."

Some items in the checklist are discussed in greater detail later in this book. But first, take another look at it and spend some time and effort on this "preflight takeoff checklist" before you take another step.

Avoiding the Documentation Deathtrap

An important part of the checklist is collecting the proper documentation. This section will expand and explain the importance of documentation as one of the most critical factors in getting your loan approved. If the checklist is a reminder of what to include, the documentation is the evidence for why you deserve the credit you desire.

Documentation is a very important word in banking. When banks were small, bankers knew every customer in such detail that often a loan file simply consisted of a copy of the loan. As generations passed, industry and culture became more complicated, and so did loan procedures and the demand for greater documentation. Three primary forces pressed banks to keep ever more detailed documentation:

1. The demand of good business practices to have a permanent record that could be reviewed by any party within the bank
2. The increased demands of auditors, regulators, and examiners to have enough information in the

file so that the individual bank officer was not the sole repository of key data

3. Increased litigation, forcing banks to have more written protection in their files

Documentation is normally hated by borrowers. In truth, it is not the favorite pastime of good bank officers either. But it is necessary, if not critical, for businesspeople to understand and master bank documentation requirements. Otherwise documentation can be a deathtrap for all of your efforts to master the use of credit.

Being able to produce proper documentation can maximize your borrowing ability. Often the ability to borrow money quickly can make or break an opportunity. Good documentation can speed your approval, maximize the amount you can borrow, lower your interest rate, and in general make your life and that of your banker easier.

An illustration of misunderstandings and problems related to documentation is that of the bank customer who entered my bank and gruffly said he wanted to pay off his loan. Now, regardless of the customer, those are welcome words to the banker! But then, as he pulled out the check to pay off his loan, he said to me, "I hope you will sleep better now."

I said, "Pardon me?" He said, "Your bank has never trusted me. You have thought me a crook, and I never wanted to cheat anybody!"

I asked him if someone had treated him badly or if he had a specific complaint. All he could say was "The bank didn't trust me." Upon further investigation, I found that this customer had borrowed money three years earlier and had paid as agreed. But with the exception of his initial loan application, he had never given the bank any updates on his financial statement, earnings, or collateral. Indeed, his file contained nine requests for current information, all of which he had ignored.

What he didn't know was that his file also reflected that the examiners had criticized his loan as being substandard because of the lack of current documentation. The file also included confidential internal memorandums from the compliance officer of the bank, indicating that the bank loan officer should not lend this customer any more money because of the exceptions. The memorandums also implied that it would be "a simple solution if the customer were asked to move his business to another bank." The bank had been forced to transfer funds out of its undivided profits over to a reserve for losses on this loan, not because the customer was late or in default, but because of the criticism due to the lack of documentation. This customer didn't realize it, but the bank had already suffered an earnings loss on his loan greater than all the interest he had paid the bank.

His mistake was in ignoring the bank's repeated requests for updated information. He seemed to think that the requests were a reflection of the bank's opinion of his character, when in reality the bank was simply trying to get basic information to document its file.

Bankers must answer to regulators, stockholders, depositors, directors, loan committees, and internal policies for evaluating loan quality. Thus, to defend a loan or present it in the best light, a banker needs the tools with which to work. To increase your borrowing ability, give the banker documentation. If you really want to impress the banker, have it ready before he or she asks, and update it periodically before it hits the exception list (the compliance department's daily report of loan files' deficiencies). One of the quickest ways to alienate a banker is to withhold information (documentation). Another quick way to eliminate your ability to borrow is to back your banker into a corner with statements like "I've got to have the money now, and I'll bring the documentation later." If some documentation on your loan request is not available, the answer will invariably be no.

Figure 6 lists examples of documentation you will need to have for different types of loans. These lists are not intended to be all-inclusive, but rather indicate some patterns that will assist you in understanding what your banker will expect.

Specific types of loans require more specific types of documentation other than just the basics of the business entity. Figure 7 provides examples of the type of documentation you'll need for real estate loans, commercial business loans, and vehicle loans.

Figure 6
DOCUMENTATION NEEDS FOR BUSINESSES

Basic Corporation Documentation

• Articles of incorporation

• Certificate of incorporation

• Corporate resolution (authorizes you to borrow; often the bank can provide a standard form)

• 2 most recent fiscal-year-end business statements

• Most recent interim business statements

• Corporate tax returns for last 2 years

• Certificate of good standing issued by secretary of state

• Minutes of board meeting where loan request was approved

• Dun and Bradstreet report on corporation

• Personal financial statement on majority stockholder if company is a closely held business

• UCC-lien search to ascertain what assets of the corporation are pledged to other lenders

- Depending on the details of your loan request, other basic documentation required by the banker

Basic Sole Proprietorship Documentation
- Trade name declaration (often the bank will provide a basic form)

- Assumed-name certificate (filed with the county)

- 2 most recent fiscal-year-end business statements (if prepared separately from personal statement)

- Any recent interim business statements

- Most recent personal financial statements and cash flow statements

- Last 2 years' tax returns

- Credit information on the company

- Other documentation requested by the banker, depending on the details of your loan request

Basic Partnership Documentation Requirements
- Partnership agreement

- Partnership resolution (usually the bank will provide a standard form)

- 2 most recent fiscal-year-end business statements

- Any recent interim business statements

- Personal financial statement and cash flow on all partners

- Last 2 years' tax returns on all partners

- Credit information about your partnership

- Specific other documentation requested by the banker, depending upon the details of your loan request

Figure 7
BASIC DOCUMENTATION NEEDS FOR 3 TYPES
OF LOANS

Real Estate Loans

- Title policy

- Appraisal (updated periodically)

- Deed of trust (or mortgage)

- Deed of trust note

- Survey and plat

- Floodplain map

- Insurance on improvements

- Copy of construction plans

- Sales contract

- Affidavit or receipt for taxes paid

- Environmental statement of nonpollution (for example, radon, asbestos, storage tank leakage, PCBs, hidden waste site)

- Lien search or title policy (to verify no other liens)

Commercial Business Loans

- Detailed inventory

- Listing of all furniture, fixtures, and equipment

- Serial numbers of all equipment

- Lien search to verify all liens

- Listing of all trade credit

- Detail of all accounts receivable

- Detail of all accounts payable

- Standard security agreement

- Monthly statement of income and expenses (bank may agree to a quarterly or semiannual statement)

- Monthly update of inventory (bank may agree to a quarterly or semiannual update)

Vehicle Loans (for Individuals or a Dealer)*
- Titles

- Power of attorney for each title

- Insurance

- Verification of odometer reading

- Physical inspection to verify title information is consistent with vehicle data (ID number, make, and model)

- Title search to verify no liens

- Automobile security agreement

- Outside statement of value if vehicle is used; invoice if new (verify value with published sources, such as yellow book, blue book, black book, etc.)

- Photograph of vehicle for banker's file

Preparing the Financial Statement

Most banks will provide a standard financial report form approved by the bank. The Federal Reserve publishes a financial statement form with an abbreviated profit and loss statement. I have used this form for years and recom-

---

*Standard documentation for vehicles, trucks, boats, airplanes; motorcycles are much the same with just minor variations.

mend it highly. But within the scope of this discussion, a far better recommendation is to use a standard format as a guide when possible, but to prepare your own statement. That will assure that you don't inadvertently agree to some boilerplate language that was placed in the statement by the bank's lawyers but that you don't wish to be bound by. However, you may not have a choice. The bank may insist that you use its form. You will then have to make a judgment.

A west Texas rancher had a similar dilemma years ago when he absolutely refused to complete his income tax return on the standard form. He had read the Internal Revenue Code and found that although he was legally obligated to report his income, it wasn't illegal to use a different form. He filed his return every year on a Big Chief writing tablet. He was consistently audited. His eccentricity drove the bureaucrats mad. But he always filed and reported his income fairly. *You* choose the form you wish to complete financial statements on.

Here are some practical tips to follow when you prepare a financial statement:

- The statement should be neatly typed.
- The statement should not omit any material fact.
- Always double-check the addition and other calculations.
- Date the statements as of the day of the figures, not the date of your signature.
- When possible on a major request, have statements prepared by a CPA or outside bookkeeper with his or her cover letter.
- A statement certified to be "without exception" by a CPA is the most desirable.
- Statements should be updated and presented to the bank annually.

- Your statement will include a balance sheet and a profit and loss statement. (A statement of sources and use of funds is desirable but optional.)
- Including assets with little actual value creates a credibility gap. (For example if your company has a warehouse full of obsolete computers, swampland in Florida, or junk vehicles, it may be best just to categorize them as "assets of negligible value," rather than to assign to them the value you wish they had.)

To illustrate the last point, consider the struggling businessman whose loan application included the following assets:

Diamond rings	$29,000
Household furniture	15,000
Art	10,000
Investment lot	20,000
Tractor	10,000

One of the members of the loan committee reviewing this application had been in the loan applicant's house and had seen his "art," noticed his wife's diamond rings, and knew the "investment" lot was a lake lot in a failed development. He said, "The rings are dirty and worth $2,000, the furniture wouldn't bring $1,000, the art has no value other than the picture frames, the lot won't bring its back taxes, and the tractor is a 1948 Ferguson that won't start. Loan denied." That customer, in trying to make his statement look a little better, lost all chances of getting his loan approved.

Financial statements are like a doctor's patient chart or a minister's Bible. They tell the banker what he or she needs to know about you financially. Oftentimes a conservative statement that shows manageable debt and prudent savings is much more impressive to the banker than a statement with millions in real estate and assets but little liquidity.

Kelly Dakken is an outstanding North Dakota banker. In Figure 8, he tells how he uses financial statements. In addition, here are some examples of what looks good:

- Accounts receivable equal or exceed accounts payable.
- Cash as a percentage of total assets is at least 10 percent.
- Cash and current assets equal or exceed current liabilities.
- The financial statement verifies there are no judgments or bankruptcies.
- Capital (reserves, savings, stockholders' equity) is 10 percent or more of total assets.
- Cash flow is adequate to service all company requirements without the company resorting to sale of fixed assets.
- Cash flow reflects a regular increase to capital.

Three businessmen decided to construct a multistory office building and applied for financing. One showed a financial statement with a net worth of $900,000. He had $400,000 in cash, $300,000 in listed stocks and bonds, and $200,000 in real estate. He had no debt. According to the second man's financial statement, his net worth was $2 million. He listed $50,000 in cash and $1.9 million in real estate and closely held companies. He had over $1 million in debt. The third man showed a financial statement with a total value of $17 million. He had $150,000 in cash, and the rest of his assets were in jewelry, real estate, and partnership interests. He had debt of over $10

Figure 8
A BANKER'S USE OF FINANCIAL STATEMENTS

DRAYTON *State* BANK

P.O. Box 369
DRAYTON, NORTH DAKOTA 58225-0369
PHONE 701-454-3317

Kelly Dakken	Ronald L. Kuznia	Pete Anderson	Joy Bakken
President	Senior V.P.	V.P. & Cashier	Vice President

August 26, 1991

Ben B. Boothe
Western National Building
8851 Hwy 80 West
Suite 201
Fort Worth, Texas   76116

Dear Ben,

A financial statement of a corporation or individual is just like taking
a snapshot picture of their financial situation at that one day in time.
A few days later or one year later another snapshot is taken which will
indicate the direction that they are going.

I use the following example: if customer A three years ago had a net worth
of $800,000.00 and customer B had a net worth of $300,000.00 but today each
of them had exactly the same financial statement which showed a net worth
of $500,000.00 which one would you want for a customer? Obviously customer
A is doing something wrong while customer B is doing something right even
though at this point in time their financial statements are exactly identical.

Also we do not allow a customer to increase his net worth based on market
value of his assets because the same assets could be devalued the next year.
Therefore the difference in net worth is related to cash flow not to changing
market values.

Obviously we still analyze financial statements using the ratios that are
taught in all of the banking schools but we feel the direction that a customer
is going is more important.

Sincerely,

Kelly Dakken

Kelly Dakken

KD/ja

MEMBER FEDERAL DEPOSIT INSURANCE CORPORATION

million. Behind the closed doors of the boardroom, the banker looked at his loan committee and said, "I would recommend approval of this loan if it weren't for the last two statements." The loan was denied.

The moral of the story is that documentation of assets should be conservative and reliable and should promote the credibility of the borrower. Bankers are experts at identifying hype in financial statements.

One cannot overestimate the importance of good documentation. For years to come, your banker will appreciate the detail, clarity, accuracy, and integrity with which you prepare your loan request information. In most cases, the banker sees your loan file far more often than he or she sees you. Let your documentation speak well of you. A lawyer once told me that he wanted to have a job where he could make money while he slept. While you are away from the bank making your business grow, *your* documentation can be making *you* money—or it can be hurting you if done poorly.

In 1988 hundreds of banks in the southwestern part of the United States were downgraded to "problem banks" because the examiners focused on documentation shortcomings. This occurred after a time when bankers had been accustomed to getting only basic documentation from their customers. Consequently, regulators in Washington began requiring much more stringent attention to documentation in the files. A banker with an excellent reputation and performance record could easily be written up for "unsafe and unsound practices" if the examiners thought he or she was not getting detailed enough documentation. It was a painful period of reeducation for the bankers. Bankers then had to reeducate all of their customers, who in many cases had had unblemished reputations with their banks.

Customers who had never missed a payment were

suddenly told that they could not borrow any more funds until they provided more-detailed documentation. The customers who failed or refused to do so simply found that they had no further credit. Many is the customer whose loan request has been declined simply because he or she did not make the effort to provide the detail the bank simply had to have to satisfy regulators. Don't let yourself fall into the documentation deathtrap. If you or your company errs, let it err on the side of providing more documentation than is necessary, never too little.

4

Preparing the Loan Proposal

"The first thing which enters my mind when a loan applicant enters my office is, 'Oh, I hope this one has come prepared,' " says John Knox McConnell, president of First National Bank of Keystone in West Virginia. A central part of your preparation is assembling your loan proposal. This chapter shows you how by providing the outline and a few explanations. You can fill in the blanks with the details of your own company and situation.

The meat of the proposal is what is important, and it should be factual, complete, and well done. But the way you present the proposal also is important. Use an attractive typed format with correct spelling and grammar. If you have access to graphics or a good computer program, take advantage of that capability. Many of the copy shop franchises will rent you a computer or do the work for you for an hourly fee. It is well worth the time and expense.

Remember, you have worked hard on personal and corporate image. But the loan proposal is the one docu-

Figure 9
COVER PAGE FOR A LOAN PROPOSAL

LOAN PROPOSAL FROM:

ABC Enterprises Inc.
4829 Madison Avenue
New York, N.Y.

Paul Martin, President

PREPARED FOR:

First National Bank of New York
James Johnson, Senior Vice President
August 1, 1992

ment that everyone on the loan committee will see. They may never see you, but they will see your proposal. Therefore it is an important part of the communication process, letting them know how professional, how efficient, and how creative you are. I once asked Duncan D. Flann, president of the Farmer's and Merchant's State Bank in Iroquois, South Dakota, about the importance of the actual loan presentation package. He replied that it's critical: "It shows how much thought went into the loan project." Jim Myers, president of the Live Stock State Bank in Mitchell, South Dakota, echoed his answer: "It is the most important item. It tells you how much thought and organization has gone into the plan."

Cover Page and Executive Summary

The first page of your loan proposal is the cover page. It gives the name and address of your company (or your own name and address if the loan is not for a business), the name of the bank, and the date of the proposal. Figure 9 provides an example.

After the cover page, you should have an executive summary. This summarizes the information listed in Figure 10. Try to keep your executive summary to a page or two.

Figure 10
EXECUTIVE SUMMARY FOR LOAN PROPOSAL

1. Personal background
2. Corporate history
3. Summary of loan request
4. Cash flow discussion
5. Collateral discussion

6. Capital discussion
7. Credit history
8. Character references
9. Sources of repayment
10. Financial statements
    a. Balance sheet
    b. Profit and loss
11. Projected statements
    a. Balance sheet
    b. Profit and loss
12. Projected banking needs
    a. Estimated deposits and accounts
    b. Other bank services desired
13. Loan term scenario
    a. Rate, payment, and payout
    b. Plan b (alternative rate, payment, payout)
14. Concluding remarks about loan, company,
    and bank

Personal Background

Next provide a brief biographical summary stressing the experience and skills that qualify you to manage the endeavor for which you are borrowing. This section should include the following information:

- Personal résumé
- Awards, recognition, or honors
- Professional education and training
- News articles about yourself

One of my banks entertained a loan application for an insurance company. The company had two principal partners. One knew the insurance business from top to bottom, and the other was a newscaster and a local celebrity, as well as an articulate salesman. The loan proposal had all of the requisite financial statements, but in addition to the cold facts, there on the second page was an 8″ × 10″ black-and-white glossy of the newscaster. The loan officer couldn't wait to meet him. In fact, the customer was effectively using the personal résumé section to create interest and open the door.

Corporate History

The next section is a chronological history of your company, highlighting some of the important strides the company has taken. If it is a new company, this section will outline the story of how and why the company was formed, and the philosophy behind the company. Here are some specific items to include:

- List of major stockholders or principals
- The philosophy of the business
- The potential for the business
- Location (photos here would be excellent)
- Recognition and awards for the business
- Growth of the company
- The past three years' profit and loss statements and balance sheets
- Newspaper articles about your company or about your industry

This section of your loan proposal affords you an excellent opportunity to sell the merits of your company to the committee. When you discuss the stockholders and partners, you can point out their standing in the community. The discussion of philosophy is the perfect place to demonstrate your belief in integrity and excellence. This

will be backed up by your operating history and the financial statements and growth you will demonstrate in those
discussions.

Photographs are important. Remember, the loan
committee will be leafing through your proposal while the
officer makes the presentation. When the members of the
loan committee see photographs or graphics that are
impressive, they will stop and give your proposal more
attention.

On the section charting the growth of the company,
select the area of your company that demonstrates your
strongest performance. For example, if you have had much
growth in number of customers, but slow growth in margin of profits from each customer, make a chart of the
number of customers. You don't want to hide the narrow
margin, but you certainly don't want to highlight it either.

Suppose your company is experiencing a temporary
cash flow or capital shortage, and that is the primary
reason you need the loan. In this section you should chart
the history of the company and point out the rapid growth
in customers and volume. This will also be charted or
explained as the key to the future of your company. The
growth rates, if continued, will pull the company profits
forward. A sophisticated banker will appreciate your direction and may also have some good suggestions as to how
to improve your profit margins and cash flow in the
process.

Summary of Loan Request

Next is the summary of your loan request. This section is
a simple summary of why and what you need to borrow.
Start the section off with a short paragraph, then provide
an itemized summary. Figure 11 provides an example.

Figure 11
SAMPLE SUMMARY OF LOAN REQUEST

ABC Enterprises Inc. is interested in [not requests or needs] a loan relationship with First National Bank. The amount of the loan is $350,000.00 over a term of 10 years for the purpose of purchasing new equipment, expanding markets, and operating capital. ABC has adequate collateral and cash flow to support this debt and looks forward to working with First National Bank.

Itemized Summary

Purpose of Loan:	Purchase new equipment, expand markets, and operating capital.
Use of Funds:	$100,000.00 for new computers, one vehicle, office typewriters, and furniture. $100,000.00 for advertising program and travel expense to expand to California market. $150,000.00 to pay initial salaries and purchase inventory during expansion program.
Collateral:	$100,000.00 money purchase interest [an item purchased with the proceeds of the loan] in computers, vehicle, equipment, and furniture from loan.
	$100,000.00 present equipment already owned [insert a list here].
	$350,000.00 accounts receivable under 60 days.

$50,000.00 other, cars and trucks.

Total Collateral: $600,000.00

Source of Repayment:	Cash flow from the business.
Term:	10 years, first payment starting in 6 months. Payments quarterly or monthly thereafter.
Rate:	Prime + 2. [If you really need this loan, price it slightly higher than the market . . . perhaps prime + 2½ but not so high that you appear desperate.]
Credit:	Credit history and references show no defaults or past dues.
References:	Will include letters of reference from John Jacobs (our accountant), Sarah Johnson (leading attorney), the mayor, and George Bush.
Balances:	Company agrees to move all company accounts to bank and estimates that the average balance will be $50,000.00. Will also move retirement accounts and accounts for affiliate company to bank.

Cash Flow Discussion

A loan applicant looked startled when I told her we would need a cash flow statement. She asked, "What is cash flow?" Her husband laughed and said, "That is what happens when you go to the mall!" He was only half right. Cash flows in both directions, in and out. Consider cash flow as like a pristine mountain lake with a small creek that fills it and a small creek that drains it. The banker wants to be sure there is enough flow to keep the lake full as well as keep the stream flowing. If the drainage creek (expenses) depletes more water than is replaced by the filler stream (income), the lake (your capital) will disappear.

In a business sense, corporate cash flow is more important than ever. There was a generation of bankers from the school of the Great Depression who came to believe that "asset-based lending" was the primary way to go. Asset-based lending emphasizes having collateral, and a lot of it. The theory is that you may lose everything else, but you still can eventually sell the collateral. That has changed somewhat with the current school of banking. Part of the change has resulted from the changes in bankruptcy laws. Current bankruptcy laws limit what a bank can do with collateral and in some instances even keep the bank from regaining its collateral in a timely manner. Another reason for the change has been a new regulatory emphasis on cash flow.

Recently I interviewed a young bank president who had previously been a bank examiner. I asked him what was the primary criterion he sought when reviewing a new loan application. He answered in two words: cash flow. You will want to address this emphasis.

A cash flow summary is somewhat different from a profit and loss statement. Whereas a P&L, according to accepted accounting rules, shows income and expenses, it also includes some "soft" expenses such as depreciation, which can distort where the cash is actually going. A cash flow statement (accountants call it a report of sources and uses of funds) shows exactly where your money is, where every dollar is used, and what is left over afterward. It demonstrates your ability to service the debt if you continue to show the performance you have in the past.

You can have an accountant prepare a cash flow statement, or you can prepare a simple one of your own. It is a simple project that will pay ample dividends for the time invested in looking up the facts. It is also a great budgeting and management tool to show you where you have been. The format for your cash flow summary can follow the example in Figure 12.

In preparing this section, you strengthen your loan request and take away a substantial objection to the loan. Best of all, you do it before the question is ever raised.

Figure 12
SAMPLE CASH FLOW SUMMARY

Cash Flow Summary for 1992
Cash on Hand January 1, 1992 $ 50,000

Sources of Funds:	
Sales	875,000
Consulting	93,000
Referral fees	7,000
Interest	5,500
Sales of assets	42,000
Royalties	22,000
Total Funds Received	$1,044,500

Uses of Funds:	
Salaries	(450,000)
Utilities	(22,000)
Telephone and fax	(35,000)
Purchase of equipment	(100,000)
Taxes	(29,000)

Interest	(75,000)
Debt service (principal payments)	(10,000)
Insurance	(80,000)
Advertising	(80,000)
Travel	(62,000)
Total Uses of Funds	($ 943,000)
Resulting Cash Balance December 31, 1992	$ 151,500

Conclusions Based upon the Cash Flow Summary: Provided the company makes the expenditures for equipment and expansion as projected in the loan agreement, on the basis of past cash flow (not the projected future cash flow), the company will have a minimum excess cash flow of $100,000.00 per year. (Note the item on equipment expenditures in this report was $100,000 paid out of operating funds on hand.) Adjusting for this extraordinary item, we will have a minimum of $200,000.00 per year for debt service.

Collateral Discussion

John Knox McConnell tells a story about a young college student who went to his local bank to get a loan for $100. The student asked the banker what it would take to get the loan. The crusty old banker said, "Collateral, boy, collateral." Promptly the college boy went back to the dormitory, picked up his 30-30 rifle, and carried it back into the bank. Employees, secretaries, and loan officers scattered as he walked into the banker's office and said, "Can I put this up as collateral?"

The banker, startled out of his wits, said, "Hell, yes, but first put the gun down."

As mentioned earlier, many bankers are asset-based lenders, and even a cash flow–oriented banker is going to request collateral. Unsecured lending practices ebb and flow with economic cycles. When the economy is booming, more unsecured loans are made. When the economy is uncertain, unsecured lending ceases. It is prudent to go into a loan request expecting and planning to provide collateral. Perhaps you will want to consider negotiating a collateral release clause containing a statement like this: "If the bank insists on collateral simply for security until credit history has been established, the borrower will require a collateral release clause in the loan agreement providing all payments are made as agreed, after a period of one year." The banker may agree to this. In the meantime, plan on having collateral in place.

Here are some more tips related to collateral:

- The proposal should list the specific items of collateral.
- Have the collateral appraised or valued by a third party with the valuation included in writing.
- Accounts receivable collateral should be based on aging of 90, 60, and 30 days.
- Inventory should be noted for wholesale and retail values.
- Equipment, tools, furniture, and fixtures are most effective as collateral when you provide photographs and an inspection letter from a third party stating that they are in good condition.
- Every banker is going to ask for "liquid collateral" (collateral such as cash, stocks, bonds, or CDs). Nearly all bank customers will respond that if they had "liquid collateral," they wouldn't be asking for the loan. Therefore, the key here is to market your other collateral in the most effective manner, one that will be the most palatable to the banker. Try not to tie up your liquid assets.
- Don't carry a gun through a bank lobby. You may get more "security" than you bargained for!

Hidden Collateral

You may well have collateral sources that you have forgotten. Here are a few ideas:

- Accumulated cash value on life insurance policies
- Equity in mortgaged real estate
- Vested retirement accounts
- Mutual funds, annuities, stocks, and bonds
- Royalty interests on minerals of real estate owned
- Book, record, or other publishing royalties or delayed payments
- Elimination of trade credit, which may release additional collateral or equipment, tools, furniture, and fixtures
- Partnership interests in investment properties (used for collateral or converted to cash)

Collateral and Character

Most bankers know that collateral ultimately does not repay loans. Good business management by people with high integrity repays loans. One of the best things you as a businessperson can do is to freely put up collateral and repay your loans in rapid succession until the banker's confidence reaches a level that will eliminate a need for collateral. While you are working toward that goal, plan on putting up far more collateral in value than your loan amount.

Since you are going to repay the loan anyway, you should have no objections to assigning collateral to your loan. This is an attitude the banker will appreciate and will build his or her confidence in you. At some point, the banker may decide that the paperwork in gathering the collateral is of more expense and more nuisance than it is worth. He or she may then suggest the release of collateral. But don't hold your breath.

Figure 13
REFLECTIONS ON COLLATERAL AND LOAN
APPLICATIONS

  ·WESTERN NATIONAL BANK

Mark E. Huckabee
President and CEO

August 2, 1991

Mr. Ben B. Boothe
P.O. Box 608
Rociada, New Mexico 87742

Dear Ben:

A book on how to borrow is a timely consideration. Let me make a few
observations. It scares me to contemplate how many borrowers we see who
know EITHER what they will use the money for or how they will repay it, but
not both. Encourage loan applicants to think through their application
asking themselves the same questions we bankers will ask.

The most important qualifications in a loan applicant in Commitment NMW.
My dad, Archie is the dean of bankers here in Lubbock with almost fifty
years experience. He has always told me that the right kind of loan ought
to be closed with a handshake, while all the documentation (although
important) won't make a bad loan good. Put another way, the current
misuse and abuse of the bankruptcy laws has placed more importance on a
borrower's character than ever before. I once had a director who said:
"Mark, I'll pledge my equipment, my cash, my assets, my wife and my sons,
because you'll not have to take it! I'll pay the loan NO MATTER WHAT
I have to do." That's what we need more of in borrowers, commitment
to repay NO MATTER WHAT.

Borrowers deal with BANKERS not a BANK. If I had to find a new banker
for my personal business today, the main thing I would look for would
be Courage. He or she would need courage before loan committees and the
regulators.   He would be able, with courage to tell me "no" and still
keep my respect. He would need courage to be able to go out on a limb
for me and leave the thousand page policy behind.

This is a people business...and more than ever good people, bankers
and borrowers are necessary.

Best of luck and best wishes,

Mark E. Huckabee, President
Western National Bank

MEH:dm

82nd and Nashville
P.O. Box 54500
Lubbock, TX 79453
806-794-8300

One of the best reflections of the attitude of most bank presidents regarding loan applications and collateral comes from Mark Huckabee, the outstanding president of the Western National Bank of Lubbock, Texas. His thoughts appear in the letter reprinted as Figure 13. Note his stress on NMW ("no matter what"). In other words, Huckabee stresses that paperwork and collateral are important, but determination to pay is even more powerful.

Lee Goodman, a great business and civic leader in Ft. Worth, Texas, told me a story that supports Mark Huckabee's point of view. Lee has borrowed over $200 million in his career so far, and with it he has developed properties worth at least $300 million. If anyone knows how to borrow money effectively, it is Lee Goodman. He recently told me his story:

"When I was thirteen years old, I wanted a calf to feed out. I didn't have the $75, and so without the knowledge of my parents, I went to the banker and borrowed the $75. It was as wild as a March hare, so I built a pen, but that wasn't good enough, so I tied up the calf to settle it down. The calf bucked and kicked and broke its neck. I was heartbroken. Furthermore, I had that huge bank loan of $75 and no way to pay it back. The banker's collateral was dead. So I butchered the calf and sold the meat to our neighbors for $73. Then on the most dramatic day of my life, I looked and there was nothing left of my investment, nothing left of the calf but a bloody hide. With tears streaming down into that bloody hide, I carried it to the rendering plant and sold it for $5. Then I took all of the money to the banker and paid off the loan.

"It was a sad experience, but the banker was so impressed that he was willing to lend to me from then on. He must have seen character in me. From that day, from the age of thirteen to the age of fifty-seven, I was able to borrow money.

"When I was in the air force, going to the Korean War, I had an old Chevrolet that was totally worn out, and I still owed $100 on it. Before leaving town, I went to the banker and told him that I would send him all of my money until the car was paid out. There was only $10 per month, so I sent it all to the bank for a year and paid it off. You know, the thought of just returning the collateral *never* occurred to me."

In Goodman's case, if it *had* occurred to him, he would never have done it. Lee Goodman is an example of the kind of person bankers seek out and back. His word is far more powerful than any written contract. As important as legal documents are in the world of lending and borrowing, the character of the person signing them is by far most important.

Valuation of Collateral

If you plan to place real estate of any kind for collateral, you should be aware of FIRREA Title 11. As a result of the savings and loan crisis of the late 1980s and the subsequent banking problems, Congress passed a law entitled the Financial Institutions Reform, Recovery and Enforcement Act of 1989 (FIRREA). FIRREA has very strict requirements for financial institutions regarding the appraisal of collateral. In days past it was considered reasonable practice for the customer to pick a friendly real estate agent and ask for a letter of appraisal on real estate. Banks often had the loan officer who made the loan write up an appraisal memorandum. But the new law eliminates that practice. Now every loan of over $100,000 secured by real estate must be appraised by an independent certified appraiser.

What does this mean? FIRREA set up uniform appraisal standards for each state to adopt. These require education and testing to provide "certification" of appraisers. This new standard is an attempt to upgrade the industry and is leading to much more detailed loan underwriting documentation. There are some advantages and disadvantages to the customer and to the bank:

Advantage: The loan applicant will have an outside
                opinion of the value of the collateral that
                he or she can use for bookkeeping, resale,
                and preparation of financial statements.

Disadvantage: The loan customer is expected to cover the
                cost of the appraisals.

Advantage: An appraisal can be a powerful legal tool
                to protect your asset from being foreclosed
                or liquidated at a below market price. It
                can also protect both the banker and the
                customer from being accused of
                manipulating or distorting values in order
                to get a larger loan.

Disadvantage: Some appraisers take six weeks or longer
                to complete an appraisal. The best
                appraisers will promise a shorter delivery
                date when required.

Advantage: If you need to have collateral released, an
                appraisal can be very useful in the
                negotiations.

Advantage: If your appraisal is done in compliance
                with the law, it is much more difficult for
                an auditor, bank examiner, or loan review
                officer to question or call the loan on the
                basis of poor or overstated collateral. In

some regions of the nation, bankers have complained that examiners have arbitrarily charged off loans (causing the bank to call loans that sometimes were paying as agreed). In some cases where banks or savings and loan institutions have failed, real estate loans have been taken over by federal agencies, then the loans have been called or the collateral liquidated at below market rates. A good appraisal in your loan file is a powerful shield against these types of "wild card" developments.

Advantage: If your bank's loan officer is promoted to another branch or changes professions, a good appraisal on file will do much to help educate his or her successor and assist you in building a new rapport and comfort level with your new banker.

We will go into more detail about the current appraisal environment later in the book. But for now, when you present your loan proposal, have the assets appraised and the appraisals included in the proposal.

Capital Discussion

Your loan proposal will need a discussion of capital. The capital, or stockholders' equity in a company, is its accumulated profits and reserves. In other words, the capital of a company is its "savings account." It is the nest egg, the foundation of financial strength. Your report needs to point out the capital of your business—not only how much, but the rate of increase and the amount of capital as a percentage of your total assets. This can be done as an individual or as a business.

To illustrate, assume that your company financial statement looks something like this:

Cash on hand	$ 50,000
Inventory	200,000
Building	300,000
Accounts receivable	800,000
Equipment	50,000
Total assets	$1,400,000
Accounts payable	($600,000)
Loans and mortgages	($400,000)
Total liabilities	($1,000,000)
Stockholder's equity	$400,000

In this case your ratio of capital to total assets is calculated by dividing the total assets into the stockholders' equity (capital). The company has a healthy 28.5 percent capital ratio ($400,000 ÷ $1,400,000 = 28.5%). Technically, that is what your business is actually worth if you liquidate all company assets and pay all company bills.

Capital, corporate equity, and stockholders' equity are all terms used interchangeably. When used on an individual financial statement, they essentially mean the same as "net worth." The calculation is the same. If your loan proposal shows a steady increase in the capital ratio (or net worth) over a period of several years, or if you can project a steady increase in this category, you will have made an excellent point. You'll be that much closer to achieving the goal of loan approval.

How important is capital to a business or an industry? When William Seidman, then head of the Federal Deposit Insurance Corporation in Washington, D.C., was asked what was the main problem of the savings and loan industry during the late 1980s, he answered, "Lack of capital." Later, when the banking industry faced problems, Alan

Greenspan of the Federal Reserve commented on the "need for bank capital." When the steel industry, the auto industry, and the airline industry all faced cyclical declines, economists cited the need for capital. In the development of the oil industry, John D. Rockefeller said that capital was his most important need. Indeed, the availability or lack of capital is a worldwide force affecting the economies of nations and industry groups and, on a local level, often determining the survival or failure of businesses. The primary reason for the failure of 99 percent of businesses is a lack of capital. With a worldwide shortage of capital, it is all-important in your loan presentation.

Credit History

Following the capital discussion, your loan proposal will contain a statement by you that your personal and company credit is good. Use a paragraph something like this:

> This is to verify that the personal credit history of
> _____ will show a record of no defaults,
> no judgments, and a consistent record of prompt
> payments. This will furthermore verify that the credit
> history of this company is flawless as the enclosed
> reports will show.

After this statement, you should include a copy of your personal credit report and business credit reports. Dun and Bradstreet and other services can provide a report on your business.

You may ask, "If it is a business loan, why should I include a personal report?" The reason is that if you are a principal or a high-ranking officer of the business, your reputation is a significant factor in the success of the business. Also, you may be asked to guarantee the business loan personally, unless it is for a giant publicly traded company.

This section can also include copies of letters from trade creditors or businesses or individuals who have carried you on a credit relationship.

Character References and Industry Recommendations

The section on character references and industry recommendations is simply an extension of the credit history, except you include letters of personal reference and letters of business testimonial. A good example of the importance of industry or customer testimonials is the story of Herb Ballew's marvelous cleansing solution. He distributed this product to major grocery store chains all over the country. From time to time he received letters from homemakers, mechanics, and all types of consumers extolling the virtues of his product. They wrote of how well it cleaned, the spots it removed, how they loved it. He created a library of these letters, and when he needed financing from a bank, he always shoved a tall stack of testimonial letters across the banker's desk.

It was effective marketing, not only to the banker, but to grocery store buyers as well. If a franchise dared to discontinue the product, its buyer was destined to get dozens of letters from customers—from Herb's library— until the buyer put the product back on the shelves. This is effective whether you produce soap, sell books, or provide computer services.

Sources of Repayment

The loan application will always include sources of repayment. Notice the plural. A traditional banker will normally think, if not ask, "If your business goes to pot, if your fondest dreams don't materialize, how are you going to repay the loan?" This is where the loan proposal will again anticipate and answer the question. You should have several sources of repayment listed, as in these examples:

- Primary source of repayment—income from sales per financial statements (estimated sales $800,000, funds available for debt service $200,000).
- Secondary source of repayment—liquidation of collateral (collateral value far exceeds loan request).
- Alternative source of repayment—factoring of accounts receivable (research indicates we could receive $ _____ if we had to use this approach).
- Backup source of repayment—cash flow and assets of guarantors of loan.
- Backup source of repayment—bringing in new investors (several have indicated an interest in buying stock in our company).

Financial Statements

Dr. C. H. Rosenburg from Ontario, Canada, needed an additional $100,000 loan from his banker. He canceled his appointments for the day; although it was costly to him, he really wanted this loan. When he finished explaining his loan application, the banker looked up over his reading glasses with a sober face and said, "Dr. Rosenburg, we are going to need a statement."

Dr. Rosenburg hated paperwork, especially what he considered "jumping through hoops" to get his loan. He leaned forward in his chair and said to the banker, "I'm optimistic!"

The banker said, with a puzzled expression, "What?"

"You said you needed a statement, didn't you? That's it!"

Unfortunately the financial statements required by bankers are somewhat different from Dr. Rosenburg's statement. A financial statement is a summary of all of your assets and liabilities at one point in time, the day the statement is signed. It is a touchstone of your status as a business or an individual. It marks a financial milestone of what you have achieved, how far you have come, or how your company has handled losses. There is a saying that the bible of a banker is the financial statement. The statement you give your banker should be neat and complete, and all totals should be checked for accuracy.

When you prepare a financial statement to apply for a loan, it is best to include every asset—even assets you may think are unimportant, such as heirlooms, or the diamond ring sitting in the vault, or the note that a long-lost customer owes you. All of your assets, when totaled up, may surprise you. If your business has been running very long, you will have accumulated inventory, equipment, accounts receivable, and royalties, and all of these count as assets. The total not only tells the banker how much you are worth, but how effective your management has been.

Figure 14 is a sample financial statement form. It is not all-inclusive (most forms aren't) but is an excellent guide when you and/or your bookkeeper build your financial statement. Also review Figure 15 (a sample credit application), Figure 16 (a sample application for a commercial loan), and Figure 17 (a sample cash flow form) to become familiar with the basic information every banker will require before an in-depth loan discussion can take place. Understand this is the information every lender will need and every borrower should have *prior* to the first loan interview.

Figure 14
SAMPLE FINANCIAL STATEMENT FORM

TO

TYPE OF CREDIT -- CHECK THE APPROPRIATE BOX   (Name of Lender)

☐ Individual -- If you check this box, provide Financial Information only about yourself

☐ Joint, with yourself and the other person ____ Relationship ____ If you check this box, provide Financial Information about

PERSONAL FINANCIAL STATEMENT OF

NOTE Any willful misrepresentation could result in a violation of Federal Law (Sec 18 U.S.C. 1014)

Name ____
Address ____   City ____ State/Zip ____
Home Phone ____ No. of Dependents ____ Bus. or Occupation ____

Birth Date ____ , 19 ____ Statement Date ____ , 19 ____
Social Sec. No ____ Bus. Phone ____

NOTE: Complete all of Section II BEFORE Section I

SECTION I

#	ASSETS		THOU-SANDS	HUN-DREDS	CENTS
1	Cash On Hand & in Banks				
2	Cash Value of Life Insurance	Sec. II-A			
3	U.S. Gov. Securities	Sec. II-B			
4	Other Marketable Securities	Sec. II-C			
5	Notes & Accounts Receivable - Good	Sec. II-C			
6	Other Assets Readily Convertible to Cash - Itemize	Sec. II-D			
7					
8					
9					
10	TOTAL CURRENT ASSETS				
11	Real Estate Owned	Sec. II-E			
12	Mortgages & Contracts Owned	Sec. II-F			
13	Notes & Accounts Receivable - Doubtful	Sec. II-D			
14	Notes Due From Relatives & Friends	Sec. II-D			
15	Other Securities - Not Readily Marketable	Sec. II-C			
16	Personal Property	Sec. II-G			
17	Other Assets - Itemize				
18					
19					
20	TOTAL ASSETS				

#	LIABILITIES		THOU-SANDS	HUN-DREDS	CENTS
21	Notes Due to Banks	Sec. II-A			
22	Notes Due to Relatives & Friends	Sec. II-H			
23	Notes Due to Others	Sec. II-H			
24	Accounts & Bills Payable	Sec. II-H			
25	Unpaid Income Taxes Due - ☐ Federal ☐ State				
26	Other Unpaid Taxes & Interest				
27	Loans on Life Insurance Policies	Sec. II-B			
28	Contract Accounts Payable	Sec. II-H			
29	Cash Rent Owed				
30	Other Liabilities Due within 1 Year - Itemize				
31					
32					
33	TOTAL CURRENT LIABILITIES				
34	Real Estate Mortgages Payable	Sec. II-E			
35	Liens & Assessments Payable				
36	Other Debts - Itemize				
37					
38	Total Liabilities				
39	Net Worth (Total Assets minus Total Liabilities)				
40	TOTAL LIABILITIES & NET WORTH				

ANNUAL INCOME

Salary, Bonuses & Commissions	$
Dividends & Interest	$
Rental & Lease Income (Net)	$

Alimony, child support, or separate maintenance income need not be revealed if you do not wish to have it considered as a basis for repaying this obligation.
Other Income—Itemize $

Provide the following information only if Joint Credit is checked above.

Other Persons Salary, Bonuses & Commissions	$

Alimony, child support, or separate maintenance income need not be revealed if you do not wish to have it considered as a basis for repaying this obligation.
Other Income of Other Person—Itemize $

TOTAL	$

ESTIMATE OF ANNUAL EXPENSES

Income Taxes	$
Other Taxes	$
Insurance Premiums	$
Mortgage Payments	$
Rent Payable	$
Other Expenses	$
	$
	$
	$
TOTAL	$

GENERAL INFORMATION

Are any Assets Pledged? ☐ No ☐ Yes (See Section II)

Are you a Defendant in any Suits or Legal Actions? ☐ No ☐ Yes
(Explain):

Have you ever been declared Bankrupt in the last 10 years? ☐ No ☐ Yes
(Explain):

CONTINGENT LIABILITIES

As Endorser, Co-maker or Guarantor	$
On Leases or Contracts	$
Legal Claims	$
Federal - State Income Taxes	$
Other -	$

SECTION II

A   CASH IN BANKS AND NOTES DUE TO BANKS
(List all Real Estate Loans in Section II-E)

NAME OF BANK	Type of Account	Type of Ownership	On Deposit	Notes Due Banks	COLLATERAL (If Any) & Type of Ownership
			$	$	
	Cash on Hand		$		
	TOTALS		$	$	
			[Enter Sec. I Line I]	[Enter Sec. I Line 21]	

(Complete Rest of Section II on Reverse Side)

BANKERS SYSTEMS, INC. ST. CLOUD, MINNESOTA
FORM PS-15   7-25-84

79

Figure 14 continued

SECTION II Continued

B LIFE INSURANCE (List only those Policies that you own)

COMPANY	Face of Policy	Cash Surrender Value	Policy Loan from Insurance Co	Other Loans Policy as Collateral	BENEFICIARY
	$	$	$	$	
TOTALS	$ [Enter Sec. 1 Line 2]	$ [Enter Sec. 1 Line 27]			

C SECURITIES OWNED (Including U.S. Gov't Bonds and all other Stocks and Bonds)

Face Value-Bonds No. of Shares Stock	DESCRIPTION Indicate those Not Registered in Your Name	Type of Ownership	COST	Market Value U.S. Gov Sec	Market Value Marketable Sec	MARKET VALUE Not Readily Marketable SECURITIES	Amount Pledged to Secured Loans
							$
			TOTALS	$ [Enter Sec. 1 Line 3]	$ [Enter Sec. 1 Line 4]	$ [Enter Sec. 1 Line 15]	

D NOTES AND ACCOUNTS RECEIVABLE (Money Payable or Owed to You Individually-Indicate by a ✓ if Others have an Ownership Interest)

MAKER/DEBTOR	✓	When Due	Original Amount	Balance Due Good Accounts	Balance Due Doubtful Accounts	Bal. Due Notes Rel. & Friends	SECURITY (If Any)
			$	$	$	$	
		TOTALS	$ [Enter Sec. 1 Line 5]	$ [Enter Sec. 1 Line 13]	$ [Enter Sec. 1 Line 13]	$ [Enter Sec. 1 Line 14]	

E. REAL ESTATE OWNED (Indicate by a ✓ if Others have an Ownership Interest)

TITLE IN NAME OF	✓	Description & Location	Date Acquired	Original Cost	Present Value of Real Estate	Amount of Ins Carried	MORTGAGE OR CONTRACT PAYABLE			
							Bal Due	Payment	Maturity	To Whom Payable
Homestead-				$	$	$				
TOTAL $							TOTALS $			
(Enter Sec. 1 Line 11)							(Enter Sec. 1 Line 34)			

F. MORTGAGES AND CONTRACTS OWNED (Indicate by a ✓ if Others have an Ownership Interest)

Cont.	Mtge.	✓	MAKER Name	Address	PROPERTY COVERED	Starting Date	Payment	Maturity	Balance Due
							$		$
							TOTALS $		
							(Enter Sec. 1 Line 12)		

G. PERSONAL PROPERTY (Indicate by a ✓ if Others have an Ownership Interest)

DESCRIPTION	✓	Date When New	Cost When New	Value Today	LOANS ON PROPERTY		
					Balance Due	To Whom Payable	
Automobiles-			$	$	$		
TOTAL $					TOTALS $		
(Enter Sec. 1 Line 16)					(Enter Sec. 1 Line 26)		

H. NOTES (Other than Bank, Mortgage and Insurance Company Loans). ACCOUNTS AND BILLS AND CONTRACTS PAYABLE

PAYABLE TO	Other Obligors (If Any)	When Due	Notes Due To Rel & Friends	Notes Due Others (Not Banks)	Accounts & Bills Payable	Contracts Payable	COLLATERAL (If Any)
			$	$			
TOTALS $							
	(Enter Sec. 1 Line 22)	(Enter Sec. 1 Line 23)	(Enter Sec. 1 Line 24)	(Enter Sec. 1 Line 25)			

For the purpose of procuring credit from time to time, I/ We furnish the foregoing as a true and accurate statement of my our financial condition. Authorization is hereby given to the Lender to verify in any manner it deems appropriate any and all items indicated on this statement. The undersigned also agrees to notify the Lender immediately in writing of any significant adverse change in such financial condition.

Date Signed _____ , 19 _____ Signature _____   Signature _____ (Other Person, if Applicable)

81

Figure 15
CREDIT APPLICATION

CREDIT APPLICATION

IMPORTANT: Please read these directions before completing this Application, and check (✓) the appropriate box below.

☐ If you are applying for individual credit in your own name, are not married, and are not relying on alimony, child support, or separate maintenance payments or on the income or assets of another person as the basis for repayment of the credit requested, complete only Sections A and D. If the requested credit is to be secured, also complete Section E.

☐ In all other situations, complete all Sections except E, providing information in B about your spouse, a joint applicant or user, or the person on whose alimony, support, or maintenance payments or income or assets you are relying. If the requested credit is to be secured, also complete Section E.

AMOUNT REQUESTED	PAYMENT DATE DESIRED	PROCEEDS OF CREDIT TO BE USED FOR
$		

SECTION A INFORMATION REGARDING APPLICANT

FULL NAME (Last, First Middle)		AGE	BIRTH DATE		SOCIAL SECURITY NO.

PRESENT ADDRESS (Street, City, State, & Zip)	HOW LONG AT PRESENT ADDRESS?	HOME PHONE

PREVIOUS ADDRESS (Street, City, State, & Zip)	HOW LONG AT PREVIOUS ADDRESS?

PRESENT EMPLOYER (Company Name & Address)		NAME OF SUPERVISOR		BUSINESS PHONE	Ext.

HOW LONG WITH PRESENT EMPLOYER?	YOUR POSITION OR TITLE

PREVIOUS EMPLOYER (Company Name & Address)	HOW LONG WITH PREVIOUS EMPLOYER

YOUR PRESENT **GROSS** SALARY OR COMMISSION	YOUR PRESENT **NET** SALARY OR COMMISSION	NO. DEPENDENTS	AGES OF DEPENDENTS
$ PER	$ PER		

Alimony, child support, or separate maintenance income need not be revealed if you do not wish to have it considered as a basis for repaying this obligation.

Alimony, child support, separate maintenance received under: ☐ Court Order   ☐ Written Agreement   ☐ Oral Understanding

OTHER INCOME	SOURCES OF OTHER INCOME
$ PER	

Is any income listed in this Section likely to be reduced before the credit requested is paid off?   ☐ No   ☐ Yes (Explain)

Have you ever received credit from us? ☐ No ☐ Yes - When?	Checking Account No. Where?
	Savings Account No. Where?

NAME & ADDRESS OF NEAREST RELATIVE NOT LIVING WITH YOU	RELATIONSHIP	TELEPHONE NO. (Include Area Code)

82

SECTION B INFORMATION REGARDING OTHER...

FULL NAME (Last, First, Middle)	AGE	BIRTH DATE	SOCIAL SECURITY NO.

RELATIONSHIP TO APPLICANT (If Any)	PRESENT ADDRESS (Street, City, State, & Zip)	HOW LONG AT PRESENT ADDRESS?	HOME PHONE

PRESENT EMPLOYER (Company Name & Address)

POSITION OR TITLE	NAME OF SUPERVISOR	BUSINESS PHONE Ext.

HOW LONG WITH PRESENT EMPLOYER?		

PREVIOUS EMPLOYER (Company Name & Address)		HOW LONG WITH PREVIOUS EMPLOYER?

YOUR PRESENT GROSS SALARY OR COMMISSION	YOUR PRESENT NET SALARY OR COMMISSION	NO. DEPENDENTS	AGES OF DEPENDENTS
$ PER	$ PER		

Alimony, child support, or separate maintenance income need not be revealed if you do not wish to have it considered as a basis for repaying this obligation.

Alimony, child support, separate maintenance received under: ☐ Court Order   ☐ Written Agreement   ☐ Oral Understanding

OTHER INCOME	SOURCES OF OTHER INCOME
$ PER	

Is any income listed in this Section likely to be reduced before the credit requested is paid off?   ☐ No   ☐ Yes (Explain)

Checking Account No.	Where?
Savings Account No.	Where?

Has Joint Applicant or Other Party ever received credit from us?   ☐ No   ☐ Yes

NAME & ADDRESS OF NEAREST RELATIVE NOT LIVING WITH YOU	RELATIONSHIP	TELEPHONE NO. (Include Area Code)

SECTION C   MARITAL STATUS

APPLICANT   ☐ Married   ☐ Separated   ☐ Unmarried (Including single, divorced, and widowed)
OTHER PARTY ☐ Married   ☐ Separated   ☐ Unmarried (Including single, divorced, and widowed)

Figure 15 continued

Figure 15 continued

SECTION D - ASSET & DEBT INFORMATION

If Section B has been completed, this Section should be completed, giving information related information with an "A". If Section B was not completed, only give information about both the Applicant and Joint Applicant or Other Person. Please mark Applicant- about the Applicant in this Section.

ASSETS OWNED (Use separate sheet if necessary.)

DESCRIPTION OF ASSETS	VALUE	SUBJECT TO DEBT? Yes / No	NAMES OF OWNERS
CASH	$		
AUTOMOBILES (Make, Model, Year)			
1.			
2.			
3.			
CASH VALUE OF LIFE INSURANCE (Issuer, Face Value)			
REAL ESTATE (Location, Date Acquired)			
MARKETABLE SECURITIES (Issuer, Type, No. of Shares)			
OTHER (List)			
TOTAL ASSETS	$		

OUTSTANDING DEBTS (Include charge accounts, installment contracts, credit cards, rent, mortgages, etc. Use separate sheet if necessary)

CREDITOR	TYPE OF DEBT OR ACCOUNT NUMBER	NAME IN WHICH ACCOUNT IS CARRIED	ORIGINAL DEBT (Omit Rent)	PRESENT BALANCE (Omit Rent)	MONTHLY PAYMENTS	PAST DUE Yes / No
LANDLORD OR MORTGAGE HOLDER	☐ Rent Payment ☐ Mortgage					
			$	$	$	
TOTAL DEBTS			$	$	$	
CREDIT REFERENCES (Paid Off Accounts)					DATE PAID OFF	

		$	

MY AUTO INSURANCE AGENT IS: (Name & Address)

Are you a co-maker, endorser, or guarantor on any loan or contract? ☐ No ☐ Yes - For Whom? To Whom?

Are there any unsatisfied judgments against you? ☐ No ☐ Yes - Amount $ If "Yes", To Whom Owed?

Have you been declared bankrupt in the last 10 years? ☐ No ☐ Yes - Where? Year?

OTHER OBLIGATIONS (For example, liability to pay alimony, child support, separate maintenance. Use separate sheet if necessary.)

SECTION E SECURED CREDIT (Complete only if credit is to be secured.) Briefly describe the property to be given as security.

PROPERTY DESCRIPTION

NAMES & ADDRESSES OF ALL CO-OWNERS OF THE PROPERTY

IF THE SECURITY IS REAL ESTATE, GIVE THE FULL NAME OF YOUR SPOUSE (if any):

SIGNATURES

Everything that I have stated in this Application is correct to the best of my knowledge. I understand that you will retain this Application whether or not it is approved. You are authorized to check my credit and employment history and to answer questions about your credit experience with me.

APPLICANT'S SIGNATURE   DATE

OTHER SIGNATURE (Where Applicable)   DATE

X   X

Figure 16
APPLICATION FOR COMMERCIAL LOAN

Application For Commercial Loan

Individual/Borrowing Company _____

Street Address _____

Mailing Address _____

County _____ Tax ID# _____ Phone (_____) _____

Type of Entity: Individual ☐ Sole Proprietorship ☐ Corporation ☐ Partnership ☐ Other ☐

Age of Entity _____ Type of Product/Service Offered _____

Amount requested $ _____ Term desired _____

Purpose of loan request _____

Loan to be secured by _____

Insurance agent Insuring collateral _____ Ph. # _____

Company's Account Nos. with Texas National Bank _____

THE FOLLOWING INFORMATION IS REQUIRED FROM THE PRINCIPALS OF THE COMPANY OR THE INDIVIDUAL APPLICANTS. AND IF MORE THAN ONE, ALL WILL BE EQUALLY RESPONSIBLE FOR REPAYING THE LOAN. USE ADDITIONAL APPLICATIONS IF NEEDED. INDICATE MARITAL STATUS ONLY IF YOU LIVE IN TEXAS OR ANOTHER COMMUNITY PROPERTY STATE.

PRINCIPAL 1/APPLICANT:	PRINCIPAL 2/CO-APPLICANT:
Your Full Name	
Birthdate	
Ages of Dependents	
Social Security No.	
Drivers License No. State	State
Are you a Permanent U.S. Citizen? Yes ☐ No ☐	Yes ☐ No ☐
Are you Married ☐ Unmarried ☐ Separated ☐	Married ☐ Unmarried ☐ Separated ☐
Street Address	
City/State/Zip	
Yrs. There	
Phone No. ( )	( )
Do You Own ☐ Rent ☐ Live with Parents ☐	Own ☐ Rent ☐ Live with parents ☐
Monthly Payments $	$
If Owned, Home Financed By	
Last Address	
City/State/Zip	
Name of Nearest Relative (Not living with you)	
Address	
Your Employer (If other than above)	
Address	
City/State/Zip	
Phone ( )	( )
Yrs. there Position	Position
Monthly take home pay $	$
Source of other income	
Amount $	$
Texas National Bank Checking Acct. No.	
Texas National Bank Savings Acct. No.	
Other Bank/Acct. No.	
Are there any unsatisfied judgements against you? Yes ☐ No ☐	Yes ☐ No ☐
Amount/To Whom	
Have You Been Through Bankruptcy or made settlement with Creditors? Yes ☐ No ☐	Yes ☐ No ☐
Where	
Have you ever had any property repossessed? Yes ☐ No ☐	Yes ☐ No ☐
Month/Year	

Personal Credit Obligations & References (for both applicant and co-applicant)

Creditor	Address	Balance Owed $	Monthly Payment $

NOTICE: REMAINDER OF APPLICATION IS ON BACK

Figure 17
CASH FLOW FOR PERSONAL FINANCIAL STATEMENT

CASH FLOW FOR PERSONAL FINANCIAL STATEMENT
Show All Numbers On An Annual Basis

	Last Year 19____	This Year 19____	Projected Next Year
CASH FLOWS			
Salary/Wages (Before Taxes)			
Bonus/Commissions			
Dividends/Interest			
Trust Income			
Rentals/R.E. Income			
(Net of Expenses)			
Royalties			
Capital Gains			
Equipment Leases			
Gifts/Inheritances			
Legal/Insurance Settlements			
Tax Refunds			
Spouse's Income			
Other			
TOTAL INFLOWS			
CASH OUTFLOWS			
Mortgage Payment or Rent			
Real Estate Taxes			
Vacation Home Mortgage			
Taxes (Income)			
Auto, Personal, Business Loans			
Charge Accounts			
Interest Expenses			
Payroll Deductions			
(Other than taxes)			
Insurance Expense			
Investments			
IRA/Keogh/Thrift Plan			
Legal Expenses			
Charitable Contributions			
Capital Losses			
Household Expenses			
Other			
TOTAL OUTFLOWS			
*NET CASH FLOW			

*CASH INFLOWS - CASH OUTFLOWS = NET CASH FLOW

_____ Date_____
Signature

_____
Please type or print name

Many standard financial forms include lengthy passages in small print containing language that increases the bank's legal protection and the liability of the customer. For that reason, you should take the time to read every word before signing *any* document. If there is something you do not understand or agree with, discuss it with the banker and your adviser.

Some businesspeople prefer not to sign a preprinted form, and opt for preparing their own. Both approaches are perfectly legal. The only potential problem is that a banker may insist on using the bank's form "or else" the banker will not consider the loan. Your judgment will have to suffice at that point.

Like our famous Dr. Rosenburg, some customers are reluctant to give financial statements, particularly personal ones. However, the banker is always going to require that you provide personal and business statements . . . if you want the loan approved. When I was the vice president of a new bank, the examiners required that the megarich town father of Ft. Worth, Texas, Amon G. Carter, Jr., provide a personal financial statement. He was worth so much in oil, broadcasting, and newspaper stock that he had adopted a policy of never giving out his statement. It simply was nobody's business, in his view. But the bank examiners had a different point of view, and they stood firm. One day Mr. Carter's Cadillac pulled up in front of the bank, and with cigar in mouth, he came in and asked for a desk with a typewriter. Every head in the bank turned around when he pulled his coat off, rolled up his sleeves, and started his hunt-and-peck typing. A secretary ran up to him and said, "Please, Mr. Carter, let me!" He grunted, "Excuse me, lady, but *no one* is going to see this *#!@! financial statement except the *#!@! bank examiners." And no one did. For years his financial statements were kept in a special sealed envelope locked in the vault of the bank.

Financial statement is an all-inclusive term that generally means not only your balance sheet summarizing assets, liabilities, and equity capital in your business, but also profit and loss statements. P&Ls are simply accounting summaries of all recognizable income and expenses, including amortized items and depreciation. This statement determines the final profit to be reported to stockholders, partners, or investors, if any. It is also the report that your banker will refer to repeatedly during the life of the loan. The banker will almost always ask for an updated balance sheet annually, but the P&L statement is often required quarterly or even monthly if you are in a volatile industry. This requirement on your banker's part is a way of making sure that *you* prepare these accounting summaries and therefore monitor your operation, as well as a way of following the company's progress.

A small business cannot afford a full-time bookkeeper or an outside CPA, but there are a number of excellent bookkeeping systems. Almost any computer system now can run basic financial statement programs that are simple and efficient.

Also, it is fairly easy to convert a profit and loss statement to a simple sources and uses of funds report. For example, note the following sample profit and loss statement:

Income:	
Sales	$500,000
Interest	50,000
Commissions	20,000
Total	$570,000

Expense:		
Salaries	$150,000	
Cost of sales	300,000	
Debt service	100,000	
Depreciation	200,000	
Total		$750,000
Net Profit or (Loss)		($180,000)

In this example, your banker and your stockholders will see that your company has had a loss of $180,000, not an encouraging thought. But the depreciation expense is not actually money out of your pocket. It is rather an accounting "soft" expense, which is simply approved to allow a business to deduct the wear and tear on improvements and equipment. This business, in fact, had a positive cash flow of $20,000, a very important item to point out to your banker should you have a similar situation. Remove the depreciation item from the P&L statement, and you have a very simple sources and uses of funds statement.

One last word on financial statements. It is against the law to falsify any fact on a financial statement. The penalties can be severe. Handle with great care.

Projected Statements

"'Tis a foolish man who tries to foresee the future," the sage said, but the business world of today calls for projections. In the letter reproduced in Figure 18, Robert L. Williams, president of Family Bank located in University Park, Illinois, tells why.

Even the Resolution Trust Corporation, the largest landowner in America, is requiring projections on new appraisals it requests for business-related real estate. Bank examiners have for years demanded that financial institutions write detailed five-year plans including expenses,

Figure 18
THE IMPORTANCE OF FINANCIAL PROJECTIONS

Family Bank

800 University Parkway • University Park, IL 60466
(708) 534-5300 • Member F.D.I.C.

Mr. Ben B. Boothe
Western National Building
Suite 201
8851 Highway 80 West
Ft. Worth, Texas 76116

Dear Mr. Boothe:

It is my belief that the financial projections are absolutely required for use by financial institutions and borrowers for three reasons: planning, comparisons, and evaluation of management and individuals.

Planning: Utilizing a definite plan, both borrower and financial institution have a basic awareness of the initial indebtedness, cash flow needed to support the debt, as well as the time required to retire the debt. I use the term "basic awareness" because, as we all know, some plans do not live up to expectation, but with initial planning both borrower and financial institution know the goals and how they expect to be achieved. Certainly this is important to the borrower; he must have a formula to repay so that he knows what he must do in order not to fail. More importantly, it is essential that the financial institution know that the borrower has a schedule for repayment and that it is a schedule that is within the realm of reason.

Comparisons: By comparing actual results with the initial plan both borrower and financial institution know what corrections to the plan are necessary to correct any negative trends that have developed. With these comparisons, the borrower, as well as the financial institution, have a better understanding of the borrower's financial position and ability to repay and can make any changes necessary to insure the well-being of both.

Evaluation: As a Banker, I use the explanation of the exception items to evaluate the borrowers. If, by virtue of recognizing any negative, as well as positive trends in his plan, the borrower has made necessary changes to correct and improve his payment schedule, he deserves and receives better terms and conditions than the borrower who has not worked up a plan. By working with the loan officer he might also qualify for a loan that would be considered policy exception, thereby giving him more latitude in his borrowing.

I should point out that, in my career, it has been a rarity for a borrower to apply for a loan showing me a plan or a projection for repayment. As a rule, the projections come only after I have explained the above and indicate that it is imperative that the financial institution has something to judge results by.
Sincerely,

FAMILY BANK

Robert L. Williams
President & CEO

91

income, and contingency plans. The Small Business Administration (SBA) requires projections on loan applications for every new SBA loan.

Businesspeople are fascinated with the future. Some of the most popular speakers and writers on the American media circuit are "futurists." These people captivate their audiences by presenting powerful visions of the future. The book *Future Shock* made Alvin Toffler a famous author even though many of his—like every futurist's—assumptions didn't and will never come true. The National Weather Service invests hundreds of millions of dollars in computers to produce weather models that seem somewhat more credible than mere guesses from pundits, even though every meteorologist knows that a forecast beyond three or four days is guesswork at best. But the media, the public, business, and governments are willing to pay, so the computerized weather forecasts go on.

With the advent of easy-to-use computer programs, projecting the future in economic terms is now a relatively fast and simple process. A myriad of alternatives and variables used to take people thousands of hours to calculate. Now modern computer programs can take a basic set of assumptions and spit out the calculations in a matter of seconds.

This area of expertise is essential for the modern businessperson. As a business leader of today, you must not only master computers, you must master the programs that will make you and your business money. For example, I made a new friend recently while traveling in Wyoming to speak to a bankers' convention. Roy Riddell has a successful chiropractic practice in Ontario. He told me that a few years ago he decided to purchase a sophisticated computer system for his office. At the time the idea of shelling out $10,000 seemed exorbitant and foolish to some of his business friends. But he chuckled as he told me, "That $10,000 computer has saved me five times more than that on billing and accounting labor."

A business trying to compete without modern tools in a world dominated by state-of-the-art technology will soon be left behind. The technology is inexpensive, powerful beyond all dreams and eminently practical and useful. Computers are no longer toys for the eccentric hobbyist, they are powerful weapons in the new economic war. Those who know how to use them will have substantial advantages.

The metaphor of a war is most powerful in the world of business today. The Chinese invented the chemical technology of gunpowder. That single innovation helped make them a world power over a thousand years ago. The British built an empire by using technology against Third World nations. The United States proved the power of technology in the recent war with Iraq. The businessperson of today who takes advantage of the technology available when preparing business applications such as financing packages or loan applications will enjoy many advantages—advantages that could mean the difference between success and failure.

Making projections for your business will require some real thought on your part. Working through this thought process, finding the ratios that apply to your industry, and studying the details are some of the benefits of having to furnish these projections to an objective onlooker. A banker who asks for projections is learning a number of things about the business, but also about you. If the bank is going to back you financially, the banker certainly wants to know that you have given thought to the future.

A simple way to make the projections is to focus on your profit and loss statement first. Plug in realistic assumptions as to what percent each of your income and expense items will increase or decrease annually. Think about the number of employees you will have, itemize the expenses, and consider how they will be affected. Consider as you grow that some of your basic overhead, such as building, rent, or utilities, will stay relatively stable or increase very slowly. Therefore, your profit margins may increase as you grow, if you keep the growth rate moderate.

In the written proposal, have three projections:

- Best-case scenario
- Worst-case scenario
- Most likely scenario (which will be somewhere in the midrange)

Have these put on a computer program and run out. Simply add or subtract the net profit or loss from your equity capital. You then have a projection of the value of your company.

Your projections should be for a minimum range of three to five years. If you run these projections out to ten years and they show an annual increase of net profit of 7 percent or more, you may be amazed at what happens. As your net margin spread increases, usually overhead and fixed expenses grow at a relatively slow pace.

But even without that effect, look at the simple numbers. Let's assume you earn $100,000 in your first year and that your profits grow by 7 percent a year. Here's what happens to your profits in the first five years:

Year 1	$100,000.00
Year 2	107,000.00
Year 3	114,490.00
Year 4	122,504.30
Year 5	131,079.60

So for the first five years, the assumptions and growth seem ordinary enough. But look what happens in the next five years:

Year 6	$140,255.17
Year 7	150,073.03
Year 8	160,578.14
Year 9	171,818.60
Year 10	183,845.90

The profits projected for the ten years total *over $1.2 million*. Not bad for a small business. That is how much your business will grow in value with only a 7 percent growth rate annually.

This is the kind of study that will attract the attention of your loan committee. Also, working through these exercises will be good for a business, you, and your staff. After all, what high-performance businessperson will not try to do better each year?

Projected Banking Needs

One of the best opportunities you will have to really make points with the bankers comes right after the projection section of the proposal. After you have shown what you expect the future to hold, then you can itemize the types of accounts you think your company will need in the future. It is a way of saying, "As we grow, I plan to be loyal to your bank, and if you will take a look at this, you can see how profitable my business can be for your bank."

In this section you can be as specific as you like. The more specific the better. Here are a few ideas, all of which will warm the cockles of the coldest-hearted banker:

- As the company cash flow increases, we will need additional accounts for:

a. reserve accounts;

b. CDs or time deposits;

c. retirement account or profit-sharing fund;

d. IRAs for individual officers and employees.

- We would like to request that the bank quote a specific rate for employees of our company who may need consumer credit, car loans, etc. We do not demand that you approve their loans but request that we have a set arrangement so that we can inform our employees.

- We may wish to pay this loan off early. If so, we would like the bank to then consider a floating line of credit that we can draw on if we need funds for a major project.

- We would like the bank to provide a special account number series and a printed check logo displaying our company name. In return, we will encourage all employees to open their personal accounts with "our" bank.

- We may wish to place a portion of company dividends into a trust, and if your bank offers trust services, we would like to discuss this with the officer in charge.

- We would like to have a corporate safe-deposit box and will also want to rent a number of boxes for other legal documents.

- We would like an arrangement to purchase traveler's checks at your bank with authorization for the bank to debit our account on short notice for business trips.

- We would like for all officers of our company to be given applications for credit cards issued by your bank.

- Does your bank offer any group accounts that have special benefits?

- On the basis of the above projections, we estimate an average combined balance of $110,000 in your bank. What type of accounts do you recommend?

The questions all beg for answers that benefit your case of wanting to be a good customer of the bank.

Loan Term Scenario

One of the great sales techniques is, Don't ask a yes or no question; give them alternatives that are both positive. Your loan proposal should include at this point a discussion of the terms, the rate, and the payment plan you expect. In most proposals we recommend that you give the bank two alternatives. The banker doesn't have to accept either, but the alternatives are a strong suggestion of what you expect from the bank and may influence the banker's final decision. For example, the wording might be as follows:

> ABC Corporation in its internal planning has concluded that a loan term of 10 years will be optimal. The start-up phase of our new expansion program is estimated to take 6 months before significant cash flow occurs, and we thus would like to start the first regular payment after that phase. [Or you may say, "We feel it most feasible to have ____ months before making regular payments to get additional sales volume under way."]
>
> Semiannual payments are preferred at a rate of prime + 2½. This will fit well within our guidelines. We would like the option of prepayment without penalty and anticipate payoff prior to term.

This sort of phrasing positions you psychologically for the next phase. Rarely do banks like to make long-term loans, and a ten-year payout is very liberal by normal banking standards. The banker will likely focus on the length of the loan instead of the initial period with no payments. Usually the banker prefers monthly payments because it gives the bank an opportunity to compound the interest. For the same reason, the customer prefers quarterly, semiannual, or even annual payments if possible. Such an arrangement lets the customer use the money longer.

Then you will want to include an alternative proposal:

> If the above proposal is unacceptable, the corporation can consider the following. With the consideration of a half point lower interest rate, we can work with a 10-year amortization on a _____-year [you decide what you can best work with, three or five years] balloon. We will begin making payments 6 months from loan closing.

Now you have set expectations and given the banker a way to approve the loan. Also, you have probably established the interest rate for your loan. The banker will likely accept one of your proposals.

Concluding Remarks About Loan, Company, and Bank

The last page of your written loan proposal will have a summary paragraph. The wording might be something like this:

> ABC Corporation believes that our company has a philosophy of service and excellence that is consistent with the philosophy of First National Bank. We believe that a business relationship is just that—a relationship. It is more than just numbers that add up. We have

demonstrated in this proposal that our projections, collateral, cash flow, and capital will justify your confidence in ABC. However, we are seeking more than that, a long-term relationship that will be profitable for all concerned. Implicit in this is a good level of communication. We hope we have made a start by this proposal. We hope and expect that First National Bank will always have an attitude that fosters good communication. We thank you for your help in this matter.

Results of a Thorough Loan Proposal

Your loan proposal doesn't need to be as long as this chapter has been. But if you will take the time and go to the effort to produce a document like the one I have outlined, several results will occur.

First, your banker will likely comment, "Few customers are this well prepared. You have done a good job of putting the facts together for us." In fact, your banker will go to the lending committee and likely brag about the proposal. I can assure you it will be passed around, and every time someone reads even a page, that person will be hearing *your* story.

Also, the banker will respect you. Even if the banker denies your loan, you will have established a basis for a continuing relationship, should it be beneficial to you.

If the loan is denied, this proposal is of such detail that it demands that the banker give you a complete and detailed response. As mentioned earlier, this response will be your map for closing the gap between approval and denial.

The process of putting the information in this proposal together will be productive for you and your staff. It can be used as a good management tool.

Finally, the written proposal is not required. It is not traditional. Rather, it is another tool in your professional effort to give you the best chance possible at approval of your financial request. If it seems too onerous an under-taking, understand this. This tool is for the person who wants to win, and this effort is for those who want every tool at their disposal for winning. You needn't include every section in your proposal. Some sections may even be detrimental. But I can guarantee you this. If you follow this outline, you have vastly increased your chances at loan approval. It is only one step of many, but it is an important step in your preparation.

Delivering Your Proposal

Any discussion about preparation for a loan presentation must deal with the verbal delivery. You have the facts before you. By now you have memorized most of them. But when you prepare for a loan interview, you must prepare as if you were giving the most important speech of your life. You must be sharp-witted, but not short-tempered. You must appear knowledgeable without appearing arrogant. You must be friendly and kind without gushing or coming on too strong. You must be able to project the image of an intelligent businessperson who knows where he or she is going and knows exactly how to get there. The banker must feel that by participating, the bank will be riding a star and making a profit in the process.

Art Johnson came into the bank one day with a loan proposal for a new project he had uncovered. He was going to invest in, of all things, ostriches. Now, this was a number of years ago before ostriches were the high-priced success they are today. A recent report in Texas told of ostriches being so valuable that cattle rustling was out, and ostrich theft in. But when this customer decided to raise them, nobody was even willing to steal an ostrich. He was well ahead of his time.

Art's approach was simple. He had a location with all

of the facilities to raise the big birds. The African laws prevented exportation of ostriches but did not prevent the removal of ostrich eggs. At that time, there were fewer than a thousand ostriches in the entire United States, and nearly all of them were in public zoos. Art had found a tribe of Bushmen who would walk through the African countryside and search for eggs. For just pennies an egg, he could get all of the ostrich eggs he could ship. The trick was packing and shipping, and getting them into the United States. He had worked out a plan to overcome all of the difficulties and last of all needed a loan to take one of his monthly trips to Africa.

By the time Art had finished telling his story, the banker was so intrigued that he was ready to go to Africa too! It sounded like a fun and lucrative way to make a living. Well, that was years ago, and while writing this book, I looked up a current ad in the classified section of my paper. It said, "Ostrich chicks and eggs. Limited supply." I called the number. "How much are your chicks?" I asked.

"Two thousand dollars each," came the reply, and the person who spoke didn't stutter or hesitate.

"Uh . . . how about the eggs?"

"A thousand each, but we only have a few left. We don't guarantee that they will hatch. You know we sell all we can get."

I saw visions of Art putting on his safari suit and jetting off to Africa, buying huge eggs from Bushmen. You see, the vision he implanted in my mind that day is still strong, largely because of his powerful manner of communicating his dream.

You may not consider yourself an "Art," but you have a dream. Think carefully about the way you wish to share that very special dream with your banker. He or she has the power to help. Your preparation will make your banker want to help.

5

Requesting a Specific Type of Loan

The previous chapter described what to tell the banker when you are looking for any type of loan. If you know what your banker will be anticipating for a particular type of loan, you can customize your request. This chapter tells you what to emphasize in a variety of situations, from buying a house to buying a manufacturing facility.

College Loans

A man wrote, "I've got two sons, both approaching college age. We have had some hope of scholarship aid, but not enough to send our boys to college. Do banks make student loans?" The answer is yes, some banks do. There are two programs specifically designed to help in such situations.

First, there is a national student loan program. This program was very popular until a government audit revealed that a high percentage of the students who participated in the program never paid the loans back. This created a political problem, and funding for the program became difficult. The program does still exist, and any college can give you the regional representative to contact. In general, the program offers loans at preferential terms and rates to help pay for basic tuition and college expenses.

The second program is the state college student loan program. Many states have a program like this. The principle is simply that specific banks throughout a state participate in loans to the student and often separate loans to parents for the purpose of college tuition and expenses. (The amount will vary state to state, and depending on which plan is chosen.) The loans are made by local banks with a payout plan that takes into consideration the graduation date and expected postgraduate income of the student. These programs require a good credit rating and copies of the standard financial aid disclosure statements. Any college financial aid department can provide the name and address of the contact person in your area.

Loan to Purchase a Retail Business

Loans to purchase existing businesses will require all of the standard information noted in the checklist earlier in the book, with an emphasis on specific areas. If, for example, the business is a retail department store with retail merchandise and fixtures, the banker is going to be most interested in the operating record and history of the business. You will need to show how good the store's location is, how the business has done for the past five years (provide tax returns or profit and loss statements), what the traffic demographics are, whether the area is growing and prospering, and what the condition of the fixtures is. The banker will also want to know the quality of the inventory in the store.

Before putting a retail business on the market, the seller often runs a sale. Therefore, the best and newest merchandise will have disappeared, leaving only older, counter-worn merchandise. A retail store can look full of inventory but be packed with shelf-worn items that look good on paper but are actually of little value.

In your loan application, don't forget to focus on items sometimes forgotten, such as the business telephone number, name continuation, clerical succession, and community relations. The telephone number of a company that has been in business for years is one of the assets you are buying. Should you lose that number, it could be a year before it is reprinted in the next telephone book, and there is a real business loss when customers can't easily call the store. You are also buying a name that has been advertised for years and is planted in the community psyche. Before changing that name, think carefully to be sure any advantages offset the loss. Clerical succession is important in a retail business. The sometimes intangible feeling of a business is what attracts some customers and should be analyzed. A careful banker will want to know that there are familiar faces in the business who have the benefit and knowledge of both the business and the customers. The banker is interested in a smooth and profitable transition.

In your loan application, also mention what steps you as the new owner will take to cultivate good community relations. Whether your business is in a downtown setting, a small town, or a suburb, community relations are important to a business. The banker will want to know that your business will be a positive part of the community.

Loan to Acquire or Begin a Professional Practice

A professional practice (business for a doctor, lawyer, engineer, or CPA) has a much different stress. There is normally very little equipment or collateral for a professional practice. For example, an existing accounting practice has value only in the number of clients and the amount of billings generated by the practice. Some furniture and basic computers and office equipment are all the assets of substance. The same goes for law firms, with the addition of perhaps a legal library. Doctors' and dentists' offices have more equipment, such as x-ray machines. Indeed, for dental loans, many bankers think of the amount to be borrowed "per chair." They consider that a complete dental work area can run anywhere from $20,000 to $50,000 per chair.

Although the collateral in these types of loans is important, the loan application should emphasize the cash flow generated by the client base, as well as a valuation of the business per client or per patient. For example, in an accounting practice, you would calculate the average billings made per client over a period of five years. If John Doe is billed $1,000 annually and the average length of time he will be a viable customer is five years, this customer is actually worth $5,000 to the practice. If the CPA has 100 customers like John Doe, his annual billings of $100,000 provide a base for the capitalization of the business. If a doctor has 100 patients and the average annual billing to each patient is $1,000, her patient list is worth $100,000. A value of the practice can be established by the banker.

The income can be "capitalized" as an approach to determining value. This is called capitalizing the income stream. The capitalization of an income stream can be accomplished in several ways. One approach that is acceptable is to find the net operating income, then multiply it by a capitalization rate. In the following example, market sources say a reasonable capitalization rate for a particular type of business is 12.5 percent. First find the net income:

Gross income of professional practice	$100,000
Operating expenses	(60,000)
Net operating income	$40,000

Then apply the capitalization rate: $40,000 ÷ .125 = $320,000. In this example, the practice shows a capitalized value of $320,000. For selling the business or applying for a loan, this value could be used to represent what the practice is worth.

Since a professional practice is a service business, the practice has value only to the extent that the professional involved is active and able to produce. Thus, the banker will be interested in knowing there is ample life insurance and disability insurance to pay off any loans that will be accrued. The banker will require that these policies be assigned to the bank. If there is no coverage, the bank will likely not consider the loan until the professional acquires enough.

If the loan is to buy a practice, a noncompete agreement with the previous owner is customary. So is a study estimating how many customers may be lost and gained as a result of the new ownership.

Loan Using a Professional Practice as Collateral

The principles that apply to acquiring or beginning a professional practice also apply when a professional needs financing and wishes to use the practice for collateral. The key in this case is to make a detailed presentation on the cash flow; accounts receivable; furniture, fixtures, and equipment (FF&E); and value of the practice. The goal is to present this information in a fashion that leads the banker to conclude that the practice has a value substantially in excess of the loan request.

Loan to Acquire a Manufacturing Facility or Use It for Collateral

In the case of a manufacturing facility, one of the major factors is the condition, value, and efficiency of function of the manufacturer's fixed assets. For example, if the company manufactures furniture, the business is going to require ample real estate, buildings to warehouse and ship, construction and finishing facilities, and a variety of specialized equipment. The loan application should stress the details of the real estate, including a current appraisal. The equipment section of the loan application should include a report and inspection by an expert in the field, reporting the condition as well as practical functions for the equipment. If any equipment is obsolete or requiring repairs, this should be disclosed.

After a detailed review of the fixed assets and equipment, the loan application should include a focus on the market for the product, the customer base, the future of demand for the product, and a specific record of past sales, collections, and accounts receivable with aging. A manufacturing facility will require extensive labor, and the status of employer-employee relations, salaries, and benefits will be of interest to the banker. Obviously, a company that is obligated to spend money on extensive fringe benefits or long-term profit sharing, bonus plans, or retirement plans will attract close scrutiny from the bank to

determine that the expense of these items does not en-
danger the security of the business and ultimately the
quality of the loan.

The loan application should also include a section
addressing environmental concerns and product liability.
A manufacturing facility will by nature have an impact
upon the environment, and a loan application that includes a Phase One environmental statement will impress
the banker. (Chapter 14 provides more guidance on addressing environmental concerns.) The loan application
can address product liability by listing liability complaints
and related lawsuits and losses with a summary of the final
outcome and cost to the company. A letter from the
company's insurance carrier verifying that insurance coverage is in place to cover said losses, along with a section
explaining the company's policy of eliminating or properly
handling liability concerns, should be included in the loan
application.

Loan to Acquire a Radio or TV Station or a Newspaper

For any kind of media loan, the emphasis will be on the
ratings measuring the viewing or listening audience or the
subscription and circulation numbers of the newspaper.
This industry is an entirely different world of finance, and
you will have to search for a bank that will handle the
application. In addition to the standard items, the loan
application will have to carry specific sections evaluating
the market area, then complete projections as to the
impact and plans of new ownership to increase circulation
or the audience.

The premium on broadcasting stations and newspapers (their excess value above the value of their fixed
assets) is very high. The reasons for this in broadcasting

have often been the expense, delay, and difficulty in getting government approval for new stations. The government by its policies has essentially assured that there is a good resale market for broadcasting stations well in excess of the value of the fixed assets and equipment of those stations. In the case of newspapers, the fixed expense and start-up costs are so high as to prevent newcomers to the industry. In addressing these issues, the loan application should include matters such as the media personalities, columnists, their contracts, and the introduction of new "stars" to the market and the financial impact. References to professional awards and recognition are important because these increase circulation, readership, and value to the franchise.

A capitalization of the income stream will be appropriate in the application, as well as a detailed listing of other sales of stations or newspapers to assist the banker in determining value. A letter from an industry broker verifying the marketability of the asset will give the banker a comfort level with regard to asset market value when making a loan presentation to the loan committee.

Loan to Buy a Golf Course or Country Club

In an exotic type of investment such as a resort, golf course, marina, or airport, it is important to establish value. The means of establishing value are found by finding some kind of service, product, or characteristic of the industry group and interpreting it into a financial indicator. In a loan application for a golf course, you will want to focus on the industry and how golf courses are valued. The stress will be upon memberships, green fees, and the general revenues of the course. When the economy is in decline, it is normal for the replacement cost of a golf course to be far higher than the comparable market value.

In a strong economy, the opposite may be true. After determining the income of the course and the number of greens, fairways, sand traps, and lakes, as well as the number and dimensions of amenities such as clubhouses, tennis courts, restaurant facilities, and dressing rooms, there is a means of comparison.

A loan review officer on the staff of the FDIC liquidation office, which is in charge of the huge portfolio of loans the FDIC has inherited from failed banks, told me that the value of golf courses is usually determined with a calculation based on the "value per green." For example, in comparing five country clubs, their replacement cost, their income stream, and their market value, a value is set based on the average price per green for comparable golf courses that have sold. So an eighteen-hole country club might be valued at $200,000 per green, or $3.6 million. Golf courses might bring a premium in some instances or areas such as Florida or southern California. When the economy is strong, a given area might command $400,000 per green as an economic tool to determine value of the course.

All of these factors will be included in the loan proposal, including an income capitalization study and extensive inspection photographs of the course and the facility. When the banker sees that the cash flow from the facility, as well as the resale value on the open market, are such that the bank's risk proves to be acceptable, then the bank can make a recommendation on the loan. In exotic types of properties, the cash flow and capitalization rates take on a substantially greater importance than in an industry or investment that is "asset based."

Loan for a Print Shop

There is a vast difference between borrowing money to acquire a country club and borrowing to purchase a print shop. Likely far more people will be buying businesses like print shops than golf courses. A print shop is a good example of a business that combines retailing and provides a service.

Print shops are excellent candidates for SBA loans, discussed in Chapter 8. There is rarely enough equipment and inventory to collateralize a large loan. Since a large portion of a printing shop's business is cash payment when the job is complete, there is usually a minimal value in accounts receivable. Most print shops invoice every thirty days, and some weekly. But these businesses, if managed aggressively, can be excellent cash generators. They require constant overseeing and management.

The items to stress in the loan application are the printing sales record for the past two years and the projected income. A review of the collection performance for the customer base will be helpful. The loan application should include a comprehensive list of the regular customers of the business and the amount of business each has produced in the past year, as well as a projection of future performance based upon their average monthly payments. A copy of the lease or rental arrangements for the location will be necessary, and the loan application should include some impressive samples of the quality and range of work the shop produces. Who knows, if you don't get the loan, perhaps you will at least get some more printing business from the bank!

Loan to Acquire or Expand an Automobile Business

If the loan is to acquire a name brand dealership for a major automobile manufacturer, a matter of interest will be contractual agreements with the national distributor. Some national companies require the dealer to commit to regular building expansion as a condition of carrying that brand of vehicle. Dealers are often under pressure to build new buildings and showrooms, putting them under greater financial pressure. Other terms of the national distributor that should be addressed in the loan application are those concerning auto inventory supply, billing and grace periods, and internal financing. The bank should, from the loan proposal, be able to quickly and easily interpret how much and what collateral the bank can take that is not encumbered by any other party. A study or comparison of other dealerships in the area, including sales figures, inventory turnover, and market price of the dealerships if available, will add greatly to the loan application. Access to other name brands or lines should be disclosed, as well as a discussion of title control, parts department performance, service department costs and income, and similar figures on the leasing department, if any.

If the dealership is a used-auto dealership, the bank will rely on the inventory to be used for collateral, as well as on other collateral such as the real estate of the business. Many used-car dealers have extensive financing arrangements. There are ways the bank can participate in that financing to assist the dealer, but the bank will also require assignment on all of the "paper" (notes receivable). Many times a bank will enter into a financing arrangement with the dealer with the agreement that the dealer will place a portion of the sales proceeds of each auto sale into a reserve account at the bank. This reserve account protects the bank against possible losses in the event of defaults. If the dealer and the bank are careful in their loan underwriting practices, the reserve account can accumulate over a period of time to a substantial amount.

The biggest exposure banks have is in the area of inventory and collateral control. The bank cannot go out to the dealership every day and inspect the cars it has for collateral. Therefore, the loan proposal should address and provide a system of inventory control and accounting that assures the bank that all collateral is under strict control at all times. To reemphasize a point that will help greatly with the loan approval process, stress in the application the volume of sales and the amount of money that will be deposited to the bank both in the sales account and in the reserve account. These figures can be substantial and can therefore be a real incentive to a profit-conscious bank.

Loan to Buy a Farm or Ranch

Farm and ranch loans often go to government-assisted lending agencies such as the Farmers Home Administration (FmHA), Federal Land Bank, or Production Credit Associations. But banks and savings and loan institutions also make these loans.

Key to the approval process is valuation of collateral. These are called asset-based loans because the proceeds and purpose of the loan go to buy fixed assets, with a small percentage used for operating expenses (at least in the acquisition process). The loan proposal should stress appraisals of the real estate as well as inspections and photographs of the crops, cattle, equipment, or other agricultural chattels. Cattle and crops are liquid collateral, so these should be itemized with a verification of market prices (newspaper price quotes, etc.) included and extended in the report.

Include a study of the balance sheet and tax returns of the borrower, showing that you are stable and have ample resources to manage the operation. Background information of your experience, training, and success in the agricultural field will be helpful, since few industries are as complex and have as many uncontrollable variables as agriculture.

Loan to Buy a House

Among the easiest loans to obtain are loans to buy a house, since the housing industry and the S&L industry have so standardized the process. Therefore, not much discussion is required here. In general, your net cash flow on a monthly basis should be at least four times what the house payment is projected to be. You should have at least 10 percent of the price for a cash down payment (although 20 percent would be better and would reduce your interest burden). You will need to be prepared to complete the standard loan application, which is an abbreviated financial statement and cash flow budget. An appraisal will require that the loan be no more than 80 percent of the appraised value of the house (although some programs, such as loans backed by the Veterans Administration or Federal Housing Administration, will finance a higher percent). Above all, the loan application should include and stress your disposable income from all sources. Income ratios are a primary factor in approval of these loans.

Loan to Acquire an Apartment Complex

Many lenders have an attitude that the real estate of an apartment complex is the least valuable aspect of the investment. The logic is that the two most important factors of an apartment complex are the quality of management and the ratio of occupancy. These are the areas the loan application should stress.

Although a comprehensive appraisal is necessary, if a loan applicant can show an occupancy rate high enough to generate funds to cover operating expenses, pay any debt service, and have funds left over for management, the applicant will have a good chance of approval. If the complex requires 95 percent occupancy just to break even, a banker will view it as a high-risk project. If the project can break even at 85 percent occupancy or less, it begins to have more investment appeal.

When the banker goes out to inspect an apartment complex, it is most impressive to find sharp and responsive management on-site. The banker should be able to see tangible results of good management. Clean, trim grounds, well-maintained apartments, and an accounting system right on top of rents, past dues, taxes, and fixed payments says much for the management of the complex. In addition, the loan proposal should specifically address the following questions:

- What plans are there to increase occupancy?
- What immediate expenditures are necessary on the complex?
- What is the average turnover rate of residents in this complex, and do you plan to lower this turnover?
- What will the market bear on rents, and how will rents be adjusted in this complex?
- What is the lowest minimum occupancy for break-even?
- What sources of funds are available if occupancy falls below that level?
- If you consider selling, what is the absorption time (anticipated time the property will stay on the market until a sale occurs) for a complex like this one?
- How strong is the market for apartment complexes like the subject property?
- What are contingency plans in the event of increases in taxes, insurance premiums, or interest rates?

- What is the projected cash flow for the apartment complex over a five-year period?
- What major maintenance will be required over the next five years?
- Are there any changes in the neighborhood or the economy that will change the nature of the tenancy?
- Have the apartments been checked for environmental safety (for example, radon or asbestos)?
- Do the apartments comply with city code, safety standards, and zoning?
- What is the remaining useful economic life of the complex?

Loan to Buy an Automobile

A lot more people will be buying cars than golf courses or apartment complexes, and there are some considerations that a first-time borrower should know. Bankers know that although profit margins in the automobile industry have narrowed with the new global economy, there are still hidden rebates and incentives for dealers. For example, new cars have 12 percent to 21 percent dealer profit included in the sticker price. Therefore, if you wish to purchase a $20,000 car, the banker realizes that the wholesale cost of that vehicle might be $16,000, and he or she will prefer to lend something less than that. Most bankers have a rule of thumb on new-car financing: lend no more than 75 percent of the sticker price or 80 percent of what is actually paid.

With this in mind, many dealers (because of their built-in overhead and profit structure) will offer better new-car financing terms than banks. It is wise to shop around for the vehicle and the financing.

The banker must take into consideration depreciation

on the vehicle. He or she will establish a payment schedule that assures that the amount owed on the automobile will never be over the depreciated wholesale value. Some new-car models will lose 20 percent of resale value the day they are driven off the lot. Other vehicles depreciate rapidly at first, then stabilize, with some occasional rare classics actually appreciating in value. The best buy is a one- or two-year-old vehicle in excellent condition, which has already suffered the "new-car premium depreciation" but still looks new.

Other than these factors, automobile lending rules are similar to those for other loans. All of the Cs of credit—credit, collateral, cash flow, character, and capital—must be in order (see Chapter 6).

One word of advice. Bankers have wholesale, retail, and loan values on every vehicle model at their fingertips. Ask your banker if you can review his or her data book *before* you go shopping. Your banker might give you some insights that will save you money.

6

The Loan Interview:
Marketing Yourself

Earlier I mentioned one of the great ironies of banking: By careful public education over hundreds of years of tradition, bankers have developed the perception that they are "keepers of the money" and that you, the borrower, must beg for a loan. Eddy Chiles, the famous entrepreneur who made millions in the oil field service industry, coined the phrase "He who has the gold makes the rules." This saying contains an element of truth. But let me coin a new phrase for you, for it is also true that in the banking business "Thy banker must lend, or he'll have no gold."

The Great Charade is that the banker must be begged for a loan and that you, the borrower, are the beggar. This charade must be eliminated if you are to have a good relationship with your banker. It is better still to get on a mental level where you have an understanding with your banker. You should enter the contract with these points in mind: "The banker has a challenge—to make good loans. I have a need for a good loan. Now let's get the two together and see how we can work as a team to fashion an agreement that is good for everyone." As soon as you can get to this working understanding, you will have removed several ego and emotional obstacles to the achievement of your goal. But what if you run into a banker who insists on playing the part of the paternalistic banker? You must decide whether to play the game, knowing well that it is an ego game that can backfire on you, or whether to find another banker.

Your Advantages

If the banker is posturing for a position of control or strength, you as the borrower can also do a little posturing of your own. First of all, you have some strengths that you should capitalize upon. You can offer to keep large balances or to pay a slightly higher rate of interest. You can create a sense that your business or entity has such great potential that it will ultimately be a major depositor for the bank. The following pages elaborate on these and other sources of power. The examples here are but a few of the possibilities.

Money in the Bank

If you followed the checklist, you will have opened an account at the bank. This gives you some leverage. You need to make it known that you are glad to have your account there, with the hint that you would hate to have to move it to another bank. New customers don't grow on trees in the current competitive environment. The more accounts you have at the bank, the greater your value as a customer. If you can influence corporate accounts, your church, civic clubs, or other organizations to move their accounts to or away from your bank, you should make that known as well. A banker will think twice before driving away a good customer.

On the other hand, if you are banking with Third National or Merrill Lynch and you want a loan from First National, you have shot yourself in the foot from the beginning. A particular irritant to some bankers is the customer who removes his or her deposits from the local bank yet insists upon asking the bank for loans. Often the small percentage advantage that a customer might gain from moving deposits to a money market fund away from the bank is an expensive lesson when a loan is denied (or approved, but at a much higher rate than if the borrower had all his or her deposits with the bank). Keeping your deposits with the bank communicates a message of loyalty to the banker. These are subtle things, rarely discussed by the banker, but they are noticed.

The Facts

Another source of strength is the sheer weight of the facts you have accumulated supporting the validity of your loan. If you have properly put together a loan proposal, the facts will weigh in your favor. Emotions are powerful, but truth also is powerful. If your business is profitable, your collateral good, your past beyond reproach, and your future projections based upon sound assumptions, the power is on your side.

Your Reputation

A great source of strength is your friends and your standing in the community. What friends do you have in high places who want to see you succeed? Billy Conn was considered one of the greatest boxers of all time. When his fan and admirer J. Knox McConnell of Pittsburgh needed a job and wanted to go into banking, he went to Billy

Conn. Now, Billy Conn was known all over the world . . .
especially after his famous heavyweight championship
fight with Joe Louis, which lasted thirteen rounds. Billy
Conn was making big money; some of his fights netted
him hundreds of thousands of dollars. He knew presidents,
he knew movie stars. He was a celebrity without question,
and all the more popular because he was also a man of
integrity and honor. Billy Conn's recommendation was
enough to cause the banker to have a sympathetic ear
toward Billy Conn's young friend. J. Knox McConnell became a very successful banker in his own right and now
operates one of the best banks in West Virginia.

Friends and contacts can increase your power with
the banker. Let me give another example. In one loan
committee I presented a loan request from an individual
who wanted to borrow using an old warehouse as collateral. The collateral was not all that great, and the customer had only mediocre credit. But the chairman of the
board spoke up with this comment: "Larry is big in the
Rotary Club. I am in that club, and everyone in town
knows and likes him. He can't afford to default on a loan.
He has too high a profile." That loan was approved by the
committee. Friends give you additional power.

The Power of Integrity

I once did a study of the thirty main sources of power in
our culture. Money, title, the car you drive, a nice office—
all of these things bring you power. So do the country
club, memberships on boards, access to media, ability to
communicate, political contacts, even the church you
attend. But one of the most powerful forces that is often
unrecognized and untapped is the power of integrity.
When your very presence communicates integrity, you
have tapped into a rich source of power.

This power is not unnoticed by a good banker. A

banker is constantly hit with schemes and projects presented by people who will take every opportunity to exploit and cheat the bank. A good banker realizes that integrity is the central power that leads to good business. When a loan applicant puts up collateral, signs legal agreements, and agrees to pay the loan back, it is all worth very little unless the borrower has good character and high integrity.

In one instance one of my banks had a loan to a man who owned a chain of auto parts stores. The company filed bankruptcy, and on that day I placed a nervous call to "Jones" to feel his pulse. I had always liked him and considered him a fine human being. When he answered the telephone, I said, "Jones, I know you are hurting now, but you have a friend in me. If there is anything I or my bank can do to help you, you know we are here."

He continued to make his payments to my bank, even though all of the other banks lost everything they had loaned him. Years later he told me, "Ben, the other banks put me out of business. They called my loans and forced me to file bankruptcy. They were abusive and unreasonable and treated me like a crook. That day when you called, it meant a lot to me. It brought tears to my eyes. You treated me like a human being . . . with respect. Like you trusted me. I'll never forget you for that." And I, the banker, will never forget that he had integrity. That is why I loaned him the money in the first place, and it was his integrity that kept him paying.

Your integrity is a big factor in your future dealings as well. If your banker doesn't see it, you need to find a way to communicate your values . . . or at least let your banker see who you really are. Your credit report tells what you look like on a computer record. Your personal integrity has to be communicated in a far different way, and your integrity will give you more power to obtain your objectives.

It is a power that is respected by the most powerful people. Supreme Court Justice William O. Douglas made a curious speech one day, a speech to the winds while he stood atop Old Snowy Peak in the Cascade Mountains. It was his outrage at the littleness of some men, and his appreciation for the power of character and integrity. He said in part:

> As I stood in the cold gale peering into the steep canyons, the froth of life seemed to blow away. I thought of vain men, pacing up and down on the platform, waving their arms, filling the air waves with their noisy complaints. I thought of clever men gaining advantages by trick and cunning. I thought of men who by manipulation got verdicts and judgments and wealth they did not deserve. . . . Old Snowy has no deceit or cunning . . . it is the great equalizer in a world where infinite evil works hard to get permanent footing.

Then he continued to point out that if he could just get all of the unethical, evil men on the top of that mountain, that

> the wind would clear the air of the vain boasts of men. The petty politician would stand naked; and in his nakedness his character would be revealed. The peddler of gossip would be deprived of his pen and his smirk; he would stand whimpering and friendless. Schemes would fall helplessly from men's lips on this rock ridge . . . judged by the harmony of his soul, by his spiritual strength, by the purity of his heart.

When you stand before the banker and the loan committee, integrity is your greatest power.

The Power of Confidence

When you are posturing for a loan, it is best not to posture as someone who is desperate, but rather as someone who sees an opportunity and is giving the bank a chance to participate in it with you. Your stature of confidence and pride in what you are and what your company is doing is a powerful tool. Many people are fearful of their banker. Some people put a banker on a pedestal.

One of the great bankers of Ft. Worth was a man named Mr. Manire. I never knew his first name. My father banked with him when I was a boy, and always respectfully called him Mr. Manire. He was important to our family, for he made the loan that put my father in business. We respected Mr. Manire, and perhaps he sensed that everyone in our family held him in too high regard. My father was always a little nervous when he went to see the banker, until one day Mr. Manire said, "Melvin, you know a lot of people think that bankers are gods. The sad part of it is that some bankers begin to believe them, and begin to act like gods. But I am no better a man than you are. Have confidence in yourself!" After that day, although my father's respect for Mr. Manire didn't wane, he felt a little less nervous about asking for a loan.

Personal confidence is a bestseller. Many times bankers deny loans solely on the basis that the person who is asking seems so nervous and insecure that the banker believes there must be something wrong. On the other hand, I can tell you that many loans have been approved as a result of the confident stature of the person presenting the facts. A key word here is *facts*. When the facts are on your side, you have reason to be confident.

The Power of Salesmanship

There is great power in being persuasive. Something that cannot be accounted for on the checklist you complete is the power of salesmanship you employ when you present yourself and the facts. Salesmanship can be used to unlock the vault doors for your business. You must learn to sell your loan application in a quiet and confident way.

I will discuss this later in the chapter, but let me provide a classic example. One of my good banking customers was Lee Goodman, prominent Texas businessman. At one time he had a net worth of over $30 million. His assets spread over several states, and he was considered by all to be a mover and a shaker. But when Lee called my bank to set up an appointment, I always dreaded the loan interview. It was not because I didn't like him; one could not keep from liking him. It was not because he didn't pay his loans back; Lee always paid. It was not a question of dishonesty; Lee Goodman was an honest man, a good human being. The reason I dreaded his loan interviews was that regardless of the constraints under which I was operating, regardless of the economy, regardless of how much he had borrowed, Lee was such a persuasive salesman that he almost always talked me into making a loan to him. Not that the loans were bad, mind you. That is not the point. The point is that bankers like to feel that they have the power and are in control. This man was so persuasive that he managed to gain control by the sheer power of salesmanship.

There is a lesson to be learned here. The cold, fisheyed banker with whom you must deal is a human being. The calculated distancing that he or she maintains may just be a defense mechanism. Your salesmanship is a powerful tool. Use it in your loan interview.

Aura of Success

The perception that you are a winner is a powerful tool. There is so much failure and grief in this world that everyone is attracted to someone who seems to be able to win success from the jaws of failure. Some people exude success.

Now, I'm not talking about the success that we see hyped so much by the motivational crowd. I'm speaking of something deeper and more genuine. The person or business that consistently practices a philosophy of business and life that results in real success creates an aura that is far beyond superficial hype.

People and businesses want to be aligned with winners. It may be the reason some people join expensive country clubs. They believe that a huge entrance fee and enormous monthly dues are worth the expense if it enables them to associate with a circle of successful contacts. But many businesspeople never join clubs, thinking that they don't have trouble associating with the successful of this world. One of the best ways to gain the respect of other successful businesspeople is through your personal diligence, integrity, and efficiency. Nobody appreciates these traits more than others who have endeavored and succeeded themselves.

Perhaps an experience from the world of banking will best illustrate the point about the power and aura of success. A local businessman came into the bank one day, but he did not come in unprepared. He had previously visited with one of our vice presidents while that VP had been out doing public relations calls for the bank. When the man came in, he acted a little coy and said, "I normally bank with the big banks." The statement thrown into the conversation was like waving bait at a hungry fish. We went after him aggressively. We checked his background, made a few telephone calls, and heard that he was a successful developer and investment syndicator. Then we invited *him* to come back to the bank.

When he came in for the appointment, he came in a late-model Mercedes, wearing an expensive suit, and ac-

companied by the president of one of his companies.
During the conversation, we learned that he had a condo-
minium in Colorado, a private airplane, and over fifty
investment entities. We were impressed. After the niceties,
we asked him for some of his loan business. He pulled out
a stack of papers from his briefcase and presented a professional and complete loan application. "I don't know if
you are big enough," he quipped. According to his extensive information, the man was worth $15 million and had
income of over $1 million per year. And he was going to
bank with us! My VP almost had his tongue hanging out,
wanting to lend this man money.

The customer requested a $500,000 loan secured by
an oil field compressor that was valued (by his file appraisal) at $500,000 but that the man had just bought (at
a bargain) for $400,000. We decided to be conservative, so
we counterproposed a loan of $400,000 provided he put
up the equipment and $200,000 in CDs as additional
collateral. On paper we had $700,000 in collateral on a
loan of $400,000 and got a deposit of $200,000 to boot.
We figured that we had made a smart business deal, for we
in fact were lending him $200,000 of his own money and
making a profit while doing so.

Then came the coup de grace. When the loan documents were prepared, instead of signing them, this new
customer scratched out large portions of the language that
he thought gave the bank too many rights against him. We
objected. His explanation: "Well, at all my other banks, I
never sign everything they prepare." We were impressed
that he had the confidence to try that. We still made him
sign our documents and felt that we had made a good
transaction.

What was the intangible contributing factor that won
the day for this customer with the bank? His aura of
success. Of course, he had a big financial statement, per-

fect credit, and he knew how to package collateral, but what really topped it all off was his style. The guy was obviously a winner, and we wanted to get in on the action. He had the aura of success and had played the part perfectly. He had successfully made a bank want to open its vault doors to him.

Playing the Part

Successfully negotiating in the borrowing jungle is like playing a part in a great play. The borrower is required to take the role of a person who has an attitude of not really needing the money but considering borrowing from this bank "if the terms are right." The implication is that there are other banks that would like to have the business.

In analyzing what it takes to play the part well and posture properly for a loan application, the example of the gentleman with the Mercedes is an excellent one to analyze. Just what did that man do so well?

- He played hard to get.
- He let the bank solicit him.
- He came with all the trappings of success.
- When he arrived at the bank, he was well prepared.
- He carried on his negotiations with skill.
- He had the intelligence and confidence to challenge the bank a little but not to the point of destroying the deal.
- He skillfully made known his past successes.
- He planted in the mind of his banker an anticipation of future success.
- He allowed the bank to make a profitable loan.

You can refine these ideas so that they fit your own situation. Subtle nuances help present an image, and borrowers need all the help they can get. Let me expand with a few tips.

Dressing for Success

Dress well. Why do you dress up for an important date? Why do families put on their "Sunday best" to go to church? What would you wear if you were going to meet a senator or some other important person? As simple as it may sound, when you are applying for a loan, it is time for you to look your best. That loan interview may be far more important to your personal life or the life of your business than the meeting with a senator.

Good grooming creates an image from the start. You don't need to be fake about it. You don't need to spend a fortune on a new outfit. But wear something neat, clean, and stylish. John came to the bank in his work jeans. The first thought a banker might have is that the customer couldn't afford better, or that he does not think it important to look clean for a business interview.

For men, nothing can beat a dark suit—pinstripes are ideal—with a white shirt and a conservative red tie. This is called a "power suit." It gives you the look of authority. The banker is likely wearing one as well, for the same reason. He wants to have the image of authority and success.

For women, an appropriate outfit might be a dark suit (pinstripes are best) with a white blouse. Please avoid anything too revealing or sexy. There is nothing that will turn a professional male banker off quicker than the perception that a customer is trying to use sex appeal to influence his decision.

Appropriate dressing is the point. If you are a rancher in Montana, a dark pinstripe might be as inappropriate as jeans covered with manure. But a clean Western outfit, a well-pressed shirt, and a good-looking hat might win the day for you.

Experienced bankers agree that what you wear makes a difference. E. J. Schnaidt, president of the Menno State Bank in Menno, South Dakota, said, "If an individual has pride in himself [or herself], this will often carry over into taking care of the handling of the loan." Roy Heetland is a CPA from Sioux Falls, South Dakota, specializing in bank services. He reviews hundreds of bank loans throughout South Dakota. He told me, "Appearance is an indication of how serious the individual is and how much importance they put on the money to be borrowed."

Persuasive Speaking

Speak with confidence, enthusiasm, intelligence, and persuasiveness. Your communication doesn't have to be in the King's English, but good grammar is a must. Think about your words. Speak slowly and carefully.

Communicate exactly what is on your mind, and volunteer nothing extra unless the banker asks for it. Don't fall into the trap of bankers like the one we will call George Ivy. He used to brag that by being silent he could force any loan applicant into talking him- or herself out of a loan. He simply let people say too much.

It has been said that most people will remember only a fraction of what you say, but how well you say it will be remembered in full. If you are not a good communicator, bring in a vice president or someone else with your company who is a good communicator, and let that person do the talking. Even Moses had a spokesman in Aaron.

The Scheduling Advantage

Set up your appointment well in advance for a day that will be to your advantage. By this time the banker should know who you are and have some background information on your business. (Remember the checklist.)

Some successful borrowers believe that the day of the week chosen for the interview is important. An apartment contractor who was hugely successful at borrowing money built his fortune up from $5,000 to over $7 million in a span of fifteen years. He swears that he did it all with borrowed money. Here is his suggestion for what day to set up an appointment:

> Always set up your appointment on Friday at 10:00 A.M., and never on a Monday. Why? Friday is a good day, the week is gone, the banker is looking forward to the weekend and is in a good mood. It is a good time to talk business with him. Never set up an appointment on a Monday. The banker is grouchy, he is anticipating all the problems of the week. Wednesday is second best if Friday is unavailable. Why? Loan committees usually meet on Wednesday or Thursday afternoons and the banker can take your application directly to committee.

Never set an appointment on the day of a board of directors meeting. The reason is that the banker is under stress and busier than usual preparing for the board meeting and has a lot on his or her mind. Hundreds of things can happen at a board meeting, many of which are bad for a bank officer. That's not a good time for you to pop in with a new loan idea.

As a friendly reminder, call the banker's secretary the morning of the appointment, just to confirm that you will be there. It might save a wasted trip.

Questions to Ask

Some specific points to make in the original loan interview are critical at the very onset. Before you initiate any discussion regarding your loan request, you should ask the banker a few basic questions:

What is the condition of the bank? Is it profitable and sound? Now, no banker in his or her right mind is going to tell you that the bank is in bad condition or is about to go bust. But you may be able to pick up some general hints as to how strong the bank is.

Follow up by asking, *how much capital does the bank have?* This is critical because banks are limited in the size of their loans as a percentage of capital. For example, at this writing, a national bank is limited to loan any one customer no more than 15 percent of its capital. Therefore, if the bank has only $1 million in capital, it could lend you and your business combined no more than $150,000. If it has $10 million in capital, it can lend you $1.5 million. Thus, the answer to this question will help you determine at the onset if the bank is capable of lending you what you currently or ultimately may need.

What is the bank's capital ratio? This is critical because federal guidelines require that a bank keep a minimum percentage of capital. A capital ratio is the bank's ratio of capital to total assets. For example, a bank with $100 million in total assets and $10 million in capital has a 10 percent capital ratio. If the bank has a low capital ratio, the bank will be far more conservative in its lending practices. For example, if a bank has a 10 percent capital ratio, it is well above guidelines, and the bank is in good shape. The banker will feel comfortable taking on new customers and backing them when they need it. But a capital ratio of 5 percent or less may be a signal that the bank is struggling. It is certainly below federal guidelines, and the bank may be unable to lend you what you need, even if the loan officer approves your credit and likes your company.

What is the bank's legal lending limit? By now the

banker will have determined that you are not the average loan applicant and that you know a little about banking. The banker should appreciate your questions, but if they put him or her on the defensive, this is a red flag for you. Again, this question gives you information that you need and have a right to know.

What is the loan officer's noncommittee loan limit? If the banker is going to get embarrassed, this is where it will happen. It is a matter of prestige in the industry to have an authorized loan limit that is high. If your officer flushes and says it is none of your business, you should simply say, "If we are to do business with each other, we are going to have to know a great deal of confidential information about each other. You will know the finest detail about my finances. I need to know your ability to work with me." If the banker still refuses, you should go on to find another loan officer. If his or her noncommittee loan limit is $10,000 and you are going to need credit in the $100,000 range, you will need a higher-ranking officer. If his or her limit is $50,000 and you will be borrowing anywhere from $30,000 to $80,000, you may want to stay with that banker. In the past five years, banks have had a trend of reducing individual officer limits. Some banks require that every loan over $20,000 be brought to a committee for final approval. If this is the case with your bank, you want to discuss this fully with your banker and see how he or she will be able to work with you in a timely and efficient manner.

What is this bank's philosophy and policy of lending now? This is important because if the bank is a very old, conservative family-run institution, its bankers may not be willing to lend much to new customers. They may have a preference for one type of loan over another. They may prefer one industry group over another. For example, many banks refuse to lend on real estate, while aggressively seeking car loans or accounts receivable loans. Also, the bank may be going through a cyclical change. For example, a lot of new loans may have come on the books with few new deposits, so management has decided to cut back on all new loans until deposits catch up with loans. Or the bank may have reached its limit in small-business loans and have decided to stress mortgage loans. You need to know what the bank's current status is.

What is the bank's policy toward my business (or industry or profession)? Some banks have a written policy that they will not entertain or encourage certain types of loans. You need to be sure your bank can and is willing to help you without any policy restrictions. If, for example, you are borrowing money to put in a new restaurant, it may be wise at this point to ask, "Do you have loan funds and resources available for a new restaurant business?" The banker will certainly hedge a little by not making a firm commitment to lend to you, but he or she should also give you some indication of the banker's and the bank's attitude.

Size of Loan Request

As a rule of thumb, it is important not to ask for very small loans, which can cause you to be categorized as a small customer. Bankers will set by memorandum a limit that they think it is OK to lend to you. For example, a millionaire once came in the bank and asked me for a $5,000 loan. I turned him down because I feared something was wrong. And I was right; he was in a cash flow crunch and on the verge of going bankrupt. Had he requested $50,000, I might not have even questioned the request and wouldn't have picked up on anything being wrong.

If you just need $5,000, go ahead and borrow $25,000. Pay back the $20,000 the next week. It will make you look good to the banker and will keep you from being categorized in a smaller range.

Knowledge About the President

Try to learn the attitude of the bank's chairman or president toward you or your industry. Get to know that person if you can. Ask a lot of questions in the community. Regardless how enthusiastic a loan officer may be toward your credit line, if the president doesn't like you or your business, you are out of luck.

The ABCs of the Loan Interview

You have done a great deal of preliminary work to get to the loan interview. You know how important this meeting is, and you know that your performance in this interview—the facts you present and the way you present them—will either open another opportunity or close it. You are prepared, and you know it. Now let me give you a perspective from the banker's point of view. If you can get into the banker's head, you have a better understanding of how to meet his or her needs. When you do that, then the banker will be willing to meet your needs.

First, be conscious of the pressures on the banker. Bankers are in a titled position that gives them prestige, prestige beyond the actual salary they make. It is not unusual for a banker to make less money than the people who borrow from him or her. So why do bankers do what they do? The prestige is an important factor. Most bankers believe that their position is an important and powerful part of the society in which they live. In many cases a bank vice president's title is an important part of his or her compensation. So treat that title with respect, and treat the banker with the courtesy and respect his or her position and self-image require.

Also remember the time pressures on the banker. A good banker has to deal with large numbers of people. He or she may be servicing $15 million in loans or $150 million in loans, and each customer requires his or her time and attention. While dealing with present loan customers, the banker also has to deal with the bank examiners. It is not unusual for bankers to spend as much as 50 percent of their time dealing with regulatory questions and meeting compliance guidelines, especially since the advent of FIRREA and other stringent banking regulations. The banker must deal with bank stockholders, especially at a community-owned bank. He or she must deal with the bank's own internal auditors. Often a great deal of time is required of the banker to acquire documentation in new files or to organize and clean up existing loan files. The banker must deal with his or her immediate supervisors, who will be continually pressuring the banker to make good loans and collect the loans on the books. He or she must deal with walk-in customers of the bank, many of whom do not have a loan request but simply want to visit. Some of these customers are practicing one of the suggestions in this book, building a friendship and rapport with the banker.

The banker must stay abreast of regulations. Periodically every banker is given a stack of regulations and memorandums from government agencies that would thwart most people. While I was a bank president, my stack of regulations averaged about two inches thick a week. And the banker, by law, is supposed to read and abide by these laws! Kenneth Littlefield, former State Banking Commissioner of Texas, had to supervise all of the state bank examiners. He told me that the average banker cannot possibly read, much less absorb and properly respond to, all of the regulations and memorandums that come out of the various banking agencies. He said the sad part of it was that "Examiners have to examine banks and interview bankers as if we really expected them to do so." Then the banker has the normal responsibilities of dealing with employees, doing public relations and sales work for the business, and going to the various banking schools to upgrade his or her professional skills. As you can see, the typical banker is very busy.

I recently walked into the office of an outstanding bank president named Gaylean McCune. As I entered his office, I recognized a familiar expression on his face. It was a mixture of "glad to see you" and "I really don't have time to see another human being." That is a standard feeling most bankers have.

A banker is apt to laugh if you mention "banker's hours." An adage used to go that a banker used a 10-6-2 system: at work by ten, charge 6 percent interest, and on the golf course by two. If that legend were ever true, which is doubtful, it certainly isn't true today. Bankers often arrive at the office to prepare for their own meetings long before "banking hours." Often they don't get out of their meetings until 9:00 A.M., at which time a number of customers and telephone messages usually are already waiting for them. They have three hours until noon, then from 1:00 to 3:00 P.M. another two hours available to the public. In other words, an average banker has only six hours in the day when you can get to him or her. Even at that, just to take care of the volume of paperwork and responsibilities, the banker may not go home until late.

I recently had the privilege of teaching a class for bank executives at Southern Methodist University's Southwestern Graduate School of Banking. In my class, consisting of bank presidents and examiners from around the United States, I conducted a survey, which revealed some interesting information. The bank executives reported that on average they were working approximately three hours more *per day* than they had worked five years ago. The biggest complaint most bankers reported in that survey was that there was such a great volume of work to do that they never seemed to have the time to complete it.

The average banker in that survey was working between fifty and sixty hours per week.

Since the person with whom you are meeting is very busy, the time he or she gives you is precious time that is competing with other demands begging for the banker's attention. To help you and the banker use that time efficiently, follow these steps:

1. Arrange your thoughts and your points.
2. Establish that the bank and banker are qualified to meet your needs.
3. Describe your enterprise.
4. Highlight your successes.
5. Note the future for your business.
6. Describe your loan requirements.
7. Then *stop*.

At this point in the interview, you have put the ball in the banker's court. It is important now for you to say nothing. Rather than letting him or her put the banker's glass eye on you and wait for you to volunteer some information that may be harmful to your case, you simply stop. Make the banker ask the questions. The banker ideally will ask questions that you are well prepared to answer and will demonstrate some enthusiasm and interest in your company. Invite him or her to visit the business.

Important: The banker does not know that you have a written loan proposal at this point. Do not take it out of your briefcase . . . yet.

The Famous Cs of Credit

At this point, the banker is mentally getting ready to grill you and run a checklist on the Cs of credit. Every banker since time immemorial has been grounded and rooted in the Cs: credit, collateral, cash flow, capital, and character. Does this sound familiar? It should, because the 5 Cs were all on the original loan proposal checklist. Figure 19 is a letter from R. W. Hawkins, one of the leading bankers of the Midwest. Notice his mention of "three Cs." Hawkins is referring to the three most important Cs—credit, collateral, and character.

In recent times sophisticated business schools have created new approaches, new names, new titles, but the basics of lending haven't changed since the merchant rulers of Italy created banking standards for the Western world hundreds of years ago. While the banker appears to be listening quietly to your presentation, his or her mind is whirling like a great computer asking for satisfactory completion of the Cs. If you complete all five of them to his or her satisfaction, you have an excellent chance of approval. If you fail to satisfy even one of them, you have reduced your chances of approval substantially.

This can be a fun part of your loan interview. Give your banker time, and if he or she is good at the job, you will eventually be asked a question about each of the five Cs. Of course, the exact words may differ. The banker may call "cash flow" a profit and loss statement or a sources and uses of funds statement. He or she may call "capital" your reserves or cash backup. If the banker has a negative attitude or is having a bad day, he or she may see the five Cs as tools to whittle you down. If the banker is positive, he or she will see them as means of helping you get the loan approved.

Your advantage is that you already know what to expect. You have the answers, and you will satisfy the banker in every regard.

What if you don't have all of the five Cs? Many borrowers want to change the rules of banking. If you intend

Figure 19
LETTER MENTIONING THE Cs OF CREDIT

SOUTHERN COMMERCIAL BANK
5515 SOUTH GRAND
SAINT LOUIS, MISSOURI 63111
(314) 481-6800

September 30, 1991

Mr. Ben B. Boothe
Ben B. Boothe & Associates
Western National Building
8851 Highway 80 West, Suite 201
Fort Worth, Texas 76116

Dear Ben,

I have enjoyed your presentations at the various state independent conventions where we have both been on the program.

I understand you have a new book coming out to try to ease the burden of both the customer and the banker when the time comes to borrow. Such a book would certainly be useful. I hope that in it you will stress that we need to know the borrower's financials for the last three years, his knowledge of whatever business he may be in, and given the supervisors' present attitude, the thought that the banker is absolutely going to ask for personal guarantees from the principals in the business and in most states, from their wives also.

You might also comment that once a banker gets to know a customer and has confidence in his ability and that he meets the three C's of credit, from that point forward the rules become much more flexible, both for the borrower and for the banker.

Sincerely,

R. W. Hawkins
President

RWH:jmd

3207 MERAMEC   CONVENIENCE BANKING SINCE 1891   7201 SOUTH BROADWAY

to get your capital from a bank, you need to know bank rules. There are other sources of capital—ranging from investment brokerage houses to mutual funds, trust departments, insurance companies, pension funds, the equity markets, partnerships, syndications, wealthy individuals, and even pawn shops—but you are in a bank. The banker is probing for weaknesses in your presentation.

The banker will first look for your obvious weaknesses. If, for example, your credit is zero or your cash flow is a negative, it will be easy for the banker to terminate your loan request. Your task is to prepare your strong points in anticipation of such scrutiny.

What if you know there is a weakness in one of your factors? For example, let's say you are weak in the collateral section of your loan. This is one of the classic loan weaknesses. The essay in Figure 20 (by Robert Sewell, an outstanding bank chairman from Texas) describes how bankers approach the collateral question.

Assume you have run your list of assets and you don't have the first tier of collateral—the collateral your banker really prefers to call "liquid collateral" (for example, CDs, listed stocks, bonds, savings accounts). You have scratched around, and all you can come up with is "accounts receivable." Your loan request is for $30,000. You have $100,000 in accounts receivable. You and the banker both know that you won't collect all of your accounts receivable. Furthermore, you and the banker both know that it may be a while before you collect any of them, and you are going to need the bulk of that money for operating expenses.

So what do you do? First demonstrate the quality of the accounts receivable. Then offer to assign all the accounts directly to the bank. This means that whenever any account that owes you money pays, the check will go directly to your banker. Then let the bank apply a percentage, one you can live with, from each payment to your loan—perhaps 30 percent (that would be enough to pay

Figure 20
ESSAY ON THE VALUE OF COLLATERAL

 EQUITABLE BANKSHARES, INC.

P.O. Box 802525   Dallas, Texas 75380
17218 Preston Road   Dallas, Texas 75252
(214) 248-7000

THE VALUE OF COLLATERAL

by

Robert H. Sewell
Chairman of the Board
Equitable BankShares, Inc.
Dallas, Texas
August 14, 1991

How important is collateral? Collateral is the main reason the Equitable BankShares, Inc. banks of the Dallas/Fort Worth Metroplex have survived the banking collapse of the '80s.

My first job behind a lending desk began in Belton, Texas in the early '70s. The first piece of advice the Chairman of the Board, Jay Kelly, gave me was "Bob, you can never have too much collateral". Has that ever proved true!

I think in understanding how important collateral is you must first understand what it is or is not. I am talking about "Real Collateral". It is not a joint venture interest. It is not something that you are relying strictly on its cash flow for debt repayment. It is not something you know nothing about...what is the fire sale price of an exavier lathe digital printing press and who would buy it? "Real Collateral" comes about by first having the borrower put a substantial amount of his own money at risk. After you have that premise covered then you combine that with the physical collateral item.

Having collateral, "Real Collateral" is what got our banks through the tough times. Sure cash flow is important...but what do you do when the cash flow goes away; the borrower loses his job; the business sales volume goes down; or the apartment project has a large vacancy rate? You turn to your collateral. This is not to say collateral will get you out whole. But "Real Collateral" will have you in a position to bring real pressure on the borrower to stay with you. No person wants to lose what "they own" particularly if they have "their money" at risk.

Banking is not a partnership relationship. I truly want my borrowers to be successful in their ventures...but I want my money back if they fail. Having "Real Collateral" is clearly the reason this organization was different from the other banks in our trade area. Yes we took some losses in the bad times but we did not take the catastrophic losses because we had "Real Collateral".

My lending career began by being required to ask for collateral and my further piece of advice to anyone in the lending business is, "If someone offers you additional collateral...take it"!

off the banker), more or less as you find feasible. This maneuver will give the banker a better sense of control and confidence.

But what if you are still in a vulnerable condition because of this weak link in the five-C chain? Your next step is to strengthen and emphasize the areas in which you are strong. You are weak in the area of collateral, but look how strong your character and credit are. Or perhaps you have a contract pending that has the potential to bring in an enormous sum of income. Now is the time to put this information on the table. It has no real tangible value at the present moment, but it may be a significant factor in your success later on. Do you have any hard contracts, letters, commitments verifying your expectations? Have them available to show the banker when the time is right.

When is the time right? Consider the interview to be like fly fishing in a mountain stream. You want to catch a ten-pound trophy, and you have only a seven-pound line. You have set the hook; now are you going to jerk the line in with all your strength? No! You will lose the fish and may lose your line as well. You must play the fish with skill. Let the banker ask you questions about the business and your loan. You have all of the information memorized, and you will give strong responses. Let the banker take notes.

If the conversation dies and he or she fails to ask any more questions, you might lead the interview a little with a statement like this: "I understand that an important criteria might be _____ [you pick the subject— your industry trends, your cash flow, your collateral, your projected earnings]. What would *you* like to know about that area?"

Ethical Considerations

Avoid every appearance of using nonbusiness inducements. "Nonbusiness" inducements are gifts, favors, or questionable activities. There are several reasons for this, not the least being that it can be illegal. One bank customer I served for years had an excellent plumbing business. Two times a year he would enter my office (about two weeks before his notes came due) and invite my son and me on a hunting trip. It didn't seem to matter what we hunted. If it was deer season, that was the invitation. Dove, then bird hunting. If no season was open, we would go frog hunting. It took me two hunting trips to make the connection between these invitations and his loans. For years I thought the invitations were because he liked me! Another customer used to try to give the loan officers expensive Western boots. Another always had tickets to the upcoming sports extravaganza. One woman (of doubtful repute, but who kept fair accounts at the bank) even brought in two young ladies and hinted that they could use a good banker. Some women mistakenly believe that a low neckline and a high hemline will buy them better terms.

Most professional bankers are amused at these methods, but they also consider them signs of weakness. Most good bankers have adopted ethics policies as a result of the law forbidding such activities. Your attitude should be that your loan should stand on its own merit. If you must resort to these methods, it is a signal to the bank (and to you) that there is a fundamental flaw in your application.

Introducing the Application

After you have basically gone through the loan application orally with the banker, bring out the written loan proposal. Introduce it with words such as these: "We have put together something I would like to show you. This information may be helpful to you as you present our request to your committee [or as you research our loan]."

Put the loan proposal on the banker's desk and go

through it with him or her page by page. If the banker seems restless, it is because you are forcing him or her to give additional attention to your request, and your proposal is structured to guide him or her to a positive response.

Verification

In the loan application process, you are going to be presenting a great deal of data based upon financial statements, projections, and basic assumptions. You can establish great credibility up front if you also bring verification. If, for example, you are discussing profits and sales, bring the sales receipts or deposit slips. If you are discussing profits, have your tax returns on hand. No one will exaggerate profits on a tax return! If you are discussing liabilities and the amount of your payments, bring copies of the note forms. Make the banker understand, early in your meetings, that what you say is true and that you can verify every figure and every financial assumption.

The Team Approach

Here's a negotiating suggestion: go to the loan interview with someone else—an employee or associate who will have a good image and help you to make a positive impression. Two people, well dressed, with a professional approach have more power. They give the banker the sense that there is more to this transaction than just you. If you have no associate, get an impressive-looking secretary or friend to go with you.

Closing Questions

When you get to the conclusion of the interview (which should take no more than thirty minutes), make the prop-

osition. You have played the fish out on the line until you
are ready to pull it in. At this point you can still lose the
fish, so be cautious and sensitive. You know you probably
won't get the banker's final decision today, but you need
to know if you have "sold" him or her. Chances are, if the
banker is enthusiastic enough about your loan, he or she
can sell it to the committee.

Begin by asking a series of probing closing questions.
Never pose these questions in a way requiring an absolute
positive or negative response. Instead, try the wording of
the following questions:

*Of the two term proposals, which do you think the
bank will prefer?* If the banker hedges or refuses to answer, then try the next question.

*Is there an alternative set of terms that you believe
your committee will agree to?* If the banker hedges
further, you should question him or her further. For example, ask for specific details, terms, rates, or loan parame-
ters. Try to determine if the banker is simply trying to
finesse the denial. You can also ask the next question.

*Are there any pertinent facts that we have omitted
or that we can provide?* If you sense the banker is uncomfortable, you need to get even more specific. It is
possible at this point that he or she can't make an evaluation without reviewing it with a senior officer, and may feel
uncomfortable expressing support for fear of being over-
ruled. But you need to know how the banker views the
proposal and whether he or she will support it.

*Do you have any reservations, and have we given
you ample opportunity to ask all questions?* If the
banker says yes to the first part of the question, you need
to probe further. If the banker says no to the second part
of the question, you need to be quiet for a while.

When does your committee meet? Here, if you have a
lot of courage, you might take the risk of asking, *Do you*

see any reason the committee would not approve our application?

If you want to be very aggressive, you can press even further: "My staff and I are prepared to come to your loan committee meeting and answer any questions or make a presentation to allow them an opportunity to get to know us better." This will rarely happen . . . but it has happened. And there is nothing like personal contact. In one instance our bank had refused a loan to a new contracting company. We were impressed with the owners, but they were young, and since the company specialized in building restaurants, we considered it too risky to approve. But the customers simply would not take no for an answer. When we explained that the committee had refused the loan, they demanded an opportunity to meet with the committee. The sheer constraints of time make this a rare occurrence, but we approved because they were such impressive individuals. Their integrity, energy, and enthusiasm were boundless! At the loan committee meeting, they made such a strong presentation that the loan was approved unanimously. Even the loan officer who had originally turned them down voted for them. They became highly successful and, as their company grew, became one of the bank's best customers.

If meeting with the committee is out of the question or an avenue you don't wish to pursue, ask for the response to your loan request in detail and in writing. Use a statement like this: "It will be very helpful to us if you will provide us with a letter outlining the terms for your approval or, if the committee has objections, the specific areas of concern."

At this point in the interview, you will know whether the loan officer is going to recommend your loan. If you came through the interview to the last three questions without a hint of the banker's attitude, something is amiss.

Before you leave the banker's office, be sure you get a commitment about response time. Make a mental note to call in two days to ask if there is anything else the banker needs to know or if he or she has any questions. Be sure to make this call before the banker takes the loan to committee.

A word on "taking the loan to committee": Some bankers have ample authority to grant your loan with no oversight, but nearly every banker requires some time to double-check your references and think about your loan. A famous dodge is the infamous "committee." Marvin Carlile, a patriarch of banking in west Texas, made every loan decision in his bank. But he always gave the "committee" the blame or the credit for any questions that needed to be addressed or any loan approval. He used the committee to delay making a decision. He called on the committee to require further documentation. He pretended to be mad at the committee at times with statements like "I'm sorry those guys are being so picky, but we need this . . ."

You can play the game to your advantage. When you present the proposal, talk about what "the committee" may want to look at. Or when you make your follow-up call, "I just thought the committee might be interested in _____." Of course, your banker may use the committee. If the loan request is for any significant amount, it will likely be reviewed by a committee. Through painful experience, many bankers have learned that having committees approve loans is an excellent strategic move in that it protects them against liability and personal accountability.

Respect for the Banker

Simple courtesy demands that you behave with respect. Respect the banker's time. Respect his or her environment. Respect his or her position. And respect his or her health. As a banker who has interviewed perhaps thirty thousand loan applicants in my banking career, I have found that simple lack of manners often distracted the conversation and made the loan applicant an adversary instead of a customer. For example, don't smoke in the banker's office. What if the banker has a lung condition or simply doesn't like smoke? Respect the items on a banker's desk. Customers have come into my office and actually leafed through items on my desk during the interview. Respect the simple dignity of the office.

One day a rough-hewn oil field worker came into my office and said, "I know all of you #*!@! bankers are crooked sons of #*!@!, but I wanted to ask you for a #*!@! #*!@! loan anyway." He did *not* get his loan. He later came in and apologized. It was his habit to go out and have a few drinks after a hot day in the sun, and that day he was a little "high." Apology or not, his lack of simple manners was an expensive learning experience for him.

7

After the Interview

Relationships are the tie that binds in good banking. It has often been said that banking is not numbers, it is relationships. One cannot build a relationship in a single interview. A good banking relationship takes time and continual effort. The moment you walk out of the bank after the initial loan presentation, you have just begun the relationship-building process.

Building a Relationship

To continue the process of relationship building, consider the following suggestions:

- Follow up on the interview by telephone in two days.
- Send the banker a thank-you note with some additional information about your business or industry.
- Be back in the bank within three days to open an account, and be sure you speak to the banker.

- Aggressively seek opportunities to see or be with influential officers or employees of the bank at community or social functions.
- Seek out an influential associate or friend, and ask that person to recommend you to the banker.
- Never, *never* ridicule or joke about the bank, banker, or banking industry.
- Send the banker an envelope with ten $1,000 bills. (*oops! Disregard the last . . . just testing you.*)

The last "suggestion" is a facetious way of warning you that under the new banking regulations, particularly FIRREA, there are severe financial penalties for breaches of good business practice and violation of banking laws. Avoid any action that even hints of impropriety. As a bank patriarch said to his officers year after year, "Avoid even the appearance of evil in banking."

The loan interview will be just the beginning in a series of communications leading down the path of a long-term business relationship that will give you and the banker a great deal of satisfaction, enjoyment, and profitability. Continue to work with the banker with an attitude that says, "Let's work together and make a good business transaction."

This working relationship is worth all of the time and effort you have invested to date. It can be enjoyable to the extent that you and the banker can help each other go to the top in your respective careers. As a good customer of the bank, you will be pushing the banker along. As a good banker, he or she will be pushing you along. It is this level of relationship that will create an enduring trust and confidence.

You only have to look around in any community and note who the most successful businesspeople are. When you do, you will find that the most successful ones have a banker, often more than one, who has over the years become one of their closest confidants. Look at a city where there is an old banker who has been there for years. You will also see a generation of businesspeople who climbed to the top with that banker or with his or her help.

As you walk out of the bank from the initial loan interview, your mind should be buzzing with plans for the future. Not just the immediate plans of following up with the interview, but plans for the future of your business, for which you have just laid a foundation.

What If You Are Turned Down?

If you handle a loan denial properly, you can strengthen the foundation of a good business relationship. Understand that most good bankers take no joy in turning down loans. To get a sample of the attitudes of bankers, I asked a convention of bankers in South Dakota what they would recommend to someone whom they have just had to turn down for a loan. Here are some of their responses:

Duncan D. Flann, president of Farmer's and Merchant's State Bank in Iroquois, South Dakota, said:

> My best advice for the loan customer of a small business who has just been turned down is to do an analysis of the reasons for the turndown. If it is legitimate, fix it, or change your plans accordingly. *Then go back and try again.* Banks do not turn down loans just for the fun of it. They are worried because of their experience of other loans like it which did not turn out as projected.

Jim Myers, senior vice president of Live Stock State Bank in Mitchell, South Dakota, advised:

> When you are turned down, step back and look at your plan and ask yourself these questions.

1. Why was I turned down?
2. How can I improve and sell my business plan to my banker? I always tell the customer *if he believes in his new business DON'T GIVE UP!*

Said E. J. Schnaidt, chairman of Menno State Bank in Menno, South Dakota:

When the banker turns down a loan, he should give the applicant advice on points which were credit weaknesses. The customer then should upgrade these and try again.

From loan officers to vice presidents to presidents to board chairmen, the answer was always the same. When you are turned down, improve your approach and go back again. It is possible that in working with the banker to find out what you both need to get this loan approved, you will have one of your best opportunities to build on the foundation for a lasting relationship. The general principles and criteria of banks in the ranch and agricultural economy of South Dakota are no different from those in Los Angeles, Houston, or Atlanta. The basic reasons for approval and disapproval, if the market is not distorted by some extraordinary factor, will be identical.

Why Some Banks Don't Lend

Occasionally people wonder why they or their company just can't seem to get credit. The reasons for the credit denial always seem the same: "Our bank just isn't making loans like this" or "The loan just doesn't meet the bank's criteria at this time." Such people may begin to wonder if there is something wrong with their industry or their business. They may even take the credit denials personally.

But often people can be essentially denied opportunities to borrow by a grapevine of bankers simply passing the word that they or their company are not a good risk. This banking grapevine emerges from the industry's tradition of powerful people making powerful decisions behind the closed mahogany doors of boardrooms, and part of a banker's power comes from his or her control of loan decisions. If people can breach these traditional barriers of secrecy and power, their borrowing potential is vastly increased. Their first step is to understand some of the reasons bankers deny loans.

Traditions in the Industry

Sad but true, banking often tends to be more cautious with regard to some industries and professions than others. As a young man I was intrigued one day when a wonderful old banker (he was eighty years old) told me to watch out for a particular customer. I asked him why, and he mumbled, "Four Ps," and shuffled off. I stood speechless, without a clue as to what he was talking about. Later in a banker's meeting I asked the other bankers sitting at the loan committee table if they had ever heard of the "four Ps." They laughed in recognition and said, "Ben, it is one of the old traditional sayings of banking that you will always lose money if you lend money to a professor, plumber, painter, or preacher."

I said, "Well, there are other 'Ps.' What about prostitutes?"

They laughed at that and said, "A banker never loses money to a prostitute. They are some of the best business-people around."

When you are seeking a loan, it is well to understand some of the traditional areas in which bankers will be cautious. Tradition can be a powerful foe or a good friend. For example, it is also a given in banking that bankers will favor loans to doctors, Certified Public Accountants, and people in the community "who have standing" or who give the appearance of being established and stalwart members of the community.

Political Reasons

It has been said that a politician has never made a profit for a bank. Yet from time to time a news story focuses on some politician who owes a bank millions. Anyone who thinks that politics do not enter into banking is foolishly wrong. Bankers will stand on the street corner and shout that it isn't true, and regulators will wring their hands as they deny that politics has anything to do with banking or bank regulation.

A perfect example of this is the period of the mid-1980s through the early 1990s. No generation of Americans has been more powerfully affected by the influence of politics on banking than the generation of the 1990s. Entire regions of the nation have been deprived of credit because political expediency called for "deregulation of the S&L industry" and then left the public and business world to deal with the consequences. What followed was regulatory politics wherein regulators intent on restructuring an industry used field examiners to change the composition of the industry through practices designed to shrink the number of banks in the industry. Unfortunately for millions of Americans, and for financial institutions, politics does play a role in the industry.

On an individual basis, bankers know that although politicians often make poor bank customers, politicians can make or break an industry group. It has even been argued with some power that political ties have some bearing on how severely examiners review a bank. This would be hard to prove except by the results, but let it suffice to make a point. If you want to borrow money, it is advisable to stay out of the cross fire of competing political interests. Certainly don't place your company or yourself in harm's way by opposing powerful political figures, unless you have influential access to the powers that be. You may not know which political friend has stock or an influence button, or is sitting on the loan committee of your local bank.

I knew a bank president who appeared on a radio interview program. While he was on the air, a caller asked a leading question that made the banker appear opposed to a leader of the incumbent political party. Just by "coincidence," within weeks the members of that party who sat on his board recommended his termination, the examiners did a "routine surprise exam," and the loan applications that he was handling were all tabled.

There is a different level of politics that may be just as important for the disposition of your loan request. That level may be the perception you give the community about the bank. For example, I recall sitting in a loan committee meeting while the board was reviewing a marginal loan application. If the loan had been a little better, it would have been fun to approve. If it had been a little worse, it would have been fun to turn down. But this loan was marginal in every sense of the word. The deciding factor for the loan decision was made when a senior officer of the bank observed, "I was at the school board meeting when Mr. Johnson stood up and praised our bank for its service to the school system. He didn't know I was listening, but afterwards he encouraged many people to vote to keep the school funds with the bank." His loan was approved by unanimous vote of the loan committee.

Many times I have sat in board meetings when someone asked about a customer, "Is he a friend of the bank?" or "Does she support the bank out in the community?" Often those little "political" influences made the difference on a loan application.

Finally there is the politics of influence. If you or your business are in the leading civic clubs, if you are active and visible in the community, if you are known as an image maker or yours is a firm that influences people, then you should consider this as power when you apply for a bank loan. You should see to it, through direct or indirect means, that the banker knows of your involvement and popularity in the community. The converse is also true. If you have a bad community image, it will hurt you when you need that loan.

Personal Life and Image

An individual's personal life and image are a part of the discussion. If a person is known to abuse spouse or children, drink heavily, use drugs, gamble, have an immoral personal life, it will have a bearing on his or her loan application. Some may declare in outrage, "My personal life is none of your business!" In a sense this is correct. But in a far deeper sense, the manner in which someone conducts his or her personal life may reflect his or her stability or attitudes regarding business in general.

And even in this age when the personal banker is becoming more and more rare, some *person* will ultimately approve or disapprove your loan request. News gets around in a big city or in a small community. That news travels fast and often by the banker's grapevine. If you ever get on the negative side of that grapevine, your life will be far more difficult in regard to banking concerns.

Inadequate Financial Statement and Documentation

Lest we forget, banking is an industry of numbers. It doesn't matter how politically powerful you are, if you are unable to put together an adequate financial statement, you might as well give up. Documentation is a key element. In short, you must take whatever steps are within your power to produce a viable financial statement and adequate and complete documentation with your loan application.

Bankers Who Don't Like You

Yes, occasionally a customer is turned down for a loan simply because the banker doesn't like him or her. If you get this message, move on to another banker right away.

Race, Sex, Age

It is against federal law for a person to be refused credit on the basis of race, sex, or age. For the most part, the banking industry has done an admirable job of complying with the law.

If you think you have been a victim of one of the rare violators, follow these steps in the order given. (1) Report the violation in writing to the bank management seeking resolution. (2) If the first step doesn't bring results then report it in writing to the bank regulatory agency in charge of that bank (FDIC, OCC, RTC, OTS, etc.). (3) If these two steps don't work, then, and only then, start legal proceedings.

Bankers Who Don't Know You

Trying to get a loan from a banker who doesn't know you makes a difficult job even harder. When the loan application for you or your company goes to committee, the banker is going to have to answer a lot of questions. This is where it is important for you to build a relationship with the banker. Don't just mail in deposits or have an employee take them to the bank. You need to personally walk through the lobby of the bank, to see and be seen. While there, you should go by the banker's office, speak to the banker, and give him or her an opportunity to get to know you. If the banker likes you and knows you, it is far easier for him or her to communicate your merits to a loan committee.

Understand that the banker is paid to be busy. He or she doesn't have a great deal of time to spend with any one person. But a regular wave, a greeting, a clipping about you from the newspaper, a short note of thanks for his or her help in some matter, all of these make a difference.

Numbers That Don't Make Economic Sense

It is almost too obvious to state, but you may be turned down simply because your numbers don't add up. It doesn't take a rocket scientist to calculate a series of numbers and determine the capability of a borrower or the capacity of a company to repay. If your financial statements don't give a clear and definitive message that your company can support the debt, that the transaction makes economic sense, don't borrow until they do.

Industry or Bank Stability

A man called me from New York City. He had kept an account at one of the nation's largest banks for most of his adult life, but when he went in to apply for a moderate-sized loan, they abruptly turned the loan down. He was shocked, then he became angry. "Ben, I can't imagine what is wrong with those people. I need a bank that will work with me," he told me with some emotion. What he did not realize was that the bank had quietly been undergoing severe regulatory criticism for some time. The bank had made a strategic error years before by investing billions in loans to Third World nations. Then, in an effort to compensate for those losses, the bank had loaned heavily in domestic real estate projects, just before a national decline in real estate prices. The regulators were all over

the bank, it was in need of new capital, and the financial
world waited with interest to see if the bank could work
through these problems.

When a bank is experiencing problems such as these,
it is more difficult than ever to get a loan approved. Policies become more conservative, loan officers become
hesitant to take risks, and the customers are the ones who
suffer, for they often think something is wrong with *them
or their application!*

While I was on a ski trip, a man on the ski lift next to
me told me his story: "My wife and I had fourteen rental
houses when an out-of-state bank bought out our local
bank. While they were experiencing regulatory pressure,
they called all of our loans—loans on properties worth far
more than the amount borrowed, and loans that were
being paid as agreed. When we asked why, they said that
the regulators insisted that they had too many real estate
loans, and our loan was considered a 'high-risk loan inappropriate to the current climate.' It nearly ruined us financially," he said bitterly.

Another form of bank instability is *merger mania.*
Industries go through cycles of expansion and contraction.
America has been in a cycle of mergers and acquisitions
for several years. When an industry such as banking is in
an expansion stage, credit is easier to acquire. When it is
in a consolidation stage, credit is harder to acquire. In the
1970–1985 period, banking was expanding faster than
ever due to a good economy and a regulatory policy that
encouraged more banks. Credit was easy to acquire. The
nation had up to fourteen thousand commercial banks. In
the subsequent period, especially from 1988 to 1991, both
the economy and regulatory policy changed. Industries
such as oil, real estate, finance, steel, automobile production, and even high technology faltered.

Part of this was brought on by federal policies, such as
the Tax Reform Act of 1986, which vastly penalized real

estate investors by removing tax incentives. This in turn caused real estate values to decline and penalized individuals and banks, which had traditionally considered real estate a stable investment "that would always appreciate."

Federal policy also brought on the philosophy of "consolidation" of the banking industry. First the savings and loan industry was "deregulated," which led to a vast expansion of powers and numbers of savings and loans institutions. But deregulation brought vast abuses, and soon the S&L industry was crippled with bad debts. Rather than make moves to save the industry, a philosophy emerged that "consolidation" was the answer. As a result very few S&Ls are left in the nation. This made the task of purchasing or financing a home during this period of turmoil much more difficult.

Then the federal government focused on the banking industry. The same people who had called for deregulation of the savings and loan industry now called for deregulation of banking. (One observer ironically noted, "Deregulation worked so well for the S&L industry, they wanted to do it to banking.") As a result, the numbers of banks initially expanded, then as problems in the economy and loan portfolios surfaced, the regulators jumped in with a vengeance. At this writing the number of commercial banks in America has dropped to 10,500. My research even uncovered a quote from a high-ranking regulator (who later indicated that he would rather not be quoted), who was asked how many banks he thought America should have. His response was shocking: "No more than 150 banks with 12 giant megabanks." The interviewer was so shocked at the prospect of a high-placed federal regulator pressing for such radical changes that he concluded, "We have seen a new day in America. A day when the federal government is committed to the idea that most banks in America should cease to exist."

This, of course, should be of great concern to the

millions of community bank customers and stockholders around the nation, but bankers by and large have been reluctant to speak out. Why? Because the people who press this philosophy also control the bank examiners, and no banker wants to expose his or her bank to tougher examinations. This problem became so acute during 1989–1991 that President George Bush called a meeting of the top bank regulators and expressed his concern that regulator actions were causing a "chilling effect" on the economy as a whole. Although regulators indicated that they would change policy direction, bankers reported that they saw little change in attitude or approach.

In Washington, D.C., during this time, a phrase has often been heard about banking: "Bankers, to compete, will either merge, sell out, or fail." As a former senator and bank commissioner of Illinois told me, "I believe that *over* 80 percent of the bank failures in America in the past few years are because of regulatory, not economic, pressures."

What does all of this mean to a business or individual who needs a loan? *If there are fewer banks and fewer bankers, there will ultimately be less competition.* Less competition in a free enterprise society leads to higher prices and less availability. Remember Velcro banks? As I said earlier, that phrase was coined in Texas relating to the massive mergers and acquisitions going on in that region. Banks were changing their names so fast that critics said they should put Velcro on the signs so that they could change the names with greater ease. Another phenomenon also occurred. Borrowers found it difficult, often impossible, to borrow from those banks. The problem became so acute that the Texas legislature actually considered a law to demand that the new banks that had come in and merged with or acquired other banks start lending money. This became the focus of a federal congressional investigation in 1991.

When a bank changes ownership, organization, or

philosophy, there is a period of transition during which loan customers suffer. It has been well documented that in areas of great consolidation, lending declines radically. As the banking crisis first surfaced in Texas and then in Boston, it was disclosed that those two areas alone had lost over $8 billion in bank capital. That extended to an unavailability of loans of over $100 billion in those two regions alone! The economic impact is enormous. For example, total bank loans in one small town in Texas declined from $90 million to $20 million in the eighteen-month period after an acquisition of the major bank in town.

If you or your business apply for an important loan and it is refused, it may be because your bank has been a participant in the "merger, acquisition, consolidation" game. Financial institutions generally prefer to keep their corporate independence. Mergers normally happen as a result of weakness, such as the need to cut expenses, a shortage of capital, regulatory pressure, or competitive pressure. Weakness also implies unreasonably conservative lending standards and often unreasonable caution to worthy customers, especially during the time just before and after the transition.

Conclusions

The statement that "the interview isn't over when it's over" has multiple applications. First, it is important that you analyze and understand any external or indirect factors that may affect your loan approval (or denial). Adjust your loan strategy accordingly, perhaps seeking out another bank that can better meet your needs. Be sure to cultivate a positive, ongoing relationship with your banker. And don't give up if you're turned down. Being aggressive and prepared, as you will be when you follow the guidelines in this book, will open the vault doors in your behalf.

8

The SBA/SBIC Alternative: Small-Business Loans and How to Get Them

What if you have applied for a commercial loan and have been turned down? All of the preparation and work did not get the loan approved. Don't despair. There will be a banker for you if the loan is structured right and if you have met the checklist criteria. When the bank's major objection is *risk*, one of the best ways to find a loan is to apply for an SBA loan.

The Small Business Administration (SBA) was formed with the intent of encouraging bankers who were reluctant to lend money to small businesses to approve those loans. (The vast majority of small-business loan applications are for new businesses.) The reluctance on the part of bankers for new-business loans is understandable. Over 90 percent of the new businesses in America fail within twelve months. Over 95 percent of the new restaurant operations fail within twelve months. These high mortality rates have taught many bankers to be cautious in lending to new or small businesses. Politicians in Washington wanted to see small business prosper and thus formed the SBA loan department. The purpose of the SBA is to improve the economy, increase opportunity for all Americans, and encourage the growth of businesses in America.

The role of the SBA has expanded over the years. It doesn't handle just small loans. An SBA loan can go up to $750,000 or more under some programs. So this department is not necessarily a "small-business" organization. The resources and assistance that this department can provide to a business manager are immense. This chapter describes how to take advantage of the SBA to achieve your goals.

You should also know that besides lending, a practical free service of the SBA is its counseling service. In a program called the Service Corps of Retired Executives (SCORE), the SBA maintains groups of retired executives who are available to assist the business manager in any aspect of the SBA loan. They offer counseling in other areas as well, including help in running a business and in establishing a bookkeeping system. Often this service makes available top executive talent and invaluable advice.

Benefits of SBA Loans

Why is an SBA loan attractive to a bank? If you can understand the advantages to the bank, you can better sell your loan application to your banker.

First, if a bank handles an approved SBA loan, the government guarantees to indemnify the bank from losses on a percentage of the loan. The amount of the guarantee varies with the type of application. For example, if a loan is to refinance an existing loan, the government will guarantee 75 percent of the loan. In other words, if the loan were for $100,000 and the business failed, the bank would have loss exposure of only $25,000, and the value of the collateral might eliminate all or a part of that loss. Therefore, the risk to the bank is minimal. For a typical new loan, the amount of the government guarantee is *90 percent*. Therefore, on a $100,000 loan, the most the local bank could possibly lose is $10,000.

The U.S. government is willing to share the risk—indeed, is willing to take most of the risk—to provide an incentive for your banker to make a small-business loan to you. The government requires the bank to keep complete documentation on the borrower, so all of the documentation work mentioned earlier in this book applies to SBA loans. Indeed, if the bank does not keep adequate documentation and the annual audit of your file discloses this, the SBA can remove its guarantee!

Another advantage to the bank is that an SBA loan helps satisfy the bank's CRA requirements. The Community Reinvestment Act (CRA) states that a bank must take steps to see that the community where that bank is geographically located is adequately served by the bank through loans. A bank must prove that it is not just sitting on its money, but is doing things to help a community prosper. There is no better way for a bank to show compliance with this law than by making an SBA loan to a local business.

Third, an SBA loan increases the capital ratio of a bank under the risk-based capital guidelines. Whereas most loans require that a bank have adequate underlying capital to support them, the SBA-guaranteed portion of a loan actually improves a bank's capital position. In calculating the underlying capital, the bank treats the guaranteed portion just like a government bond. Therefore, instead of a bank investing $500,000 in government bonds, which have no risk and pay 8 percent, why not invest in an SBA loan, which may pay 12 percent with no risk? During times of economic decline, capital is a critical factor for banks, so SBA loans will have greater appeal.

An SBA loan is also a marvelous means of providing credit to the community beyond traditional banking standards. This can create a great deal of goodwill and interest within a community. It will not hurt you to remind your banker of this as you discuss your loan.

Finally, the rate of interest banks can charge on an SBA loan is limited to New York prime (the traditional interest rate charged to the best, or 'prime,' bank customers by the major banks in New York City) + 2.75 percent. At this rate, the bank can get a good return on its money while the customer is assured of not being charged an excessive rate. There is a fee of two points for the guarantee, which goes to the SBA, not the bank. All other closing costs related to an SBA loan can be added into the principal of the loan if the customer prefers.

Now consider your position. Assume that you applied for a loan, and a large part of your collateral was in the form of inventory, furniture, fixtures, and equipment. A bank usually prefers liquid collateral such as CDs or government bonds, but you did not have any liquid collateral. The bank therefore denied your loan. Now you look into a Small Business Administration loan with a 90 percent guarantee. Suddenly your loan will take a whole new perspective. Rather than liquid collateral, the bank will now be able to enjoy a government guarantee on a loan that will also increase the bank's capital calculation. A loan that was impossible for the bank to approve suddenly becomes a feasible business proposition. By using an existing government program, you have turned a lemon into lemonade.

There are other advantages for the borrower as well. We have already mentioned that the interest rate is limited to 2.75 percent above New York prime. Another advantage is that whereas a bank might prefer a term of three to five years on a standard commercial loan, the advantage of a government guarantee makes a longer loan term feasible. The term might be for seven to fifteen years, so that payments are lower and you have greater flexibility. The table below summarizes terms of a typical SBA loan.

TERMS OF A TYPICAL SBA LOAN

Rate	New York prime + 2.75%
Term	5 to 15 years
Payments	Monthly amortization or quarterly payments; occasional 20-year amortization with 5-year balloon
Collateral	Inventory, furniture, fixtures, equipment, land, and anything else available such as vehicles, stocks, bonds, savings
Guarantee	Personal guarantee routinely required on all loans
Government guarantee	Varies according to the type of loan: 75% to refinance, 90% for new loan, or the SBA will "blend" a loan guarantee if a portion of the loan is refinance and a portion new, in which case the percentage will be averaged
Other features	There is a strong secondary market for the guaranteed portion of SBA loans. Although it will not affect you, your bank might sell the guaranteed portion to an investment group or pool. This can be very profitable for your bank and releases other loan funds back into the community.

The regulatory attitude toward SBA loans benefits the borrower as well as the banker. If your loan is paid as agreed, the chances of regulators criticizing the guaranteed portion of an SBA loan are much less than for a standard commercial loan. A loan that is not criticized is obviously one to be desired by the bankers, and it certainly lessens the chance of a borrower having a loan called because of regulatory pressures.

How to Get Started with an SBA Loan

To get an SBA loan, the first step is to call the regional SBA office nearest you. Ask them to send the general brochure and information packet. After you have reviewed this material, call and ask to speak to an SBA officer. Ask him or her to explain the program to you, and verify that there have been no changes in terms. Also ask the officer what the status of SBA funding is. Occasionally funding runs dry, so be sure SBA funds are available. Then ask if the office handles direct SBA loans. Some SBA offices do, although most prefer that you go through a local bank for SBA applications. Request a list of banks that make SBA loans in your area.

With this list, make your next series of telephone calls to those banks. In each phone call, simply inquire about the status of the bank and if they still make SBA loans. If so, you can set up an appointment to see the banker.

The preparation for an SBA loan is somewhat complicated, in that much of the same information that you accumulated on the checklist earlier in this book must be completed on government forms according to SBA format. Anyone may fill out these forms, but since there are specific things the SBA likes to see, many people hire a CPA or an SBA loan packager to complete the details of the packet. The fee for this service will vary depending upon the time required to complete the forms. Many packagers will complete the SBA application form and create a packet for you for a fee starting from as little as $1,000, depending upon the size of the loan and the time and labor involved. A packager who has a good business will also have a rapport with the banks that actively make SBA loans and with the SBA as well.

Red flag! Select a packager carefully. Avoid any service that wants you to pay the full fee for the service in advance. There are people in this business who run advertisements, take a thousand dollars up front, and then never deliver any service. A reasonable down payment or deposit is acceptable, but avoid the bait-and-switch artists who will take your money, then three weeks later, when you expect your application to be complete, tell you, "Sorry, your loan is not of SBA approval quality." Ask for bank references of your SBA packager, and ask for a list of clients who have successfully used his or her service. Make a few phone calls to the packager's customers, and speak to at least one bank that has funded a loan for that agent. A small effort in research can be most helpful to you at this stage.

Occasionally a bank will be willing to complete your SBA loan application. However, it will probably require a fee for doing so. The fee will be about the same as that of an outside loan packager.

Time Factors

Usually the wait for approval of an SBA loan is longer than that required for a standard bank commercial loan. You can expect that it will take at least two weeks to complete the application forms, and then from the time the SBA receives the completed forms, another six weeks until you receive a decision. The SBA's printed information mentions a six-week turnaround time, but in most cases it takes longer than that. So you are looking at a time frame of at least eight weeks.

If time is a critical factor, there is a way to shorten the time delay for approval of an SBA loan. The SBA certifies some banks as approved in-house SBA lenders. This authorizes the bank to review the documentation and to approve and fund the loan before it sends the loan package to the SBA. These banks are SBA specialists, so they move much faster than a loan packager or the SBA. Often they have a direct computer link with the SBA and can move very efficiently. The regional SBA office will give you the names of these banks.

Where to Close the Loan and Make Payments

An SBA loan is funded in the same way as every other loan at your local bank. In fact, most people do not realize that the local bank actually puts up 100 percent of the funds for the loan. The only differences are the paperwork and the guarantee that is provided by the SBA. In most cases, the only time SBA funds are actually used is in the event of a loan default. The SBA then issues a check to the bank for the guaranteed amount.

Therefore, the transaction should take place in your lending bank. You will make payments just as you would on a regular loan, and you will send all documentation to the local bank.

Speaking of documentation, your paperwork is somewhat more critical for this type of loan. Try not to omit anything. There is no room for editing in this area. Figure 21 provides a sample checklist for preacceptance of an SBA loan application. After wading through that list, you should not be discouraged. You have already gathered 95 percent of the information to meet the initial loan proposal requirements presented earlier in the book. And it is an important effort that can lead to approval of your SBA loan.

The bank or the SBA will provide all of the basic forms required, but handle these with great care! In one instance, it took a customer of one of my banks some six months to get all of the forms and papers filled out and completed in accordance with SBA requirements. He kept filling them out incorrectly and having them returned.

After you have sent in the initial loan request and packet of forms, it is not unusual for the SBA to request further documents or expanded information. If there are specific obstacles, your bank officer can call the SBA directly and speak to them. Also, there is no law against your speaking to SBA officers. But remember that SBA offices are normally understaffed and their employees are working under rigid time constraints. The mentality of these officers is that of people buried by a giant paper game. If you get the paperwork done right, then everything else will probably fall into place. If it is of any comfort, once you have had one SBA loan approved, the subsequent loans are not as difficult.

David Long of the Dallas regional SBA office is one of the people who make dealing with the SBA a pleasure. David, an ex-banker, understands credit and what makes a good loan. Several years ago, when I was in his office to present a customer application, he showed me the success and loss statistics of the SBA. To my surprise, the SBA's loan performance was as good as that of many banks. One might think that the SBA is a lender of last resort. Many have a misconception that it is a government giveaway program. Anyone who has ever tried to get an SBA loan approved will be disenfranchised of those ideas. SBA officers are knowledgeable and thorough.

The approval of an SBA loan for your business is a compliment to your thoroughness and attention to detail. Thousands of businesses in America thrive and operate successfully, employing even more thousands, because they have financing made possible by the Small Business Administration. Some banks have become so impressed with the SBA that they will entertain nothing but SBA loan applications. These banks believe that by using the program, they are doing a favor to the customer, the community, the bank, and the economy. And this program is available to almost any American who has a credible loan application.

Figure 21
REQUIREMENTS FOR PREACCEPTANCE OF AN SBA
LOAN APPLICATION

☐ Application (Form 4) completed, signed by applicant and preparer. (Note that items 8, 9, and 10 must be completed.)

☐ Lender's Application (Form 4-I) financial spread and credit analysis.
  • Lender is requested to supply a cover letter that briefly identifies the nature of the business and its strengths and weaknesses.
  • For new businesses, lender's credit analysis to include a breakeven analysis and working capital analysis.

☐ Credit Report for the business and principal owners.

☐ Description and history of the business and benefits from loan.

☐ Source and amount of owners' equity injection (required for new businesses).

☐ Signed and dated year-end balance sheet and operating statement for _____ years with supporting *signed and dated* year-end tax returns.

☐ Balance sheet and operating statement dated within 90 days, *signed and dated*.

☐ Schedule of debts, with complete explanation of any debt that is to be refinanced with this request.

☐ Reconciliation of net worth, where applicable.

☐ Listing and aging of accounts receivable and accounts payable.

☐ Projections, both P&L and cash flow (where applicable), for three years with supporting assumptions. Assumptions to be supported by a business plan, market analysis, and market strategy (required for all new businesses).

☐ *Signed and dated* current personal financial statements of proprietor, partners, officers, and stockholders owning 20 percent or more of the business, with supporting *signed and dated* personal tax return for most recent year-end. (Spouse's signature required.)

☐ Statements of affiliates (latest yearly financial statements *signed and dated* of all businesses owned, operated, or 50 percent or more controlled by principals of this business), supported by the most current year's tax return, also signed and dated.

☐ Management résumés (include experience, education, training, etc.).

☐ Copy of lease, where applicable.

☐ Statement of Personal History (Form 912) for all owners, officers, directors, stockholders owning 20 percent or more of stock, and key management personnel.

☐ Request for Counseling (Form 641), completed and signed.

☐ Statements Required by Laws and Executive Orders (Form 1261), signed by all owners, officers, directors, guarantors, and stockholders owning 20 percent or more of stock.

☐ Certification Pursuant to Immigration and Nationality Act (Form 1261A), signed and dated.

☐ Compensation Agreement (Form 159), signed by all parties where applicable.

☐ Resolution of Board of Directors (Form 160), completed, where applicable.

☐ Copy of assumed name certificate(s), partnership agreement, or corporate charter and incorporating bylaws (whichever applicable).

☐ Certification Regarding Debarment, Suspension, Ineligibility and Voluntary Exclusion (Form 1624), signed and dated.

☐ Franchisor's financial statements, FTC disclosure statement, and a copy of the franchise agreement (for a franchise).

☐ Other: _____

Collateral Requirements

☐ Schedule 4-A, completed and signed.

☐ Serial numbers of applicable items.

☐ List of items to be purchased and their cost.

☐ Appraisal and most recent tax appraisal.

☐ Other: _____

Construction and Real Estate Requirements

☐ Copy of deed of trust (or mortgage) and warranty deed.

☐ Appraisal of real estate.

☐ Plans and specs on new construction.

☐ Copy of construction contract with turnkey *firm* cost quote.

☐ SBA Form 601 completed, signed by contractor and applicant.

Change of Ownership and New-Business Requirements

☐ Copy of buy-sell agreement.

☐ Current owner's year-end balance sheets and operating statements for last three fiscal years.

☐ Pro forma balance sheet as of day of ownership change or start-up.

☐ Other: _____

SBA Lending Policies and Practices

The SBA will not entertain loan applications in some areas:

- *Broadcasting*—The SBA will not accept applications for radio, TV, or other broadcasting media. Because these industries are highly government-regulated, the SBA involvement might represent some kind of conflict of interest or breach of law.
- *Publishing*—The SBA will not accept applications related to publishing companies.
- *Financial institutions*—The SBA will not accept

applications related to the financing of banks or savings and loan institutions.

- *Politics*—The SBA will not get involved in loans for political parties or political purposes.

Like banks and S&Ls, the SBA may not discriminate on the basis of race, sex, age, or ethnic group.

The SBA has a variety of programs to benefit communities and business. For example, one program of the SBA will lend to assist a community in an industrial development or a business purpose sponsored by the community, provided that the effort produces jobs and stimulates the economy. Another program of the SBA provides loan guarantees for the purpose of generating economic activity in depressed areas of cities. Often these loans are the best hope in some areas for urban renewal, and too often these loans are not fully utilized by the public and business community.

A Case History

Here is the story of a fictional new business that used SBA financing.

John Parker of Philadelphia had worked as an executive for several plastics companies. He had been a competent employee, working his way up to a position of respect in the industry. At the age of forty-five, he saw an opportunity to start a new plastic injection molding company when another company decided to liquidate a large supply of equipment and inventory at below-market prices.

Although his credit history was excellent, Mr. Parker knew he could not borrow enough money on a standard commercial loan with his bank, so he investigated SBA loans. He found that there was a location for his planned

company within an "economically distressed" part of
town, and also that the SBA was sponsoring a loan program to attract new jobs to that area. After a great deal of
research, he prepared a detailed loan proposal to submit
to his bank. The projected location was an area out of his
bank's lending territory, so his banker was at first negative
about his application. But with continual pressing on
John's part, the banker took the loan to committee and
(you guessed it) on the basis of the SBA guarantee, the
loan was approved in the amount of $500,000.

John's company is now a thriving business that em-
ploys thirty to forty people, generates a good profit, and
has been a good investment. John has since expanded his
business with additional SBA loans. The bank, noting his
success story, has started an SBA department and now
makes dozens of SBA loans every month.

Ideally, this is how the SBA is supposed to work.
Opportunity meets ambition supported by a prudent government program and funded by a local bank.

Final Comments on SBA Loans

The forms and documentation requirements of the SBA
are continually being amended. Get the latest forms and
information from your local SBA lender or the regional
SBA office. The government is glad to provide information
and copies of all forms at no charge.

Don't let the forms intimidate you or discourage your
progress. You can obtain help from several sources: your
banker, the SBA staff, SCORE volunteers, professional
loan packagers, and even your personal CPA.

Small Business Investment Companies

A Small Business Investment Company (SBIC) is a company licensed by the SBA to provide financing to small

businesses. The general public is for the most part un-
aware of the SBIC program. It was formulated as an off-
shoot of the Small Business Administration to provide a
hybrid loan service for companies and individuals who
could not locate conventional financing. There are only
368 SBICs in the nation, but they have over *$1.4 billion* in
loans outstanding.

How SBICs Work

A group of investors, a bank, or a corporate entity decides
to form an SBIC. They put up a minimum of $1 million,
and the SBA agrees to lend the company as much as four
times their investment, or $4 million. Therefore, if a com-
pany contributes $1 million and the SBA lends four times
that amount, the SBIC would have $5 million available to
businesses. Assume that XYZ Company cannot find conventional financing but needs $500,000 to acquire a new
business or to expand current operations. The SBIC could
provide the $500,000 in a combination of loans (using
XYZ's assets as collateral) and equity. In other words, XYZ
Company might receive $250,000 in loans, and the SBIC
might purchase $250,000 of XYZ stock directly from the
business, placing a total of $500,000 cash in the treasury
of the business.

When an SBIC invests in a company's stock, the SBIC
normally requires that it have one or more seats on the
company's board of directors so that it can monitor its
investment. The advantage to the owner of the company is
that the business doesn't have to pay interest on the funds
from the sale of stock. The advantage to the SBIC is that if
the company prospers, the SBIC can sell the stock for a
significant profit.

The program is more a venture capital program than
a lending program, but it provides the venture capital to
companies that might not otherwise be able to afford to

enter the public equity markets. Occasionally SBICs have made many times their investment as the companies grow. An SBIC provided the initial capital for a young computer company with the unusual name of Apple. As the world knows, Apple Computer has become one of the success stories of the computer industry. Another company that received start-up funding from an SBIC is Federal Express Corporation, now a leader in delivery services.

SBICs are owned by investment groups, other companies, and even banks. Banks own 38 percent of SBICs because this vehicle provides them with a legal way of becoming involved in venture capital projects. SBICs also provide ways to accommodate customers who normally would not qualify for traditional loans in commercial loan departments. These loan applicants are often deemed too risky for trust-department loans.

Getting SBIC Financing

When you are looking at the possibility of using SBICs to acquire capital, the manner in which you negotiate your loan and equity may make an important difference in the future of your company. If your company provides a board position in return for equity capital, it is important that you have a clear understanding and good communication with that individual, allowing the company to grow and prosper in the best possible way. In this regard, using an SBIC is somewhat like bringing a minority partner into the business. The SBIC participation also may provide additional expertise and consulting, which can make a positive difference in company direction.

A possible disadvantage may be the paperwork and documentation involved in acquiring an SBIC loan. But this should be no more onerous than for a standard SBA loan. The reporting requirements, although tedious, can also be an advantage if the business uses the opportunity to really review the numbers and the direction of the business. Finally, it might be considered a disadvantage to issue additional stock and dilute your ownership in the company. But capital is king, and the additional funds that will be available without any interest expense should more than make up for any dilution disadvantage.

Since there are relatively few SBICs, how do you find them? Contact your regional SBA office or the SBA in Washington, D.C., and they will provide the information.

Every few years, someone in Washington decides that the SBIC program should be done away with, and an investigation follows. The weight of facts and the power of the many success stories generally prevail, and the program is given another funding reprieve. For the business or company that has been unable to find financing, SBICs are a practical answer to a void in the lending marketplace.

9

Seeking Out a Bank of Last Resort

If you have given your loan application to several banks, tried the SBA approach, and *still* haven't found a bank that will lend you money, consider the following experience. A well-respected banker was in an investment group that needed a multimillion-dollar loan for a commercial building. He had all the details in beautiful proposals with complete documentation but still could not locate a lender to make the loan. The credit was fundamentally sound in every particular. He sent the loan package to and had interviews with over forty banks and savings and loan institutions, still without luck. Some institutions were over-loaned, some did not make real estate loans, some considered the loan too large, some considered it too small, some institutions considered the property out of their territory. The reasons for the refusals were endless. In this case, the proposal was good; it was simply a matter of finding the right lender.

Finally, after two years of searching, the man found the right bank. It was an institution that had developed a very low loan ratio and needed to put new loans on the books. The lender not only provided everything the loan proposal called for but a little more. How did the group finally locate the right bank? One of the investors in the group mentioned the project to a banker at a church gathering.

It would be nice if there were some kind of find-a-bank service that could catalog which banks are offering what services at any given time. But there is no such service. Often the only way to find out is through continual probing and questioning, using telephone, letters, and the famous business grapevine.

Banks are continually changing in their needs, services, and ability to perform. That makes it more difficult for commercial and individual loan customers to function. Often bank executives themselves know which banks are seeking particular types of loans or which banks have just had an influx of deposits and need to lend some money. It is a good idea to know a few bank executives you can call and talk to informally about what is going on in the industry.

Be persistent. Seek out all the sources for your loan. They are many, and funds are available to meet your goal. Here are a few sources to consider:

- *Local community national and state banks*—It has been said that locally owned community banks are more likely to provide a high level of personal service than you will find elsewhere.
- *Local savings and loan institutions*—Although the S&L industry has been buffeted, those that have survived are lending money.
- *Big regional "megabanks"*—If you can ever break through the political barriers and into the confidence of officers at the big banks, you will have a powerful source of funds.

- *Credit unions*—Many credit unions are growing faster than other institutions, because they have been hurt less by regulatory changes than other institutions. Each credit union has strict charter guidelines, so call first to see if they can handle your type of request.
- *Savings banks*—Call first and see what their policies are. There are many savings banks in the Northeast. Some are well over a hundred years old.
- *Insurance companies*—The money from your insurance premiums goes into investment pools that lend out a specified percentage of the fund. These pools prefer larger loan applications, usually in excess of $1 million.
- *Trust departments*—The same bank that turned you down in the commercial loan department may have a trust department that is looking for good loans.
- *Pension and retirement funds*—These funds are constantly seeking good ways to invest their money. If your proposal is sound, they are worth investigating.
- *Association funds*—Union groups, teachers' groups, railroad groups, all have funds set aside for their association purposes. A union group may have a large pool of reserves for purposes of contingent member support. A teachers' group might have a payroll deduction fund. Often these groups will lend funds on a short-term, well-secured basis.
- *Corporations*—Corporations go through periods of being cash rich. Occasionally, if you know the right person, they will lend for a short term.
- *Wealthy individuals*—Those who are blessed with having nothing to do but watch their investments are always on the lookout for reputable businesses

to back that will make them money. A word of caution here: be careful that *you* don't get bought out in the process.

- *Partnerships*—Many people don't need a loan as much as they need a partner. A partnership is where two or more parties agree to assume and share the risk. A good loan will stand on its own merits with a minimum of risk. But in most partnerships, both partners still have risk and liability for all of the debt. Therefore, if your partner flakes out, you still have the liability.
- *Friends, associates, or relatives*—The danger with borrowing from colleagues or loved ones is that you run the risk of losing a close relationship if things don't go well, and sometimes even if they do. The advantage is that these people know and understand you best. Good communication is the key. Many businesses have gotten off the ground with seed money provided by friends, associates, and relatives.
- *Foreign investors*—These are difficult to establish because there are so many communication, trust, legal, and logistical obstacles. Find a nation that is prospering, and focus on locating a source of financing within that country. In recent years, Japan, Germany, and Holland have been excellent sources of new capital for thousands of American businesses. How do you make contact? Go to a public library and find a list of the International Chambers of Commerce. Then through the chamber of the nation you have chosen, locate banks and investment brokers. Or get the names of leading bankers through the *International Bank Directory*, and write letters of inquiry asking for referrals.

- *Doctors and attorneys*—The medical community in particular has prospered over the years, and many doctors, as individuals or as group practices, have large sums of money at their disposal. They often hire managers to invest their money. This is a good source, but it may take valuable time to make credible contact.
- *The SBIC alternative*—As you read in the previous chapter, SBICs have many advantages. This hybrid source of funding is available to loan customers who cannot find other satisfactory financing.

Finally, don't forget to listen. Use your social and business contacts to help you locate the right lender. At a Rotary Club meeting or a church gathering, you may unexpectedly find the source of credit right for you. In the meantime, if you would like to start a find-a-bank service, give me a call. The idea could make someone rich.

10

Using a Loan Agent/Consultant

In some situations, using an outside consultant to assist you with your loan application might be a powerful help to you or your business in getting your loan approved. In most cases, it is preferable for the individual or the owner of the company to establish the all-important rapport with the banker. But a loan agent can sometimes be of invaluable assistance. For example, the busy businessperson starting a new concern may simply be *too* busy running the company to put together and present a complete loan presentation. His or her time may be far better spent making money and letting an experienced consultant assemble the details. Complicated or technical loans such as SBA applications often are "packaged" by consultants.

Large corporations almost always have a team of accountants and lawyers who put together their loan presentations. Using such experts can be a valuable help for the individual and the small business as well. Perhaps you are not a good communicator, are a poor negotiator, or do not understand how to put together a projection or a P&L statement. Bringing in a professional can also generate energy and insight into the behavior of others.

There are numerous qualified loan consultants— some past bankers, some accountants, some retired CEOs of large corporations—who can provide valuable advice and experience at a reasonable price. Fees for this type of service vary with the consultant, but most work on an hourly basis and charge from $75 to $200 per hour. If you are fortunate, you will find one who may work on a fee contingent upon loan approval, but if you do, you will find that the final fee is much higher than for an hourly consultant.

Benefits

One consideration, if you use a loan consultant, broker, or agent to represent you, is the perception it presents. First of all, a consultant will present a professional image to the banker. When you have gone to the trouble and expense of hiring an outside consultant, there is no doubt that it should impress your lender. He or she will realize how important this loan is to you.

Also, one of the basic tenets of negotiating is that often the subject has far more credibility if someone else says something good about the subject than if the subject says it about him- or herself. An excellent example of this concerns a speech I made before a large bankers' convention. A former congressman in the audience approached me after the speech and said, "Man, that was dynamite! If you will give me copies of your material, I'll get it to the President." I looked at him with some doubt and said, "There is *no way* the President is going to pay any attention to me!" He grinned and said, "He will when *I* recommend it to him."

Within a few weeks, I saw a newspaper report wherein the President made a statement that was almost identical to the material I had provided. I called my friend: "Did the President get my material?" He smiled and said, "Yes, and you may be hearing more about it in the newspapers."

Now, in a very real sense, the fact that a third party represented me made the presentation far more effective than if I had sent it off to the President of the United States myself. The same principle holds true for you when you are borrowing money. While you have much credibility as the owner or borrower, it is sometimes more powerful if a third party extols the good aspects of your business or management than if you try to do it yourself.

This will not relieve you of the importance of establishing a personal rapport with the banker, but it will certainly add another bullet in your shot at loan approval. This is perhaps more true if your first loan request was denied.

Another positive aspect of using a professional to prepare your loan package is the insight that objective observation from an outside professional may inject. Although no human will know more about your business than you, the owner, often you are so involved in the day-to-day operating details, the problems of management, that you may lose a larger perspective. The perspective of an outside professional may instantly focus on a positive aspect of your business that you had not considered. In one case, I was working as a consultant for an old, established bank with an excellent financial statement and a good profit ratio. But the bank staff appeared to be almost inundated with their daily work load. I closed the office door of the bank president and said, "I would like to speak to you confidentially. If you will consider initiating two programs, we can solve two problems that could save your bank a great deal of money." He looked at me with some curiosity, and as I explained, a wave of relief showed on his face.

"It is so simple, why didn't I think of that!" he exclaimed. "You didn't think of it because your mind was so full of your day-to-day challenges," I replied. In the end, he told me that those two suggestions may have saved his bank over a million dollars. In this case, the perspective of an outside consultant proved to be valuable to that executive. In some cases, another viewpoint can be helpful to your company as you build a loan proposal.

Selecting a Consultant

When selecting a consultant, you will need to get this basic information:

- Ask about his or her past successes.
- Verify references.
- Obtain a written disclosure of the fee schedule.
- Require a written contract and agreement that specifically outlines your expectations and job description.
- Ask to review a sample of work done for other clients, and see if it appears professional and impressive.
- Interview the consultant, and probe to determine his or her competency and knowledge of banking and loan documentation. (Use the checklist in this book as a guide.)
- Consider whether you like the consultant. Is he or she impressive to *you*? If the consultant can't impress you, he or she will have a harder time with your banker.
- Ask for a preliminary "verbal outline" of the consultant's strategy for preparing your loan presentation.

All of this information should be free to you as a part of your initial interview with the consultant.

Next you need to consider whether using a consultant is economically feasible. Is the money you will spend on this professional worth the time it will allow you to concentrate on your business? Will the consultant substantially increase your chances of loan approval?

A good loan consultant can often take a mediocre or marginal loan package and present it in a credible format. Often, it is well worth the price to hire an outside agent to prepare your package just for the knowledge and a sample packet, which you can use in future loan presentations. In the final analysis you, the borrower, need to determine if a loan consultant is practical, considering your needs. As borrowing and lending requirements grow ever more complex in the changing bank world, many borrowers will answer in the affirmative.

=== 11 ===

When Your Loan Is Approved

The telephone rings. Your secretary tells you it is the banker on the line. Your heart skips a beat. You pick up the telephone. "Hello."

"Hello, this is Cameron Wright from the bank."

"Yes, Mr. Wright." At this point you brace yourself for the news.

"I am glad to report that your loan has been approved."

You are momentarily speechless.

"You may come down to the bank any time, and we will have the loan papers ready for your signature."

"Uh, that's great," you say weakly.

"The loan committee asked me to convey their compliments on your proposal and documentation. It was thorough and well done. It made our job easier."

By now you are thinking that all of the work was worth it. "Well, thank you."

"When will you be in?"

"I'll be there at 10:00 A.M."

"We'll have the papers ready."

"Good-bye."

What mistake did the borrower make in the conversation? It seems that you got everything you asked for. But in some cases borrowers are so pleased to be approved that they fail to ask a few very important questions.

What to Say to the Banker

This critical point in time can be very powerful. The banker knows this. The period when the loan is approved but yet unclosed can still be a period of negotiation. Consider it like the time a real estate agent has a customer interested in a property but the deal is not yet closed. Oftentimes many critical issues are brought out at the closing table. Or it could be compared to a lawyer making final arguments to a jury. Often those last points are critical to the case. There are a few questions the customer might ask at this point.

Which of my proposals did the committee approve? Remember, you presented an original written proposal with your preferred request and an alternative. Be sure you understand what the bank is authorizing.

Were there any alterations to my proposal? Bankers and loan committees are notorious for approving loans but with so many "minor" alterations in their favor as to cost the customer money. Therefore, you need to understand how any changes will affect you.

At what interest rate? This question may seem redundant, but there is another bank technique you must be aware of. Your proposal mentioned a float above prime rate, so ask, "Whose prime?" Often the prime rate in New York is a full point higher or lower than in a different region of the nation. Historically, New York prime has been the lead indicator and has been the base for most major banks all over the country. Local banks often set their own prime rate. Be sure the "prime" that is attached to your loan is to your advantage.

How will the interest rate be calculated on my loan? A word of caution here. There are several ways banks calculate interest. One way is "add-on," which is usually the most expensive and is normally calculated on a 360-day year. In this calculation the interest for the entire term of the loan is calculated and added onto the principal of the note, then the total is divided by the number of months. This becomes your payment. Here's an example:

Loan	$1,000
Rate	10% add-on
Term	24 months

$$10\% \times \$1,000 \times 2 \text{ years} = \$1,200$$

$$\$1,200 \div 24 = \$50 \text{ per month}$$

Remember, you also paid the interest up front, so although your "add-on rate" is 10 percent, your true interest rate is higher.

A second way of calculating interest is simple interest based upon a term. Some banks calculate simple interest using a 360-day year, and others use a 365-day year. The reason is twofold. In the old days of banking P.C. (pre-computer), bankers reasoned that since there were 12 months in a year, it would be simple to figure interest on a 360-day year, or a 30-day month. That was the public explanation. What bankers often failed to tell the customer was that by using a 360-day year, the bank actually made a little more money each day of accrual than if it calculated interest on a 365-day year.

Here's an example of the calculation on a 360-day note:

Amount	$1,000
Rate	10%
Term	2 years (loan due at maturity)

In 730 days (365 × 2), you will have paid 10% × $1,000 = $100 for the first 360 days, then $.27 per day for the additional five days for each year. So your true payment of interest over two years is $202.70. Another way to calculate it is just to figure $.2777 per day for 730 days, or $202.72. (The difference is a rounding error.) The same loan calculated on simple interest at 10 percent would be $100 per year, or a total interest of $200, or $.2739 per day.

Simple interest is less confusing, will keep your bookkeeping simple, and is less costly. It may sound like small change, but as your business grows and so do your lending needs, it makes a difference.

Are there any prepayment penalties? Most commercial banks will answer no, but it is good to ask.

Are there any closing costs or fees? One of the biggest complaints borrowers from the savings and loan industry had in the heady boom days before the great fall was that large mortgage loans often had huge closing costs that did not appear until near closing. Not only were there standard fees for appraisal, title policy, and attorney, but also loan origination fees, loan processing fees, commitment fees, and a host of fees with names too numerous and creative to count were added to the loan package. Some commercial bankers have adopted similar policies in the interest of profits. They are very congenial about adding these fees into the loan amount "so these fees do not come out of your pocket" and so they can charge interest on the fees. In spite of the numerous regulations regarding truth in lending and disclosure, often the disclosures are so complicated that they discourage one's attempts to understand. Better just to ask your banker and get a straight answer.

What happens upon maturity of the loan if unforeseen events indicate that I can't pay it off? This is the time to understand the banker's attitude. Is the bank going to repossess all of your collateral? Will your banker be willing to let you reduce the loan and put it on a repayment program? Certainly, you do not go into a loan with the intent of defaulting, but you do want to understand all of the risks involved.

What if you move to another bank? How will that affect this loan? At this point, it is good to have the banker give you a written understanding of the loan to which you can refer if he or she leaves. Consider a customer we will name "T. Bone." T. Bone had a loan he was paying, but with some effort. His banker respected his integrity and always made allowances when the loan payments came in late. The banker and the customer had a good enough relationship that they trusted each other. Both knew the other would do his best to help in the troubled times. The banker left the bank, and our friend T. Bone got a call one day from the new banker assigned to his account. The message was not a friendly one. His loan was being called; he would pay in full immediately or face a lawsuit, judgment, and repossession. T. Bone was shocked. To pay off the bank, he had to liquidate property that had been placed for collateral at a distress sale value far below what he thought the property was worth. The outcome of this matter might have changed if there had been a correspondence file indicating that the customer had always paid, and that the bank would work with him so long as he was able to pay in good faith and was not over a specified number of days past due.

The Big Question

Your loan has been approved! It is now time for the most important question of all: do you really want it? This is your last chance to reevaluate before you become obligated to a legal contract that could lead you to substantial success or great failure. Remember, more people file bankruptcy as a result of borrowing too much money than for any other reason. Do you really want to borrow this money?

A brilliant CPA in Boston became quite good at finding profitable investments. As his reputation grew, some of his wealthy clients asked him if he would keep an eye out for good investments for them. The economy was good, with real estate prices going up, so the CPA (we will call him Sam Sovereign) started putting together shopping center developments, apartment complexes, and office building investments. These deals were all too large for any one investor to handle, so Sam Sovereign put together joint ventures and partnerships and "cut his clients in." Sam took the responsibility of obtaining the loans. He would sign the loans as managing partner and always personally guaranteed them.

He had mastered the keys to managing credit, and there were several bankers in Boston who were willing, if not anxious, to handle his loan requests. It seemed that Sam could do no wrong. Every investment was profitable, and each time Sam's group sold one of the developments for a profit, the investors just let Sam keep the money and invest it in another project. One day Sam woke up and was

managing over $30 million in investments. At least that
was their value on paper. He had loans of about $21
million on the various properties, all of which had his
signature and personal guarantee. Sam's reputation became such that even the largest banks in Boston knew him
and solicited his business. He became overaggressive in
his borrowing practices.

In one case Sam and his partners put together an
investment group to start a concrete business. They
needed concrete trucks, a building, a batch plant, and
several hundred thousand dollars in operating capital.
Sam went to a company that sold concrete trucks, with an
agreement that he would buy the trucks, but on a one-year
lease-purchase agreement. They agreed, and he purchased
a fleet of trucks. Then Sam found a bank that had repos-
sessed a concrete batch plant. The bank wanted out, so
Sam came in as a "white knight" and said he would purchase the batch plant from the bank if the bank would
finance the deal and also lend him an additional $200,000
operating capital. The bank, faced with a potential loss,
saw Sam the successful businessman as a savior, and they
also saw a way to make a profitable loan. Sam then found
a building and leased it, with a term of three months' free
rent and an option to buy the building at the end of a two-
year lease.

In this case, Sam had put together a new company
and gained control of $900,000 in assets for himself and
his partners without putting a penny of money down. Sam
knew this entire group of deals did not follow conservative,
prudent business practice, but those were heady times.
Sam also realized that on all of the leases, contracts, and
loans, his name was on the bottom line. His bankers
usually required that his partners sign guarantees, but
occasionally the bankers would say, "If Sam Sovereign's
signature is on the loan, it is sufficient for us."

The economy began to falter. Real estate values started to decline. New construction slowed to a grinding halt. Sam quickly put the real estate on the market, but the properties didn't sell. He reported to his partners that although there was not a good market to sell the real estate, they could hold out on the rental income from the properties and the income from the concrete batch plant until the market turned. The economy didn't cooperate, and real estate prices went down even further. Owners of large real estate projects all went through the same mental process. They knew that to survive they would have to attract tenants, which required that leasing rates be lowered. Before long the rental income was not enough to cover the debt service. The concrete company was not doing well because investors were afraid to build new structures in an economy that could not support existing construction.

Sam called on his investors to put up additional money to service debt, which they did for a while, then one by one they began to drop out. The ones who dropped out first were those who had not signed personal guarantees on the loans. Sam checked his holdings. He now had $22 million in loans on properties appraised at $19 million. Sam was technically bankrupt, and his financial future was going down as more and more investors dropped out, leaving him with the liabilities. Some of the banks extended terms, lowered interest rates, and made a diligent effort to work with him. A few banks under pressure called their loans and ended up repossessing partially vacant office buildings.

Sam's legal counsel recommended that he file bankruptcy and let the banks have all of the collateral. But Sam had too much integrity for that and continued to work with the properties. He sold his airplane, he sold his vacation home in Colorado, he drove a used car and made great personal sacrifices. Bit by bit, going through virtual hell, he found a new tenant here, a buyer there. Every time he sold a property, he applied all of the proceeds to his debt. All this while he was trying to carry on his CPA practice, which caused him to work long and late hours regularly. Three years later, Sam reported that he now had loans of $2 million on assets valued at $2.1 million. His personal net worth had been wiped out—all he really had was his home—but he had fought through a terrible economic cycle and survived.

Sam determined to devote himself to his CPA practice. He concluded that the perks of having control of millions of dollars in assets were not worth the work, stress, and pain that came with it. Sam Sovereign survived, but he learned a valuable lesson. Mastering the secrets of debt is a two-edged sword. It can bring great rewards, but it must also be handled with great judgment and care. In Sam's case, he was responsible enough to take care of the creditors who were loyal to him. In spite of a poor economic cycle and overaggressive borrowing and investing, he kept his reputation and self-respect intact. He also gained the undying respect and admiration of the bankers who had backed him. The doors of the vaults of those bankers whom he repaid rather than filing bankruptcy may again open up to him . . . but in the future, Sam and his bankers will be more prudent.

Sam's story illustrates the point of this chapter and the questions better than anything. Now that your loan is approved, is it wise, is it prudent, is it the right thing for you and your business? Do you really want to consummate it? These are words of caution, but caution when borrowing money—especially when it can affect your life to the good, or the bad—is worthwhile.

Remember the old saying: "Be careful of what you ask for, for you may get it!"

12

Safe Ways to Dump a Bad Banker
Without Ruining Yourself

You have your business, you have your loan, things are going along until you begin to have problems with the bank. At first it may be little things, for example, the bank's bookkeeping department does not balance your checkbook, or a forged check clears your account. Perhaps your IRA statement has the wrong balance. Little things continue to happen. Your employees try to cash their paychecks, and the banker refuses or charges an exorbitant fee. Your canceled checks are not all in your statement. Your loan payments are calculated incorrectly. By now you are a little fed up. The task of a bank is to handle and account for money, and your bank doesn't seem to be doing a very good job of it.

In a move to clear up the problem, you decide to go into the bank and speak to your officer about the problems. He or she listens and takes a few notes but when you leave, you have the feeling that the banker, or that bank, just isn't going to give you the personal attention you expect.

Then it happens. The bank cashes a forged check on your company account, and when they find the problem, they refuse to honor their mistake. They charge *you* a service charge for the research time to uncover their mistake. You worked hard to build a banking relationship. You worked hard to create a well-documented loan file, and you have always honored your commitments. You call your banker again, but he or she doesn't seem responsive. Another bank in town has been courting your business, but you are reluctant to move, for fear that it might jeopardize your loan relationship.

It is obvious that something has to change . . . so what do you do?

Determining What Must Change

Determine whether you need a new banker or a new bank. It may well be that your bank is fine, that you just have an individual who has become overwhelmed with other responsibilities. Perhaps the banker has other, larger customers and simply can't give your business the attention he or she once did.

You worked hard to build a good relationship with this banker, and you certainly don't want to throw that away. Therefore, it will be time well spent to go in one last time, with your banking problems detailed. That conversation is your best last attempt to evaluate the banker and to determine whether the problem is with the banker or the bank.

It could be that the bank has adopted new policies that have caused the banker to do things differently. For example, it is not unusual for a bank to increase service charges. Most officers have the authority to waive or refund service charges, but sometimes they don't. In deciding whether the problem is your banker or your bank, find out whether the bank is experiencing a high turnover of employees and staff. This may be a reflection of other problems.

If the problem is the banker, the easiest solution is simply to call the president or the department head and tell that person confidentially what your problems are. State that you would like to be assigned to another officer who will take care of your business. At this time it is important to specify what you expect out of your banker. In this manner you don't have to move your entire account structure and loan structure to another bank.

An old farmer had banked with his small-town bank in Iowa for forty years. It was the bank of his father and his grandfather. He found a farm he wanted to buy to add to his other holdings, and applied to the bank for a loan. The farm economy was bad, and the bank was "loaned up." It had loaned as much as policy would allow. The bank therefore turned down the farmer's loan request. The banker expected the customer to get mad and leave to do business with another bank. So the banker asked him, "What are you going to do?"

"Well, if this bank won't make the loan . . . I just won't borrow any money anywhere."

Your business may not have the flexibility or the choice that farmer had. You may need the loan desperately and would like to know why the bank can't offer this service. If you understand what the problem is, it will help you see what your options are.

Understanding the Source of the Problem

Dozens of things can affect the level of service a bank offers. One of the most common is a change of management or ownership. This change almost invariably causes a period of transition difficult for banker and customer alike. Often new owners like to replace the staff with people *they* have hired and trained. Unfortunately, replacing or reducing staff creates a period of orientation time in which customer service suffers.

Often present management is forced to make changes in policy. The simplest example of a visible policy change that affects you is in the area of service charges. A bank experiences increasing overhead or losses and can't make up the difference in loan fees or investments, so it increases service charges. Some banks pay their entire salary expense from the income of service charges.

Occasionally a bank will change its philosophy. One of the largest banks in the nation bought out a regional chain of banks in Florida. There was a public outcry from thousands of customers, who suddenly found that they couldn't get loans, yet they paid high fees for every little service from traveler's checks to notary service. This was an example of a simple change in philosophy. Nobody liked it, but the policy direction had been dictated at the home office several states distant. The policy was to disregard customer loyalty concerns, to forget the personal service, which is costly in time and labor, to look only at the bottom line. The result? The customers suffered.

Occasionally a bank will find itself under regulatory pressure to change policies. Banks have literally been taken over quietly by regulators and had their internal policies changed dramatically upon memorandum by examiners. In these cases, the customer does not know what is going on. What banker in his or her right mind would advertise that the examiners are concerned about the bank? The customers first feel it when some new policy causes them grief or costs them money. These issues are illustrated by a story told by a banker in Montana. His bank, which was considered a good bank, was examined, and during the course of the examination, the examiner became very critical. The bank then had to endure *five years* of stricter regulatory procedures, even though it was well capitalized and making a good profit. I asked the bank president if it had an impact on his customers. "Oh, yes," he said. "They didn't know it, but we were being tougher than ever, requiring things that we normally wouldn't, because the examiners had us under their magnifying glass."

Often outside influences, far beyond the control of either the banker or the customer, have a direct bearing on the service level and the ease of obtaining loans. The letter in Figure 22 provides a good example.

Picking a New Bank

Care and patience are important words when picking a new bank. You don't want your current banker to think you are leaving mad, and you especially don't want your banker to resort to forcing you to pay off your loans when you move. Perhaps it is time for you to invite to lunch that other banker who has been courting you. In strict confidence, explain the problems you are experiencing, and set forth what you expect in a bank.

If the banker responds positively, go through the same questions you asked in the initial interview of your original banker—questions about the ability, quality, and philosophy of the new bank. Be sure the banker understands all of your needs. One day a customer came into one of my banks and opened accounts with several hundred thousand dollars in the name of his business. Soon thereafter, he applied for a loan. Our loan limit to any one customer at the time was $500,000. This customer wanted to borrow $600,000. We could not help him. He had opened all of those accounts for nothing. It was beyond our legal ability to lend him what he needed. He could have saved some time and labor by asking us up front what our legal lending limit was.

Figure 22

DESCRIPTION OF OUTSIDE INFLUENCES ON BANK POLICY

GEORGE WM. BERRY, PH.D.

702 COLORADO, SUITE 103
AUSTIN, TEXAS 78701-3036
FAX (512) 477-1432
(512) 477-3143

January 23, 1992

Mr. Ben B. Boothe, President
Ben B. Boothe and Associates
8851 Highway 80 West, Suite 201
Fort Worth, Texas 76116

Dear Ben:

On a number of occasions, you and I have discussed how the combined influence of politics and economics impact the banking industry. During the early 1980's, Texas experienced a great economic boom because of the oil and gas shortage, favorable tax investments in real estate, oil and gas, and encouraged "growthmanship" for financial institutions.

The Department of Energy had stated unequivocally that it was the policy of the Federal Government that the United States shall be FREE from dependency on foreign oil. Prior to 1986, real estate and oil and gas received favorable tax treatment under the Internal Revenue Code.

The Texas boom was effectively killed by the Tax Reform Act of 1986 and the change in attitude toward foreign oil. These decisions were made in the political arena.

This background information is mentioned because banks are subject to extreme regulations by the various government agencies. These attitudes shift. Today, it is difficult to obtain real estate loans in Texas because of the great number of foreclosures. We have a continued overhang of real estate inventory because of RTC and FDIC.

Bankers and bank customers should be attuned to the changing political and economic environment. Customers may want a real estate loan but may have to use other types of collateral to obtain funds. Understanding the political and economic environment in which we live will aid each of us.

Sincerely yours,

George Wm. Berry, Ph. D.

GWB/jr

Gradually Withdrawing

One of your biggest complaints may be that your current bank is not giving your accounts enough attention. You can use this to your advantage. Gradually draw the funds out of your accounts, and don't make any more large deposits there. Open new accounts elsewhere. When you change bank depositories, be prepared to change lenders as well. Be certain that you have laid the groundwork to move your loans to the other bank on terms at least as good as the terms you already have.

When you are thinking of making a change anyway, it is an excellent time to let a new bank solicit your business. Offer to move your loans if the bank can beat your current rate of interest and terms. It has been said that the dog doesn't care for a dead fish until the cat tries to get it. It could be that by careful negotiation, you can move your banking business at great advantage, or, if your present bank learns that you are moving your business, it may improve its service and terms as well. In any case, you win better bank service.

One large borrower didn't like the service charges at his bank. He also felt that they were not efficient or, as he said, "on their toes" in bookkeeping. He kept his loans at bank A but gradually drew his accounts down to a bare minimum and banked with another bank. It was two years before bank A noticed.

Keeping Your Options Open

Most people will benefit by having one main bank to do most of their business, but it is also good business to keep a second account and relationship with another bank, just in case. For example, Bob Jones opened an account at a savings and loan institution in Colorado while he was building a mountain home there. The S&L where he had his account made a mortgage loan to him for the mountain home. The same month he also opened an account at a local bank. One day he got a notice in the mail that the S&L had been closed by the government. He was lucky—and wise—to have had another banking relationship already established in that town.

By handling your banking needs in the manner that I have described, you multiply and diversify your financial potential, rather than let it be destroyed. When you are asked where you bank, your reply can honestly be "I bank with several banks." That's not a bad reply in any setting. Note that all banks will want you to do all of your business with that bank. That is understandable and fair . . . if they justify your business with the level of service you demand and require. Knowing you also bank elsewhere gives your banker an incentive and a challenge. And when bankers have more incentive to offer the best service possible, they will.

13

What to Do if Your Loan Goes Bad or Your Credit Rating Is Poor

"Things happen" said the bumper sticker on the car of a shopping center developer in Boston. Often, though every detail of a loan looks good on paper and in financial projections, the unexpected happens. Suddenly the loan of which you were so proud has gone bad. Indeed, it was reported that in the states of Texas and Massachusetts alone, in the period between January 1989 and March 1991, over $11 billion in bank capital was lost. That represents perhaps $150 billion or more in loan funds that were no longer available, just in those two regions. Few, very few people predicted the severity of the economic declines in those large, formerly prosperous markets. Bankers and customers alike were caught by surprise. The bankruptcy courts were packed to capacity with huge backlogs on the dockets. Businesspeople caught in a cycle of declining property values and declining business suddenly found that they could not pay their loans and that banks were unable or unwilling to lend them more or even work with them on outstanding loans. The loans went into default by the thousands.

What do you do if it happens to you?

The first thing to keep in mind is the long-term effect your course will have on your career, your future, your business, and your reputation. The quick way out is to file bankruptcy and run away from your obligations. With the bankruptcy laws of today, that course is an easy way out. And then come the lawyers who consistently recommend it as a business strategy.

Filing Bankruptcy

Bankruptcy is an alternative, but one that has several negative connotations. When you file bankruptcy, you have most certainly ruined your chances of acquiring other funds for some time to come. Bankers who have been hard hit by defaults have little sympathy for a business or an individual who files bankruptcy. A banker in Colorado was noted for physically throwing a preacher out of his bank when the preacher disclosed that he had filed Chapter 7 bankruptcy. (His timing wasn't very good either, for he mentioned it right in the middle of a loan application.) The banker was heard quoting scripture as he pulled the preacher by the scruff of his neck through the lobby. Secretaries reported hearing the banker say, "You are a minister of gospel! You should be ashamed—haven't you ever heard the scripture 'Owe no man anything'? Get out of my bank and stay out!"

Bankruptcy, like other bad credit, will stay on your credit report for a minimum of seven years. That is not the worst of it. It will stay in the memories and files of bankers far longer. Essentially, when you file bankruptcy, you are escaping responsibility, but the price you pay is that you are effectively locking yourself out of the credit system for some time. Whereas bankruptcy in England and Europe is considered not only a business disgrace but a social disgrace as well, in America some have tried to make it an acceptable form of financial management.

Essentially this is what happens to the banker when an entity files bankruptcy. If, for example, you have a company that makes widgets, the banker has to come in, pick up the pieces, perhaps run your widget company, and hopefully liquidate the mess you left. Since the bank must deal with problems like this, it should be clear why bankruptcy participants do not endear themselves to bankers.

Bankruptcy law has been manipulated by unscrupulous lawyers to achieve everything from breaking union contracts to avoiding payment of alimony. It has in turn put a terrible strain on the banking system—such a strain that some people believe the current bankruptcy laws are responsible for the failure of large numbers of financial institutions. Whereas the law was originally written to be a salvation of last resort, to "save the family farm" or to protect someone who is devastated, for example, by medical bills, in recent years it has been distorted and abused with great effectiveness. So when your loan goes bad, don't file bankruptcy.

Positive Courses of Action

There are some positive things that you can do if your loan is in trouble. First, talk to your banker. Go in and tell him or her every detail. Strongly emphasize your intention to deal with the bank in good faith.

Ask the banker if he or she will refinance your loan, defer payments, lower interest rates. The banker, when he or she realizes that you are behaving in good faith and trying to avoid bankruptcy, should conclude that some help from the bank now may save the entire ship from sinking.

Never let your communication turn negative, and never be embarrassed to stay in touch. A customer became past due on a loan, and for thirty days the bank made every effort to contact him by mail, telephone, even telegram. Finally the bank had no choice but to hire an attorney and initiate legal proceedings. After the first correspondence from the attorney, the customer came walking into the bank. His demeanor was like that of a dog dragging his tail between his legs. "You didn't have to sic a lawyer on me," he said.

"Mr. Smith, let me tell you something," said the unsmiling banker. "All you've got keeping you out of the biggest lawsuit you have ever seen is communication. As long as you are communicating with me and showing good faith, this bank can help you. When you stop that, we have no choice but to take legal action."

The customer said, "I didn't want to talk to you because I was embarrassed." That day he learned to get over his embarrassment and to start working with the banker who wanted to help him.

Don't give your affairs to an attorney, unless you want to go to court. When I was a child, I had an air gun, a prized toy. One day I pointed it at a friend. He looked at me and said, "Never point a gun at anyone . . . unless you intend to use it." He then grabbed the gun and gave me a working over not to be forgotten. If you want to spend your money on attorneys and your time in court, that is your choice. But remember, banks have deeper pockets and can hire better attorneys.

There is no doubt that an attorney is necessary for advice on many issues. But the day when you turn your financial affairs over to your attorney and he or she takes control of the events in your life instead of you, you are in for an unpleasant journey. Attorneys are trained to be hired guns and to give legal advice. They are not trained businesspeople, and often good legal advice is very poor business advice. For example, whereas taking bankruptcy may be the best legal advice you could ask for, it could be the worst business decision you ever made.

Keep Paying

Keep paying on your loan regularly, even if it is a token amount. A senior vice president of a national bank borrowed $79,000 to invest in a shopping center project. Suddenly three disastrous things happened that he could not have foreseen. First his bank failed. Next he lost his high-paying job. Finally, the investment manager (the senior partner of the shopping center) skipped the country and left him holding a debt for $79,000 with no way to pay for it. He could not find a bank job anywhere and finally started a company painting apartment complexes.

He made quite an impression on the bank officers when he came in every Friday (in his overalls and painter's hat, spattered with paint from his shoes to his forehead) and handed the banker his checks for the week. All he asked was that the banker leave him enough to operate on. Some weeks his company paid $50 and others several hundred dollars. In light of his continuance and persistence, the bank did everything in its power to help him, not only by deferring interest, but also by referring jobs to him and encouraging him in every way possible.

Keep Believing

No matter how overwhelming your financial problems are, never fail to believe that you can survive and work through them. Lee Goodman, a prominent businessman in Ft. Worth, Texas, built a company worth more than $35 million over a period of twenty-five years. When one of the famous economic downturns hit Texas, he suddenly saw people he had trusted failing all around him. People quit paying. Investment associates filed bankruptcy. His cash flow dropped to the point that he had to start liquidating assets.

Five years later, his net worth had fallen to a negative $3 million. Yet he still came to work with a smile and never gave up faith that he could work his way through. As one of his bankers, I always appreciated Lee, because in spite of all of his losses, he never failed to pay his bank note. He became an inspiration to an entire community, in that he would not give up.

Slowly Lee's debts began to fall, and his business began to improve. Bankers who had been afraid when the economy was failing began to realize that this was a man who would fight to do what was right, to his very dying breath. Lee Goodman lost millions before the cycle bottomed out, but then he began to bounce back. He went through all the financial upheavals without filing personal bankruptcy and without spending all of his energy and money on lawyers. He tried to spend his creative energy looking for creative ways to survive. And he did. If you think you have problems, consider how much he lost, and he still came back successfully.

Set Priorities

Prioritize your income and expenses. An old rancher in Wyoming had always managed to turn a profit. Year after year his ranch did well when others didn't. Finally one of his neighbors came over to see him to ask his advice. "I just can't seem to make it work. Look here at my records. What do you think?"

The old rancher looked at the figures and said, "Well, young feller, 'pears to me that you don't know your algebra very well."

"Algebra? What does algebra have to do with running a ranch?"

"Well, you done let your gross habits exceed your net income."

"Just what does that mean in English?"

"Well, the way I see it—and you asked an' all, I'm not trying to be meddlesome—you've got two choices. Either increase your net income or reduce your expenses." With that advice, he walked off.

When your loan goes bad, it is time to reexamine everything in a new light. It is time to list every expense and categorize each in order of priority. Then review the opposite side of the ledger, itemizing all income sources. You must then review every asset and determine which ones should be liquidated first, in order to create capital for reducing indebtedness, on which to operate.

You may be required to change your lifestyle and make a radical change in the way your company does business. But if you can successfully pull it off, you and your business will benefit for years to come from the things you learn. Much of the ability to make it happen is your willingness to make the hard decisions. Some will be painful, and some will affect people with whom you are close. But those very people will understand that you are in a struggle for survival. More than likely, you will gain the respect of everyone around you when you are willing to sacrifice and do what is necessary to save your company from failure.

You may have to resort to creative means of generating cash flow, and that creative effort may be your greatest victory. For example, a tent factory was in dire straits and resorted to making parachutes to generate temporary cash flow. The government heard about the business and placed an order for hundreds of parachutes. Eventually making parachutes became more profitable than making tents.

Examples abound. An oil company lost 85 percent of its business supplying oil field pipe. To stay in business, the company started making storm shelters out of oil and water tanks in inventory. And an old grocery store could not compete with the giant food chains that took most of the old store's retail grocery business, so the manager started cooking hamburgers in the back of the old store. His hamburgers made Kincaid's a world famous luncheon stop in Ft. Worth. Magazines and newspapers nationwide have featured Kincaid's for its huge, tasty hamburgers. A farmer on the Great Plains could not generate enough profits growing traditional crops. With the help of a doctor who was intrigued by grapes, the farmer planted a vineyard. Soon the farmer and doctor were producing fine domestic wines, wines that have won awards even in France.

What Not to Do

Years ago a man from Armenia moved to the United States. He worked hard as a tailor, and after many years of saving, he decided he would buy the building he had rented. Still more years passed, and he bought the building next door. As he grew older he accumulated a tiny estate in small retail buildings. He sent his sons to college, and one of his sons decided to build an apartment complex.

The apartments became a financial success, and after a number of years, the son, like his father before him, decided he would expand. He developed a ten-floor office building. But this did not work out nearly as well as his apartment complex. Before long he realized he had negative cash flow and the office building was not leasing up fast enough to save him. Instead of going to the bankers who had financed him, he hired an attorney, filed bankruptcy, and walked away from the investment.

Some fifteen years later, I was handling a banking transaction, and this man's name came up as one of the parties. I called a banker in the town where the man lived, and he simply said, "Oh, everyone here knows that he is a flake. Why, fifteen years ago we financed an office building, and instead of trying to stick it out and make it work, he stuck us with it. I'd stay away from him if I were you."

We did some further research on the fellow and found that he had been the principal investor in several aborted developments. His pattern was established. He would draw up elaborate plans and sell the loan as an impressive package. No local banks would deal with him, so he went to cities on both coasts and finally resorted to borrowing from foreign banks. But if the project did not begin to bring in cash within a short period of time, he would file bankruptcy. He had, in fact, filed bankruptcy several times. Somehow, through his Armenian and New York banking connections, he managed to find lenders and investors. But none were local banks!

As fate would have it, I found myself in his city, and while eating at a restaurant I saw him sitting with a prominent businessman. I overheard him say, "Sure, I've done it several times. Go ahead and file bankruptcy. It is the cheapest way out. Stick them before they stick you." That was all I heard. I'll never forget his words, because one month later in the national business press, a story ran. The very man with whom he had been talking had just filed bankruptcy. In the process this second businessman nearly broke three banks. Bankruptcy was his game . . . on the advice of another flake who had taught him the game.

There is no way to know or understand how many businesses or individuals are injured by people with that kind of philosophy. Nor is there any way to estimate how much their way of doing business costs the society in general. Certainly it drives up interest rates, makes credit harder to acquire, creates problems of unemployment, and takes money away from the stockholders and banks that were unfortunate enough to back them in the first place. Clearly the example just given is not the way to build relationships to help you master the credit game and gain the trust and backing of lenders when you need them.

The Importance of What You Do

Why all of the emphasis on what to do if you *don't* succeed and the loan goes bad? It is simply this. The way you handle your banking relationships when the worst has happened will determine the banking relationships you are able to develop in years to come. The banking grapevine is a powerful conveyor of information. If you are ever labeled as a failure without character, the chances of your future financial success with banks are slim.

The examples of Lee Goodman and the son of the Armenian immigrant tell how two men faced financial loss and loans that went bad. One of the men handled the situation irresponsibly. He is almost sure to be without bank credit from any bank within five hundred miles of his home base. The other man handled similar challenges with spirit, determination, integrity, and creativity. He has so impressed bankers who thought he would never make it that he will always have the goodwill and gratitude of the bankers he paid even when the going was tough.

Lee Jacobsen is one of the best bankers in Nebraska. In the insightful letter in Figure 23, he talks about saving credit in hard times. His views support the position I have taken here.

Repairing Credit Already Gone Bad

A banker's trade is dealing with credit, money, and people who have learned the successful use of both. Often

Figure 23
ADVICE ON SAVING CREDIT

Columbus Bank
and Trust Company
MEMBER F.D.I.C.

Mr. Ben B. Boothe
Boothe and Associates
Western National Building
8851 Hwy. 80 W
Cowtown, Texas 76116

Dear Mr. Boothe:

During good times debtors and creditors work companionably
side by side, with debtors willing to accept any proffered
terms set before them, asking few questions regarding
repayment schedules and collateral pledged. However, when
that dreaded prospect of economic down turn or the actual
fact hits the lending industry, debtors find themselves in
the position of having insufficient cash flows to meet
their debt obligations. Inevitably, the resultant squeeze
gives birth to growing thoughts of bankruptcy to ease the
pain. Imperatively, now is the time for the debtor to run
toward his financial institution to seek immediate council,
not run away in avoidance. All the facts and figures
should be presented to the lender along with an open mind
to all possible solutions, no matter how heart rendering
the final decision may be. From a business standpoint,
this form of action makes sense, but emotionally is
difficult to accept. Unfotunately, debtors don't realize
that most creditors are more than willing to work through
rough times. This is especially true when a creditor sees
the debtor really trying to keep the lines of communication
open plus sees him working to fulfill his commitment to
repay.

Bankruptcy is <u>seldom</u> a suitable solution. Everyone loses
except the attorneys who represent the two estranged parties.

Sincerely,

COLUMBUS BANK AND TRUST COMPANY

Lee Jacobsen
Vice President, C.L.O.

LJ/mm

2501 13th Street • Columbus, NE 68601 • (402) 564-1234

bankers deal with people who have accumulated large sums of money *after they have suffered terrible financial setbacks*. Some of the practices and traits of these successful people are worth reviewing.

One of the most prominent traits of successful people is their persistence and determination. When it comes to money matters, people who face obstacles such as bad corporate or personal credit often want to give up. Some of these people have said, "I went through a bankruptcy, and all of my hopes financially are gone," or, "I went through a divorce, and it nearly ruined me and the business." Indeed, trying to start a banking relationship or a new business with bad credit is much harder than starting with no credit at all. The person with bad credit has had problems in the past and will have to face them realistically, recognize them, and deal with them head on. But successful people will not let these obstacles stand in the way. They keep looking for solutions, and in their search they will find that there is a pathway to wealth. This pathway consists of eight steps, even if your credit has been bad in the past. Figure 24 illustrates these steps.

Step 1: Build Good Credit

Credit repair is only one of eight steps that will "jump start" you on the financial high road. Understanding the proper use and abuses of credit is critical to rebuilding your credit. Wealthy people use credit to make money. A cardinal rule is to borrow money only when it will help you acquire an asset that will not only service the debt but make a profit as well.

The poet Ogden Nash quipped, "Wise advice for the banker who will heed it, only loan money to those who don't need it." Here we think we can give even better advice to a person wanting to repair and use credit prop-

Figure 24
THE STAIRCASE FOR REBUILDING CREDIT AND
CREATING WEALTH

        8. Invest in humanity.
      7. Exercise self-discipline
         and patience.
     6. Invest money wisely.
    5. Invest time wisely.
   4. Study wealth.
  3. Pay yourself first (save and
     reserve).
 2. Budget in detail.
1. Build good credit out of bad.

erly: "Wise advice for the borrower who will heed it, only borrow money when the investment will feed it." Never borrow money for personal luxury items. For those, use cash out of your standard of living. If you don't have the cash, just pretend that those items are beyond your standard of living . . . for perhaps they are!

One day a businessman came to my office in utter despair. His business was on the rocks, as was his marriage, because of financial stress. The business had gone through a bad economic cycle, then medical bills had caused a series of past-due payments that had led him into a "black hole of credit." To buy himself time, he started running his business by charging everything to the hilt. When all of his trade credit was at capacity, he resorted to short-term personal bank loans. When he could borrow no more, he loaded up his twenty or thirty personal credit cards to their limit. At this point, when he could borrow no more, he found that he still did not have the cash flow to service his payments. He could pay the business operating expenses, but his debt service was overwhelming. In a matter of six months, he had ruined a perfect credit rating, which had taken years to establish. Now his company suppliers would not ship to him except by COD. The "black hole of credit" was sucking him slowly into bankruptcy. He came into the bank with his wife.

"Mr. Boothe, we want to rebuild our credit. What can we do?" They told me their story, one that I've heard many times. They had the best of everything, all purchased on credit. Luxury cars bought with friendly financing at the automobile dealership. The finest of furniture purchased with credit cards. A beautiful home financed by a generous savings and loan institution. They had even bought a new swimming pool and ordered business inventory with credit cards. As I looked over some of the past-due statements they had stacked on my desk, I realized that all of the thirty credit card accounts were "loaded," and their average interest rate was over 19 percent. Nearly one dollar in every five they paid out was for interest. And they were "cash broke."

They were constantly being hounded by bill collectors. The business was debilitated to the point that they were spending a majority of their time—time that could have been used to build the business—in dealing with credit problems instead. On the surface, it appeared that this couple was hopelessly sliding toward disaster. While they described their problems, they continually snapped at each other about small items: whose fault it was that they had lost this customer, why one bill wasn't paid, who ordered what, and why it was a mistake. They were going down the tubes, partially because of plastic credit.

I said, "I'll help you, but only on one condition: that you do everything I say." They agreed, and we shook hands on it. I thought to myself, "Fixing this financial mess is going to be a challenge," but as I studied these people, something about them signaled character and determination. They had made mistakes, but they were good people. It seemed worth the investment in time to try to pull them out of the financial fiasco they had created. "Now I'm going to give you a few simple instructions. You will follow them without delay and without discussion, OK?" They both nodded silently. "The first thing I want you to do is lay all the cards on the table, figuratively and literally."

The husband spoke up, "But we've told you the truth. We haven't hidden anything."

"OK, you've laid the figurative cards on the table, but now I mean literally. Lay all of your credit cards on the table." They looked at each other in some surprise and began pulling credit cards out and putting them on my desk. The stack grew—cards of every color, cards for computer stores, department stores, a number of gas cards, prestige cards, gold, silver, and platinum cards. When the last card was on the desk, while they watched wide-eyed, I began to cut every card into tiny pieces.

Before I was through, they were both becoming emotional. Those cards had been points of prestige and ego. They had been their key to immediate gratification. The gesture was not only to cut the cards but to cut their emotional bonding to credit. It was a symbol like the short haircuts administered to new recruits at army boot camps. The couple experienced a powerful moment while in my bank office that day.

I then dictated a letter to my secretary while they sat and listened: "Mrs. Filewood, type a letter to every one of Mr. and Mrs. Doe's credit accounts. It will say, 'We appreciate having done business with you, but we have destroyed our credit card and request that you cancel this account. We wish you to honor no new charges to the account. Please remove us from your mailing list and send no replacement cards. We are enclosing payment in full and trust that you will report us paid as agreed.' "

In a little while they both signed thirty letters, which the bank mailed for them that day. Included in each letter was a cashier's check for the payoff of the loan.

But real credit repair takes more than just cutting up your credit cards. A new pattern of business habits must occur. The next step starts you on that path.

Step 2: Budget the Business and Your Personal Finances

While the letters were being typed, I did a quick calculation with the couple and found that a debt consolidation loan would save them a substantial amount in interest fees. In exchange for the debt consolidation loan, I took many of the assets they had purchased with the debt as collateral.

Then we spent the next hour making a business and personal budget. The business budget itemized every possible expense to the smallest detail—postage, envelopes, printing, utilities, rent, inventory, labor, insurance, sales tax, even petty cash. Next we prepared three scenarios of income based on the worst quarter, the best quarter, and the average quarter for the year, and projected these figures to an annual basis. After determining what the business could realistically produce, we projected how much they could afford to draw out of the business in dividends or salaries to pay themselves. With this figure in mind, we then prepared a family budget, also detailed— health expense, entertainment, gifts, house payments, all credit payments, food, utilities, clothing, auto maintenance, income taxes. We even budgeted Mother's Day gifts and allowances for the children.

I explained, "Make budgets for both family and business. *Successful people stay informed about their income and expenses and know where they stand finan-*

cially at all times. You can't know where you are going financially unless you know where you are now."

They agreed to adhere to the budgets as sacred law. When they managed to spend less than the budget through wise management, they were dollars ahead— dollars they could use to pay off debts or invest to increase their income. I asked them to work up a monthly budget report and to review it together before sending it to the bank. (For a banker's comments on budgeting, see the letter from Loren Jilek, president of Farmers State Bank of Lester Prairie, Minnesota, in Figure 25.)

We next reviewed the credit report of the business and their personal credit. The business report was not all that bad. That was because many trade creditors are hesitant to report bad credit too soon, for fear it will cost them a customer. But their personal credit was a shambles. Fortunately, the majority of the reports showed only minor past-due payments on the credit cards we had just destroyed and paid off. The other expenses, such as the house payments and furniture payments, were included in the budget.

The couple did not realize that bad credit stays on a credit report record for seven years. I pointed out several ways to deal with a bad report:

- Eliminate any future late payments.
- Start rebuilding the report with nothing but positive credit.
- Have a third party, such as a credit counselor, attorney, or CPA, challenge the bad reports and ask for confirmation. Often bad credit is reported by mistake, and the law requires that when challenged, the credit bureaus have to recontact the creditor and reconfirm the credit within thirty days. If the reconfirmation is not forthcoming, the credit bureau

Figure 25
COMMENTS ON THE IMPORTANCE OF BUDGETING

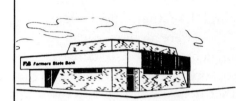

Farmers State Bank

P.O. BOX 128 • 500 CENTRAL AVE. • LESTER PRAIRIE, MN 55354

Oct. 23, 1991

Ben B. Boothe and Associates
Western National Building
8851 Hwy. #80W
Suite 201
Fort Worth, Texas 76116

Dear Ben:

As a banker, I consider budgeting a very important part of the goal setting
process. The customer needs a plan in order to be successful. Budgeting is
one of the very first steps of a workable strategic plan. Through budgeting
the customer indicates that they are knowledgeable in their business and this
provides us with the background to determine the quality of credit. No
budgeting or poor budgeting is a sure way to create obstacles to the borrowing/
lending process.

Best Regards,

Loren E. Jilek

Loren E. Jilek, Pres.

PHONE 612/395-2515

has to remove the questioned item from your file. It is not unusual for the reconfirmation letters never to appear.

- If there are "judgments" on your credit report, these must be addressed. A judgment is the result of a court process whereby the court declares that you have a debt of record in the county.

A judgment may be a lien against your real estate or other property that is subject to public liens. This has to be paid before you can receive proceeds from the sale of that property. In other words, if you sell such property, before you get a penny of the proceeds, the judgment must be satisfied. The creditor who originally loaned you or your company the money must be paid in the judgment amount as defined by the court.

When businesses or individuals sue and gain a judgment, normally they consider it a loss. If, for example, you have a judgment with XYZ Corporation for $25,000 that has been on the books for several years, you have two ways of removing it. Either pay the $25,000 and ask for a release, or try to negotiate an agreed settlement. In the majority of cases, a judgment can be settled if you call the creditor and say that you would like to make an offer for settlement. Would the creditor accept $5,000 cash in exchange for releasing the judgment? You might be pleasantly surprised! The amount will have to be negotiated, but this is an effective means of eliminating judgments.

When you have the release, see that it is immediately recorded and reported to the credit bureau. How do you get the $5,000? It is simple. If your banker is trying to work with you, he or she knows that a judgment supersedes a collateral interest. He or she may be willing to lend you the money, provided the bank gets a clear lien on your property for collateral.

After paying off the credit card accounts, making budgets, and reviewing the credit report, the next step is to make a series of positive credit moves that do not increase your liability but show a definite turnaround in your credit history. Borrow small amounts, place the funds in a reserve account, and then in a short time use the reserve account to repay the loans, verifying that each transaction is being reported to the credit bureau. Often, a banker reviewing a credit report will notice that at some point in the seven-year report, a definite change has been made. If the evidence is strong enough, the banker may be convinced that the original problem was simply a temporary one, rather than a reflection of your permanent credit habits.

Step 3: Pay Yourself First

In your business and in your personal budget, pick a percent of your gross income—perhaps 10 percent of your personal income or 5 percent of your business gross—and put the money aside into a savings reserve. Consider this percentage the first priority after bills are paid.

When you get your paycheck, if it is for $200, save $20. If the business has sales of $5,000, put $250 in a reserve account. Put the money where it will be hard to get. You might consider putting it in a time deposit account or a certificate of deposit.

You will find that you will hardly miss the money, but over a period of time, that 10 percent will become the springboard from which you can become a millionaire. In other words, this 10 percent will be your nest egg, your secret hoard of funds to help you realize your aspirations. Consider this example. On a meager income of $24,000 per year, $200 per month will equal $2,400 per year. If invested at a return of 15 percent per year (which is possible with some effort), in twenty-eight years the nest egg will be worth $1,130,509. An income of $40,000 per year with savings of $4,000 per year ($333.33 per month) will be worth $1,021,312 in just twenty-four years. Now, these examples don't take into consideration raises, bonuses, or increases in business. Increase the annual contribution by 6 percent per year, and the time factor drops dramatically. The road to financial security is paved with good credit, good budgeting, paying yourself first, and investing wisely.

Step 4: Study Wealth

Another step to successful credit and financial management is to study wealth. Study those who have obtained wealth and the way they did it. Only a minority have inherited wealth; most wealthy people make it through their own efforts. These people possess something others don't: the positive attitude that they are winners! They don't feel that the world owes them anything, but that through hard work, honesty, and good positive imaging, they can make things happen. The value of attitude in turning around a bad credit situation is impossible to measure, but it is important. Successful people don't sit back and watch but use their great discipline and determination to move from accomplishment to accomplishment. These people don't have the time or inclination to spend their energy criticizing others; they simply maintain positive goals and keep marching forward.

Step 5: Invest Wisely in Your Time and Work

Few people create good credit, a good business, or wealth just from an ordinary effort. You find very few people who become wealthy from their salaries alone. Invest your nest egg as it begins to grow. Most people find that as their salary increases, so does their cost of living. As a business grows, so does its overhead. Almost by magic, a $300 or a $3,000 increase in income seems to disappear. Consequently most money is made by doing something extra, such as buying an old property, renovating it, and selling it for a profit.

There are hundreds of ways to make an extra effort to increase the potential income of yourself or your business. A man who owned a flying business delivering executives to business meetings found that he could increase his income by taking aerial photographs while en route, then selling them to the landowners below. A woman took her hobby of making pottery and turned it into a retail business. The section of the store that carried her hand-thrown pottery increased the sales of the store by 20 percent. A multimillionaire who owned a chain of nursing homes loved antique automobiles. He began collecting them and soon had a warehouse full of vintage cars. By converting the warehouse into a museum of antique cars, he turned his hobby into a profitable business. Two individuals in a partnership that built restaurants paid the expenses for their managers to take an annual hunting trip and retreat. They found that their staff became highly motivated by these retreats. Thereafter they started charging other companies to participate. It soon became a source of additional income the partnership never expected. A banker had to design new computer programs for his loan department. The programs were so successful that he placed an ad in the trade journals and made thousands by selling his brainchild to other banks.

Step 6: Invest the Fruits of Your Labor—Money—Wisely

When your extra effort generates "extra" income, the money can be poured back into good investments . . . to take advantage of the "magic multiplier." The magic multiplier describes the process of letting excess money make money for you and begin a financial snowball effect. Just as debts can snowball into a black hole, so your extra earnings can also snowball, having a great positive effect as well. Remember, too, nothing can improve your credit like cash and good investments!

You wouldn't go to a dentist for a foot problem, and you wouldn't ask a bus driver to pilot your airplane. Therefore, when you have funds to invest, do it wisely, with the advice of those who know money best. Find competent, successful, and trustworthy people to advise you, and avoid salespeople with a vengeance. There will always be those who will take your money, saying that they will turn it into a million.

Remember a basic rule of finance: higher rates reflect higher risk. If you are seeking a return of 10 percent but some institution is paying a bonus rate well above the market, it may be because the institution is in trouble and needs the deposits. Or if a mutual fund or stock is paying well over the market rate, be careful. A customer had ten $100,000 certificates of deposit in one of my banks. The market rate at the time was 10 percent. He insisted on more. Another bank offered a rate of 12.75 percent, and he rushed to put his money in that bank. In a matter of months, the other bank failed. He had forgotten the basic rule of finance.

Your investments are the financial reflection of your life—the hours you have toiled and the worry you have invested. When you *do* (and you will) have extra money to invest, make your choice of investments a serious effort of deep and considered thought, using the best advice of the most trusted and knowledgeable people you can locate. Study as if you were studying for a final exam. In truth, it may mean more to you than any college exam you were ever faced with.

Step 7: Exercise Self-Discipline and Patience

Individual and corporate discipline is one of the greatest tools for credit management and building wealth. A perfect example is that of "Status Sam." His company had to have new cars for all of the officers every year. Of course, Sam had to have another one just as big for his family as well. He and his business always seemed to be cash tight. "Prudent Paul," his best friend, had a business in which management watched every cent. No personal entertainment, no perks, they just paid good wages. That was how Paul ran his personal budget as well. Paul never bought inventory, a car, or anything, until he could pay cash. He didn't grow as fast as Sam, but when the chips were down, he always had cash. Over the years Paul's business became four times larger than Sam's. Paul borrowed occasionally, but only when doing so made him money.

A business or an individual, particularly when young, will find that a little less debt and a little more cash can grow into thousands with time and good management. It is essential to realize that conservative investments of small risk are far better in the long run than high-risk, speculative investments. Most wealthy people obtained their resources over many years of exercising good judgment. Rare indeed is the person who made it overnight!

Step 8: Cultivate the Intangible Extra: Interest in Others

Finally, remember that good credit comes with high integrity. As integrity and good credit lead to success through good management, wealth often follows. Wealth is often complemented and given more impetus when accompanied by a goal of helping society. If one has an attitude of wanting to help humanity—to help other businesses, to help other individuals—this attitude seems to add energy to life and even increase one's business power. It is an intangible extra that empowers and energizes.

Armand Hammer started out as a young, idealistic doctor with a desire to feed the hungry in Russia. His integrity and idealism impressed Lenin and a whole series of Russian leaders. For over fifty years, he was one of the few people on earth who could walk into the offices of the leaders of Russia and the next week get an appointment with the President of the United States. It wasn't because he was a wealthy oilman. That was not what empowered him. It was his idealism that opened doors and allowed him to achieve great wealth and worldwide influence. He thought of the world as a global family in which we are all members.

Hammer learned a secret that you can learn too: Life is far more than just money or profits. Of more importance are human relationships and the impact we have on people. Those who focus on wealth simply as a financial game to accumulate numbers may have a good time. They are competitive, daring, professional, and sometimes even ruthless. But the few who have mastered this principle have added another aspect to the formula.

Consider your interest in helping others as like that old gasoline commercial touting a secret additive developed to give the car a special boost. An altruistic outlook provides a passion that energizes your work more than any numbers game. It creates a vehicle by which every act, every project gives you resources to help fulfill some human need—to feed a hungry child, build a school, create a cure for cancer, bring peace to a region, promote international goodwill, promote understanding, bring a smile to a child, educate an illiterate person so that he or she can practice a trade or profession, or bring the power of a written language to a tribe whose language has never been written. The list is endless.

Some of the great business leaders of our society, such as Andrew Carnegie, have had tremendous impact on our culture because they mastered the principle that good credit comes with high integrity. One flamboyant west Texan who knew how to make money by the thousands tended to give his money away to good causes almost as fast as he could earn it. Once he told someone that one of the ways he motivated himself to make money was to make a financial commitment to some charity or good cause. It brought out his creativity to make more, and it made his efforts fun! He made and gave away millions, all while having a good time in the process.

Interest in other people will add a positive factor to your ongoing financial growth. You may wonder what this has to do with borrowing money. The answer is that a banker has to evaluate the overall person when making loan and business judgments. The person who is well rounded and who demonstrates extraordinary qualities can't help but impress the banker and improve his or her opportunity for successful banking relationships.

14

Behind the Closed Doors
of the Boardroom

It had been a long and exhausting meeting. The chairman's expression was grim. The long board table with its elegantly polished surface, which brought out the walnut wood grain, was not a source of joy this day. The luxurious setting of paneled walls hung with expensive art did little to ease the tension that filled the room. The tension seemed so strong that the walls might blow out. This was the day of the examiner's report on the bank's loan portfolio.

A federal examiner sat at one end of the long board table, the bank directors sat around it, and the bank loan officers sat on chairs that had been brought in and scattered behind the directors. The chairman sat opposite the examiner.

The examiner cleared his throat. "Hmmmm. Ladies and gentlemen, the conclusion of this report is simply this. You will have to charge off $4.5 million in loans immediately. This will require a capital injection. There are ten

235

directors here; that will cost you approximately $450,000 each unless you can raise it from other sources. We will give you ten days to provide us with a written response as to your specific plans. If you don't comply, the bank will be closed, and you will lose everything you have invested in the bank over the past ten years. We cannot make any firm statements as to legal liability, but there will be an investigation as to whether there has been any criminal activity or malfeasance."

One of the directors spoke up. "Now listen here. You and your other examiners have charged off loans that have been and are paying as agreed. You have taken loans with appraised values well in excess of the loan amount and classified them as substandard. You have crippled this bank by being overzealous in your examination standards. Our underwriting standards are just fine."

The examiner flipped through his notes. "If that is so, what about the Nancy Williams note? It shows no current appraisal." The directors looked at the loan officer who serviced that loan. The loan officer squirmed uneasily as he responded, "Well, Nancy Williams is a good customer. She pays on time. She didn't want to get a new appraisal because we got one when the loan was first approved three years ago."

"That is where you erred. You should have required a current appraisal. Because you didn't, we have charged off 50 percent of the loan and placed the rest as a substandard asset." The examiner continued to turn pages. "Oh, yes, here is a loan to a motel owner. There is no certified profit and loss statement, and no balance sheet."

Everyone looked to the vice president of the bank. "Well, that's a problem, you see. This customer is a good friend of one of the major stockholders of the bank, and our stockholder said if we required those things, he would pull all of his and his friend's deposits . . ." His voice trailed off near the end of the sentence as the directors glared at him.

The examiner went on: "We have found account after account that doesn't have current documentation. Whether or not the loans are paying is irrelevant. We expect documentation. It is basic to good regulatory review."

After an hour or so of this, the meeting with the examiner adjourned. A secretary told the bank president, "Mr. Jones is here to see you with his new loan application."

The bank president excused himself and told his directors, "If you like, go ahead and convene the loan committee meeting, and I'll be back as soon as I see a customer."

As Mr. Jones started out his loan request, the banker said, "I see that this is a real estate loan. Of course, you know we are going to have to require an appraisal." The customer turned red in the face. "What? An appraisal will cost me $800. Everyone knows what the property is worth. What is wrong with you bankers anyway? Are you trying to send one of your appraisal friends some business? This is the stupidest thing I have ever heard of. If you really think I will sit here and listen to this bull, you have another thing coming! I'm moving my business." The customer stomped out of the bank as the bank president sat speechless for a moment, watching him go.

He walked out to his secretary's desk and said, "You know, sometimes you just can't win for losing." The bank president returned to the loan committee.

One of the directors said, "I saw Mr. Jones walk out of your office. Problem?"

"Well, yes. He wanted a loan on that property just south of Ridge Road, and when I told him we had to have an appraisal, he got mad and left."

"I know that property," said the director. "It is worth double what he needs to borrow. Why didn't you go ahead and make the loan?"

Then the chairman spoke up. "We are in a time when common sense of what will make a profit and what is good for a bank sometimes takes a back seat to satisfying the paperwork demands of the regulators. This is a good example of our bank losing a good customer because of that."

In this age, there is a fine line between satisfying the demands of regulators, the demands of good business practice, and the demands of customers. This is one of the lines a bank and its bankers must walk.

Appraisals

One of the areas that requires sensitivity and responsiveness from the person who wishes to borrow money on real estate is the area of appraisals. As the economy goes through cyclical recessions, the subsequent fall in real estate values always leads to closer scrutiny of real estate loans. Regulators have relentlessly attacked the documentation and underwriting standards of banks. Bankers throughout America have reported examiners writing down real estate loans as much as 50 percent, citing a "bad real estate market." Often these write-downs have seemed arbitrary, especially when the bankers or S&L officers feel that they know better than anyone what the value of their real estate should be. Write-downs seem even more arbitrary when the loans are being paid as agreed by the customer. And this is happening thousands of times, to the consternation of bankers, who then are penalized for having good loans on the books. This, in turn, makes life harder on customers who borrow.

For example, if a $100,000 loan is written down 20

percent by a regulator, the banker must endure a $20,000 expense and put that money in a "reserve for potential losses," even though the customer may be current and know nothing about the examination. It's easy to see that this would take away the incentive for that banker to make any more real estate loans, and the banker would look for ways to get *that* customer off the books, even if it meant calling the loan.

Or consider the famous examiner "Juliet." Juliet was well known in one region for writing down real estate loans by 30 percent. Therefore, consider a $100,000 loan on your house. Juliet would write it down to $70,000, your banker would face a hit of $30,000, and you might find your banker not quite as friendly when you next walked into the lobby. If you needed a real estate loan at a bank Juliet had recently visited, your chances would be about as good as those of Saddam Hussein joining the Friends of George Bush Committee. If the banker knew that the bank might face a loss of 30 percent if he or she made a new real estate loan to you, your loan would never be approved.

When this sort of regulatory environment is in effect, the overall economic impact to a given bank, community, or region can be substantial. For example, it is estimated that in New England alone, some $45 billion in loan funds were unavailable in 1991 simply because of the subsequent problems banks suffered there. Many observers believe that a large percentage of the bank closings were regulatory driven. This was confirmed even by the President of the United States in an October 9, 1991, article in the *Wall Street Journal*: "The administration attributes the limp economic recovery partly to a 'credit crunch' that is making it difficult for companies to borrow. In the past it has blamed regulators for being too harsh on banks."

Because many institutions have failed as a result of

their inability to fight off the regulators or defend good real estate loans, financial institutions have resorted to increasing appraisal guidelines to improve their ability to defend their real estate loan portfolios. Unfortunately, many appraisers are unfamiliar with bank regulations or the workings of financial institutions, and they have sometimes contributed to the problem. In a knee-jerk reaction to the negative press, many appraisers have resorted to using distress sales to establish "fair market value." This distorts the market and worsens the dilemma the banks face. It is just as much a distortion to use distress sale values to set market value as it is to use inflated values. Unreasonably low appraisals hurt not only loan customers, but also financial institutions.

To complicate the situation further, in requiring that all loans of $100,000 or more have an independent appraisal by a qualified certified appraiser, regulators have sent a strong message. Regulators in Washington want more comprehensive appraisal practices, and they will get their way. It is much like the days when banks first started requiring credit reports, truth-in-lending statements, financial statements, and then profit and loss statements. With the advent of each, there were howls and rumblings of protest, but all this documentation is standard practice now. The new appraisal standards are also becoming standard practice.

This was brought on by the abuses that occurred in the savings and loan industry when regulators chose to deregulate the industry. As a result, all kinds of abuses occurred, not the least of which was a number of cases where unscrupulous appraisers with limited or no qualifications wrote appraisals that were inflated or blatantly false. In some cases financial institutions did their own appraisals, overstating values for various unscrupulous schemes. When FIRREA was passed, it standardized and eliminated those type of abuses and got financial institutions up to speed in the appraisal area. To avoid regulatory criticism and as a matter of prudent business, bankers and customers will take early steps to acquire good appraisals on all real estate loans. Those who don't will simply be out of luck.

What does this mean to customers who need credit from banks? If you are considering real estate loans, plan on getting comprehensive appraisals early, with possible periodic updates to protect your position. The appraisal must be from an independent source (not a friend, partner, stockholder, customer, or employee). A good piece of real property with a legitimate independent appraisal confirming a value well in excess of the loan request can do much to pave the way for loan approval.

Some banks have extensive REO (real estate owned as a result of repossession) holdings. By law, these must be reappraised annually. REOs can be a source of good investment bargains and preferred financing from the bank. The bank will often be interested in speaking to a customer who will take over these properties. For some banks, the liquidation of REO properties can help boost earnings as well as relieve regulatory pressure.

An appraisal will give the customer the tools to acquire funds, give the bank a greater comfort level, and can limit legal liability for both the customer and the bank. Of course, a side effect will be fewer write-downs on loans that have good appraisals. Furthermore, it just makes good sense to have good, professional documentation of the value of real estate properties. The day is coming when every businessperson will have a CPA, lawyer, and appraiser. Consider this—would you rather use your appraiser or the bank's?

Environmental Concerns

Another new trend that will be important to future loan packages is the focus on environmental concerns. Since the waning days of the peace movement of the sixties, momentum and interest in environmental issues has grown in America. This movement has not left the banking industry untouched. While the industry has been conservative and traditional, the pressures of social, cultural, and regulatory conscience have had an impact. Therefore, in your loan application of the future, whether it be for a large manufacturing facility or a small gasoline station, you should address environmental concerns.

Environmental Inspections

Several federal regulations have placed the bank under risk of criticism and penalties if it does not show that it has taken prudent steps to verify that environmental review has taken place. Regulations now require that any loan under the auspices of a federal agency must at least have a Phase One environmental inspection. Loans covered by this regulation include any real estate loan handled by the RTC (Resolution Trust Corporation) or FDIC, as well as loans guaranteed by the Small Business Administration.

Environmental inspections have been classified as Phase One, Two, and Three. A Phase One inspection can be made by an inspector who physically visits the site and inspects for visual and obvious environmental hazards. These inspections are usually not extremely expensive ($200 to $2,000 in most cases, unless it is a major undertaking). The inspector provides a written report, checking off a preset list of areas reviewed, and certifies his or her findings. This level of inspection might include items such as a check of Environmental Protection Agency (EPA) records for levels of radon in buildings. The inspector will

interview people familiar with the site to determine
whether the site has ever been used for dumping or chemical storage.

In one instance our consulting firm, Boothe and
Associates, was engaged in an appraisal assignment for a
bank that was in the process of repossessing a furniture
store. In the course of the appraisal field research, we
documented that the vacant land west of the building had
once been the site of a gas station. Buried fuel tanks were
still there, under the parking lot. These tanks obviously
had not been tested for leakage in years. This type of
situation could have created a great deal of liability and
expense for the bank, because once the land became the
property of the bank through foreclosure, the bank would
by law be liable to clean up the lot and to remove the
tanks and polluted soil or seal them against any environmental damage. Any cleanup costs would be the expense
of the bank. The bank in this case decided not to fore-
close, just to avoid the potential liability.

Another aspect of a Phase One inspection is to research the possibility of the property containing any apparent or obvious problems, such as lead paint or asbestos. A Phase One inspection will contact utility companies
to determine if and what levels of PCBs are present in
electric transformers. The proximity to high-voltage power
lines is a concern. Of course, the inspector observes obvious hazards related to chemicals, smoke, fumes, animal
wastes, and sanitation problems.

Your loan presentation should include some reference
to the attention you have given these concerns, and you
should indicate your willingness to engage a Phase One
inspection if your loan is in the required category. From
another perspective, if you are about to purchase a building or a house, you should *want* to know if there are
environmental problems. Your negotiating skills may be

tested to see if the seller is willing to pay all or a part of any inspection or test to determine that the building is environmentally safe.

Rarely is a Phase Two inspection required with an initial loan application. This level goes beyond simple field investigation and visual research to require actual laboratory testing. The inspector takes samples and registers professional laboratory results from soil tests or water pollution sample tests. These reports are much more expensive and usually require a qualified engineer.

An excellent example of a Phase Two inspection is a case involving a neighborhood in Dallas. A field test took lab samples of the soil in the neighborhood near a lead smelter. Results of the soil test showed that the soil was highly toxic and perhaps responsible for the degree of illness among children in the area. If you were a loan customer about to invest in that area, both you and your banker would be very interested in these types of test results.

The Phase Three inspection goes into an even greater degree of detail and environmental evaluations, including consulting for cleanup. If you are involved in a loan application that will require this level of inspection, my advice to you would be to forget the loan and go on to another project. There are a myriad of federal regulations involving environmental pollution and the financial responsibility for those involved.

The parents of a young Chicago executive purchased a farm as a retirement retreat. Although they had no knowledge or involvement, an oil company had buried on the farm several fifty-gallon drums that contained toxic chemicals. The parents of the young executive died, and he inherited the farm. A few months later, he got a letter from the EPA citing him for violation of environmental laws. He was required to clean the site at an expense of several hundred thousand dollars. He was innocent of any wrongdoing, but he got the letter, for he was the owner at the time the problem was "uncovered."

To ensure that environmental concerns will be taken seriously, the government has made doing so a matter that can affect individuals and companies financially. Joseph Iacuzzo, managing director of the Environmental Assessment Association, highlights this in the letter that appears in Figure 26.

Your banker will appreciate your attention to this area and will respect the thoroughness of your loan application if it addresses the subject. Hopefully, your property will have no environmental problems. But if you are involved in buildings, real estate, agriculture, petroleum products, plastics, mineral and chemical production, electronics, or even a matter as simple as purchasing a home, caveat emptor.

Radon in the Home

The matter of radon pollution in homes has been known and documented for many years by scientists and government regulators. It became well publicized when a specific house was shown to have had a radon level over one thousand times the normal or safe level. To further bring the issue to the minds of the public, some energetic person decided to test the radon level in a building owned and staffed by the Environmental Protection Agency. The building was found to be polluted by radon, creating much chagrin and embarrassment to officials there.

Radon pollution is an issue that will have an ever greater impact on loan approvals as lenders become educated about the problem and its financial implications. There is no doubt that the collateral value of a property will drop substantially if it is found to be hazardous.

Radon is a colorless, odorless gas that is emitted as a result of radioactive elements existing naturally in the soil. The gas is normally dispersed into the atmosphere at a

Figure 26
WORDS OF CAUTION ABOUT ENVIRONMENTAL MATTERS

ENVIRONMENTAL
Assessment Association

8383 East Evans Road
Scottsdale, Ariz na 85260-3614
Tel: (602) 483-8100
Fax: (602) 998-8022

Joseph M. Iacuzzo
Managing Director

Ben Boothe
Boothe and Associates
8851 Hwy. 80 West
Cowtown, Texas 76116

Dear Mr. Boothe,

The Environmental Assessment Association exists for the purpose of helping the lending and real estate industries understand the critical importance of the effects environmental issues have on lending practices. There is no escaping the fact that the astute lender, investor or broker must have some basic knowledge of environmental hazards and their impact on values.

Environemntal regulations promulgated by the various Federal regulatory agencies, such as the FDIC, OTS, OCC and the Federal Reserve Board are either in place or being drafted. Lax enforcement due to Federal and State examiners lack of training with regard to environmental issues are being addressed as new programs to provide the training are being developed and implemented.

There are few issues that are growing in importance the way that the environmental issues are progressing. Lenders absolutely must understand how they will be affected by environmental problems and learn how to interpret and cope with the situations that they will be facing in the near future.

The Environmental Assessment Association, as a professional organization, provides it's members with basic information in a clear and concise format. This is the type of material that lenders need to survive in the changing environment.

Sincerely,
ENVIRONMENTAL ASSESSMENT ASSOCIATION

Joseph M. Iacuzzo
Managing Director

level that is harmless to human life. The problem begins when it is trapped in a commercial or residential structure by walls, windows, and doors. It normally seeps into a structure through tiny cracks or openings in the foundation. If the structure is not well ventilated, radon can become dangerous. Some research reports have indicated that it is a thousand times more harmful to the lungs than cigarettes or x-rays, as the tiny radioactive particles are breathed in and have enormous destructive power to the sensitive linings of the lungs.

Why has the government not taken stronger steps in this area to protect the public? As one employee of the EPA "unofficially" said while I was researching radon, "Radon has such broad implications for the financial industry that we consider it a hot potato. If the public were really informed as to how widespread the problem is and the apparent health risks, it could create great turmoil in the real estate industry in areas known to have high radon levels. This could have an impact on thousands of loans. It is a political issue, and we prefer to keep a low profile."

Most mortgage companies now require a radon test or an environmental statement on every home loan application. Commercial banks have been slow to require testing on commercial real estate property, but are quick to require aggressive corrective measures when a problem is uncovered, especially when there is a possible banking loss or lawsuit.

Protect yourself and your loan by preparation. A radon test kit can be acquired at most major hardware stores for a few dollars. Those few dollars are a small expense compared to the ultimate potential price of lung cancer contracted by someone you care for or work with. Furthermore, what banker wants to take collateral that might decline in value extensively if some environmental problem is disclosed later?

15

The Ten Commandments of Managing Credit and Creditors

Banking and the subject of borrowing can be dry. But throughout this book we have stressed the importance of quality communication for a successful banking relationship. Mark Twain once said that the most serious subjects are best taught with the spice of humor. Present these "Ten Commandments" to your banker and I guarantee that he or she will laugh. Your banker may even take the Commandments to his or her board of directors. Certainly you will be remembered with goodwill. This chapter will also make a great plaque to put on your wall to read every time you have to borrow money.

I. THOU SHALT NOT BORROW UNLESS THOU CANST REPAY.

II. THOU SHALT GO TO THY BANKER PREPARED WITH TABLETS OF FACTS AND FIGURES WHICH SHALL PLEASE THY BANKER'S HEART.

III. THOU SHALT HAVE NO OTHER BANKERS BEFORE THINE OWN.

IV. THOU SHALT NOT LIE TO THY BANKER, THE PERSON WHO LENDS THE MONEY FOR THY DAILY BREAD.

V. THOU SHALT NOT WAX ELOQUENT IN CRITICISMS OF THY LENDER, FOR THY BANKER'S HAND MAY SMITE THEE, AND THOU WILT FIND THYSELF IN THE GUTTER OF NO CREDIT.

VI. THOU SHALT GIVE THY BANK TITHES SO THY BANKER CAN MAKE A FAIR PROFIT AND SO THY BANKER WILT SAY, "IT IS WELL THAT THIS PERSON BANKS WITH US."

VII. THOU SHALT ENTER THE SANCTUARY OF THE BANK WITH RESPECT AND SPEAK KINDLY TO THY BANKER SO THAT THOU WILT BE PLEASING IN THY BANKER'S SIGHT.

VIII. THOU SHALT NOT ENTER THE COMPANY OF HARLOTS, WICKED LAWYERS, AND THOSE WHO WOULD LEAD YOU IN THE PATHS OF BANKRUPTCY AND DEFAULT. BUT RATHER THOU SHALT LOVE THY BANKER WITH ALL THY HEART AND PRAY THY BANKER'S MERCY AND BLESSINGS WHEN THE SHEKELS WANE.

IX. IF THY BANKER PROVES UNFAITHFUL, THOU SHALT GO TO THY BANKER WITH TWO WITNESSES AND SAY, "PRAY THEE, MONEY CHANGER, WHY HAST THOU FORSAKEN ME? I BEG THEE CHANGE THY HEART, FOR I HAVE BEEN THY SERVANT ALL THESE YEARS." BUT IF THY BANKER'S HEART IS HARDENED FOR LOAN DEMAND IS TOO HIGH AND THY BANKER MUST NEEDS BE RID OF THEE, THEN SPEAK NOT WITH ANGER, BUT RATHER BRUSH THE DUST OFF THY FEET AND SEEK OUT A BANKER IN ANOTHER PLACE WHO WILL CHERISH THEE ALL THE DAYS OF THY LIFE.

AND WHEN THY FIRST BANKER FINDS OUT THAT THOU HAST GONE TO ANOTHER, AND AGAIN

COVETS LOANS SUCH AS YOURS, THY FIRST
BANKER WILL REPENT AND COME TO THEE,
RENDING HIS OR HER GARMENTS AND SAYING,
"COME BACK, GOOD AND FAITHFUL SERVANT, FOR
I WAS WRONG. MY LOAN RATIOS WERE BAD, AND
THE ANGELS OF THE REGULATORS WERE HOT
UPON ME. BUT I HAVE SEEN THE ERROR OF MY
WAYS, AND MY TEMPLE IS YOURS. THERE STANDS
IN MY VAULT A GREAT PILE OF SILVER AND GOLD
AT A REASONABLE RATE."

THEN IN THY HEART THOU MAYEST WANT TO
SAY, "BEGONE FROM ME. FOR WHEN I WAS
HUNGRY, YOU FED ME NOT, AND YOU IGNORED ME
IN THE COUNTRY CLUB. BUT NOW THAT I AM RICH,
YOU COME TO ME, THROWING DUST IN YOUR HAIR
AND WAVING GOLD CARDS AND FREE CHECKING
AT ME, BUT MY HEART IS HARDENED." BUT THE
WORD OF THE PROPHET IS "THOU SHALT NOT SAY
THOSE THINGS." RATHER THOU SHALT SMILE AND
WITH KINDNESS SAY, "DO NOT WEEP SO, BUT
KNOW THAT NOW I HAVE ALL I NEED. MY NEW
BANKER LENDS AT LESS THAN A TITHE. WILL YOU
DO BETTER THAN THAT?"

AND WHEN THOU HAST SAID THUS, THE
BANKER WILL SHUDDER AND GNASH HIS TEETH,
AND WITH GREAT WAILING IN HIS HEART WILL
SAY, "YES. COME HOME AND WE WILL GIVE UNTO
THEE A BETTER RATE, AND WE WILL NOT
FORSAKE THEE AGAIN."

AND THOU WILT SAY, "OH, DEAR FRIEND, I
WILL COME HOME TO THEE IF THOU WILT MERGE
NO MORE AND CHANGE NOT THY NAME AGAIN,
AND NEVER AGAIN FAIL TO KNOW MY NAME OR
CHARGE MY ACCOUNT A SERVICE CHARGE." (BUT
THIS SHALT THOU KEEP IN THY HEART, THAT THY

FIRST BANKER ONCE BEFORE LEFT THEE WHEN
THE FAMINE CAME, AND THOU SHALT KEEP SOME
OF THY GOLD IN ANOTHER PLACE.)
        THY BANKER WILL AGAIN GNASH HIS TEETH,
BUT TO THEE HE WILL SMILE AND SAY, "HERE MY
CUSTOMER WAS LOST, BUT HE IS FOUND AGAIN.
HIS DEPOSITS WERE GONE, BUT THEY ARE BACK."
(THY BANKER MUST REPORT TO THE BOARD THAT
HE BROUGHT YOU BACK TO THE FOLD.)

X. THOU SHALT RUN THY BUSINESS WITH INTEGRITY,
    FAIRNESS, AND HONOR AND SPEAK WELL OF ALL
    GOOD PEOPLE AND WORK WITH DILIGENCE. AND
    THOU SHALT LIVE EACH DAY AS IF IT WERE THY
    LAST, PAYING THY DEBTS AND GIVING TO THE
    POOR.

IF THOU OBEYETH ALL OF THESE COMMANDMENTS, THY
HOUSE SHALL GROW STRONG, AND THE MERCHANTS WILL
HAIL THEE IN THE STREETS AND SAY, "THERE GOES A GOOD
PERSON, BLESSED ABOVE ALL. THAT PERSON WALKS IN RIGH-
TEOUSNESS, WITH HIS BANKER BESIDE HIM."

16

A Look at the Future: Things You *Can* Bank On in a World of Change

During the Great Depression, a great banking tragedy penalized millions of Americans. An entire generation (later called Depression children) carried the scars of that time. America's financial industries had been controlled by a few rich and powerful institutions. Banks were "deregulated" and could invest depositors' money in stocks, bonds, real estate. In some cases banks invested large proportions of depositors' money in the stock market, until the fatal day when the market went up no more. Then powerful men such as J. P. Morgan issued orders to sell, and sell quickly, while publicly proclaiming their support for and confidence in the market. A panic followed—a panic that ground the financial industry and the economy of America to a halt. A few huge entities had become so powerful and so enmeshed in the financial structure of the nation that when they got into trouble, the entire nation was affected. Then when the nation's central bank should have been increasing liquidity, it for nearly five years reduced liquidity in the banking industry. This resulted in a liquidity crisis throughout the nation. Money was not to be had by business, banks, or the public. This deflationary period we now call the "Great Depression."

The absence of credit was one of the symptoms of this depression. With no credit to oil the wheels of industry and business, a generation of people had to learn to survive without money, or with much less than they ever had before. America was almost reduced to a barter system like it had endured a hundred years earlier.

Every family has heard parents and grandparents tell the stories of that time. My grandfather traveled from Girard, Texas, to New Mexico for weeks at a time, just to drive a tractor for fifty cents a day. When he came home, his body was covered with great blisters and boils. Grandmother lanced the boils on his weary body while the children watched. They were trying to save the little 160-acre farm they had bought and financed through their bank five years earlier. Three of the four children—boys six, eight, and ten years old—worked in the fields, chopped cotton, and then later picked it.

My grandmother tells me about putting a cotton sack over her shoulder and picking a bale of cotton in 101-degree weather. She had put baby Jim, the youngest, on a blanket on the ground at the edge of the field. She was not accustomed to this kind of labor, but they could not borrow operating expenses to pay hired hands. Though she had been raised in a good home where this kind of labor was not necessary, she was determined to do her part to keep the family in food and clothing, and to pay the bank. When in exhaustion she walked back to the edge of the cotton field, where baby was sleeping, a large rattlesnake was coiled up right beside Jim. She killed it with a hoe, and the baby was unharmed, but she later declared, "How I hated life on the farm."

As I see it, her hatred wasn't really focused properly. Her hardship was brought on by the economy, their lowered standard of living, and the difficulty that the lack of credit created. It has been said that our nation will never see those types of cycles again. Indeed, after the Great Depression, an entire series of laws and regulations were passed by a Congress determined to learn from the experience and protect the nation from recurrence. The McFadden Act, the Douglas Act, the Bank Holding Company Act, and a whole body of laws were created to insulate the banking industry from ever again being dominated by a few giants—giants like J. P. Morgan, and the businesses he controlled in the 1920s, which in the event of giant mistakes could destabilize the nation's economy.

But in the past twenty years, a generation of whiz kids have come up with what they consider a new philosophy. Their philosophy is summarized in a conversation I once had with Bill Seidman, former head of the FDIC and RTC: "When we get through with banking, we won't have many banks like we do now." Richard Breedon, head of the Securities and Exchange Commission (and an outspoken official on banking issues), has publicly suggested that banking be totally deregulated, that deposit insurance be eliminated, that banking be relegated to the status of any corner business without the many government protections we have come to appreciate and rely on since the Great Depression. Initiatives coming from the Treasury Department have been intended to accomplish many of these goals. It appears that the future will reveal a banking world with many mergers of unlikely partners, with a net result of fewer but larger (and possibly less efficient) bank organizations. Daryl Barklow, president of the Illinois Community Bankers, comments on this trend in Figure 27.

Figure 27
COMMENTS ON THE TREND TOWARD BIG BANKS

EDSB
EAST DUBUQUE SAVINGS BANK

Daryl D. Barklow
PRESIDENT & CHIEF
EXECUTIVE OFFICER

September 27, 1991

Ben Boothe
Western National Building
8851 Hwy 80 West, Suite 201
Fort Worth, Texas 76116

Dear Ben,

The subject matter is vast and many subjects are hard not to write about, but the nearest and dearest to my heart right now is, the "Big Bank Versus the Small Bank" and the impact that will be created if we allow the industry to be consolidated.

Bigger is not always better and, especially so, when we discuss money brokers. Banks are really money brokers. People make deposits at a lower rate, and Banks lend the money back out at a higher rate, the differential being the gross profit for the Bank.

If the industry is consolidated down to 150 major financial institutions in the U.S., the term 'money brokers' will become 'power brokers'. Greed seems to set in, when the money and the power is left in the hands of a few big banks.

It seems to me that there is nothing wrong with the banking system now if 'too big to fail' is eliminated and the community banks are allowed to serve the consumer.

Sincerely,

Daryl D. Barklow
President

DDB:sh

242 WALL STREET, P.O. BOX 259, EAST DUBUQUE. ILLINOIS 61025-0259 • 815/747-3173

255

What the Future May Bring

The immediate cycle ahead bodes for management policy and style to move away from the personal and individualistic approach to banking. For a while at least, the industry may well become dominated by "numbers crunchers" intent on fulfilling whatever policy directives come from their home office in order to achieve the statistical goals of the megabank "master plan."

A banking world may emerge where this example may be the norm: At 9:00 A.M. the vice president in charge of the commercial lending department receives a fax from the home office, which says, "Our bank group has had a strong influx of international loans to fund lately, so fewer funds are available for allocation to your region. Statistical study shows that your branch is three points too high in manufacturing loans. Take appropriate steps to decrease loan ratios in your area."

By 9:30 A.M. every loan officer receives a memorandum that says, "Home office is pressuring us to make no more manufacturing loans. Comply immediately."

XYZ Corporation has had perfect credit and a good account with the bank for years and even stayed loyal when the bank changed its name, merged, and became a branch of Mega-National. The corporation has presented a comprehensive loan proposal and up until today thought the loan was sure to be approved. Senior Vice President Lisa Chang is somber in their meeting. "I'm sorry. Your loan application is denied. You may wish to reapply in ninety days. We have been told by the home office that there are no loan funds available for manufacturing facilities at this time." XYZ suddenly finds that it has a credit problem in its own community, never realizing that the reason may be that the home office has approved a group of loans to manufacturers in Japan.

Across the street, a competing manufacturing company that has presented not nearly as good a loan proposal may be approved for a loan because its bank's home office just wired, "We have had $4 billion in loans paid off, and the regional bank branches should use all due diligence to make good-quality loans in the interest of increasing company profit."

New Technology

Change will be the watchword for the traditional world of banking for the next cycle. Think of this as "the new world order of banking." The future of banking is bringing a broad array of new services and technology applications that are fascinating at least. Consider some of the following new ideas being considered by some "progressives" and in some places test marketed.

Bank by Laptop or Desktop Computer

A businessperson may be able to access every account, every loan from his or her own office through a telephone modem. The result is almost instant information. The customer can transfer funds among accounts simply by pressing a button.

The new technology of banking may make the arrangement of branch banking and huge central bank buildings obsolete. Why spend millions on physical branches when a customer can get the same service with a laptop computer?

Borrow by Computer

Soon the loan application will be presented on a computer screen in some of the very offices where loan officers now sit. All facts and figures will appear immediately on the loan officer's desk. Many loans will be approved or checked by preprogrammed computer statistical guidelines.

Bank by Telephone

A bank-by-phone service has been marketed in several regions. The customer conducts transactions by pressing a few telephone digits. So far the service has not been well received by the public.

Checkless Society

The banking industry has for years been trying to eliminate the massive paperwork of dealing with billions of checks. Truncated accounts (no return checks) have been accepted with reservations in the credit union business. The future generation will finally be a checkless society, but not in the form of truncated accounts.

In this new generation of banking, customers will simply make all transactions by a credit (or debit) card or computer input. Credit cards issued by the bank will have microscopic memory functions, which will keep an ongoing memory of your various account balances and will be updated every time you use your card. The bank statement will be transmitted by computer. If you want copies of all transactions, they will be transmitted to you on your own printer. Or for an extra fee, the bank will mail a printed statement.

Remote Banking

There will be a day, perhaps in ten years, when a bank customer will be able to access the bank by using a handheld computer. It may be a remote computer that can access the bank through a cellular phone hookup so the customer can handle banking transactions from any location, whether it be a mountaintop or the customer's fishing boat. I call this "Dick Tracy banking," with an image of a wristwatch-sized bank access transmitter that can handle deposit transfers, credits, or debits. If there is a problem with your account (you become overdrawn or past due), an immediate signal will be transmitted to the "watch." This is not a "watch" you want to lend to your teenager in the mall at Christmas shopping season!

Video Banking

In September 1991, Personal Financial Assistant, Inc. (PFA) of Charlotte, North Carolina, announced it had invented a service whereby all important officers of the bank are "cloned" through video, with their standard presentations on trust services, loan application requirements, CD requirements, and every major bank service. The letter in Figure 28 describes how this works. The customer goes to a booth in a mall or shopping center, presses a button for the desired service, and then pushes buttons in response to the questions the "video clone" poses. Thus, bank officers are multiplied electronically. One must suppose that the next step will be customers sending their banking requests by video to the loan committee. I interviewed PFA's president, Richard D'Agostino, who told me the service was offered in seventeen languages.

In Europe the company is negotiating to put "video branches" in post offices throughout some nations. Consider going to the post office to mail a letter and coming home with a new-car loan! When reading the letter in Figure 28, consider the implications of this new technological application.

Figure 28
DESCRIPTION OF A VIDEO BANKING SERVICE

PERSONAL FINANCIAL ASSISTANT, INC.

October 28, 1991

Mr. Ben B. Boothe
Ben B. Boothe & Associates
8851 Hwy 80 West, Suite 201
Fort Worth, TX 76116

Dear Mr. Boothe:

We appreciated the kind words about PFA in your letter to Richard D'Agostino. The PFA technology is very exciting and timely in the today's volatile environment that exists for the banking industry. The PFA System addresses key banking issues, ie. improved customer service while accommodating today's lifestyles, increased market share, identifying new revenue streams and reducing the cost of retail distribution and labor.

The PFA System has been described as "revolutionary for the delivery of retail products" by the <u>American Banker</u>. The PFA System provides the ability to perform <u>banking transactions</u> (such as account openings, credit card applications, mortgage applications, insurance, etc) <u>anytime, anyplace</u>. The PFA System resides in a modular unit in which a diverse set of products <u>can be electronically delivered but administered by remote centralized personnel.</u> There is <u>no keyboard or touchscreen to confuse or intimidate the customer.</u> The customer, using the telephone in the modular kiosk, is automatically connected, <u>**verbally and visually**</u>, to the proper back office personnel. Quality customer service is integrated with automation, cost effectively. PFA Units can be positioned anywhere; <u>malls, supermarkets, colleges, corporations</u>, etc. The PFA System will do for bank platform transactions what ATMs did for teller transactions.

The PFA System is installed at Banc One in Ohio. PFA has, on contract, several of the largest financial institutions in North America, with planned implementations in 1991.

Sincerely,

Ginger W. Wise
Director, Sales and Marketing

4235 South Stream Blvd. · One LakePointe Plaza, Suite 100 · Charlotte, NC 28217 · Phone 704/357-8004 · FAX 704/357-3769

Master Full-Service Computer Service

Existing computer programs will take care of all of the
accounting, investments, filing of tax returns, and all
bank matters in *one master program*. The program
generates and sends the customer a consolidated monthly
statement of his or her net worth, tax status, and bank
balances. These programs have been used by some exclu-
sive financial service organizations. They will be marketed
to upscale customers who can afford to pay the fees for the
first few years. Then, with the evolution of competition,
they ultimately will find a mass market.

Cashless Society

A cashless society is coming, but it's a long way in the
future. It will be available in degrees, but the most educated and sophisticated customers will be the ones to
adopt it first. A cashless society will imply that every
transaction is made by an electronic debit or credit to an
electronic ledger rather than by an exchange of hard
currency for goods or services. Credit cards, computer
terminals, fax machines, or laser transmitters may be the
tools of this culture. A large segment of our society is not
prepared to accept a cashless society, but with "megabus-
iness" courting and hoping for marriage with "megagov-
ernment," watch out.

   The vast implications of adopting a cashless society—
instant electronic transfers with no float and no room for
error—boggle the mind. For the banking industry, massive savings in overhead would result. In addition, there
are political, social, cultural, educational, and economic
implications. Questions of privacy and personal rights will
come into play. The power of government to tax and
monitor personal matters will also be in play.

The Changing Role of Nonbank Businesses

As the legal structure of banking changes, nonbank businesses will offer more and more of the services now considered part of "traditional banking." More corporations will take on the traditional role of banks by cashing payroll checks, providing savings and pension accounts, and making loans. These services will be without federal insurance and will be backed only by the financial strength of the corporation. Despite the risk, many people will use the services.

The Changing Role of Government

The government will get more involved in banking. Banking and money represent power. The trend of deregulation will not overcome the unyielding temptation of the government to gain the power represented by banking. A large segment of the banking industry will become nationalized in every sense of the word. This nationalization will be brought on by a dramatic event, such as the failure of some emerging megabank. To avoid a national panic, and to continue to provide some level of service to the public, the federal government, unable to find any banks big enough to buy the megabank, will have no choice but to take the beached whale over, own it, and attempt to run it.

If the performance of the RTC is any example, massive inefficiency will result, along with even more massive gridlock and punishment to the economy. This new "nationalized banking beast" could grow into an octopus-like family of nationalized banks owned and operated by the federal government. I see bank lobbies painted Government Gray, with service much akin to what you get in a post office. Slow, bureaucratic loan committees will ponderously review loan applications, and the inefficiencies will be magnified to a scale unheard of in today's banking world. Loans at these banks will take months for review and approval, if it comes at all. Files of the bank will be accessible by other government agencies such as the IRS and the FBI, and the considerations of privacy will be gone.

A Broadened Role for Banks

Banks will engage in numerous professional and corporate activities now reserved for professions and other industry groups. Here are some examples:

- *Accounting and tax preparation*—Banks will computerize tax models from your checking accounts and file your tax returns electronically.
- *Real estate sales*—Banks will locate and serve as real estate brokers for your real estate investments.
- *Insurance*—Banks will sell, underwrite, and offer every conceivable kind of insurance.
- *Appraisals*—Banks will take over the appraisal function for all types of real estate.
- *Stocks and bonds*—The traditional role of the stockbroker will be taken over by the banking industry. There may be special sitting rooms in banks where customers can come and watch the market.
- *Annuities, retirement plans, mutual funds*— Rather than using an outside service, the public will simply go to the bank, which will have a series of its own annuity funds.
- *Securities underwriting and equity offerings*— The bank will handle these transactions through a network of other banks, often completely eliminating the need for participation in the traditional stock markets.

- *Corporate ownership of banks, bank ownership of corporations*—Banks will become increasingly owned by and owners of nonbank-related business enterprises. The lines that separate banking from private industry will slowly disappear.

One of the stages of bank evolution will be the appearance of a "minibank" in every large supermarket. Since this is a center of activity and regular volume, the exchange of currency and credit is a natural in such a store. In ancient times, the markets always became the centers of commerce, and they will again. As the checkless and cashless society evolves, these minibanks will become centers of groups of computer terminals. These terminals will be available free to the public as a customer service to attract business.

A new bank service that will appear will be the "mobile bank." This will be a bank on wheels that can drive to any public gathering. On one side people will walk up to the mobile terminal or bank window and conduct banking business. On the other side customers will have the convenience of drive-up banking. These banks will even be staffed with loan officers, so individuals can apply for loans of all kinds. These mobile banks will not only be used for public gatherings but will also become the bank for outlying communities that no longer have their own banks. The mobile bank will come into towns on a regular basis— perhaps one town on Tuesday, the next on Wednesday, and so on—to service the financial needs of the community. Although larger loan requests will still require a personal visit to the bank offices, smaller consumer loans will be handled well at these mobile banks.

The position of consumer loan officer, and many other lending positions, will be largely phased out. These positions will be taken over by a computer program and terminals that can be placed anywhere there is telephone service and electricity. Some banks have already experimented with computerized loan applications. Although the customer loses all semblance of personal service, the computer applications have at least as good a performance rating as those of their human counterparts. Any loan application can be faxed or sent electronically by computer modem to a home office, where a clerk will simply signal back approval or denial.

Trying to Keep Up

Sometimes prophecy and imagination cannot keep up with technological development. Even as I am writing this, an article from the business section of a large newspaper reports, "The latest in 'High Tech . . . High Touch Banking.' " A company has just developed another "Video Bank Connection" where a customer can connect with his or her banker and speak by television to apply for a loan. Therefore, the customer never has to leave the office or home, but just dials the banker's number. All financial information would be faxed to the bank in advance of the "video appointment."

Consider the implications of a bank without a lobby, where people never enter, never really shake hands or touch a banker. Consider all of your transactions being handled electronically with an image on a screen. Of course, if you happen to need a loan when the power is out or your TV needs repair, you may just be out of luck. The implications for total electronic banking are powerful and lead more than ever to a society based in home units, rather than huge central office business centers.

Based on studies of ancient cities and foundation remains, students of culture and sociology report that the centers of traffic were the centers of commerce, business, and influence. In other words, if there was a wide path to a building, the place where the people went was the center of activity and influence. In our culture, downtown sections are often built around a central business section in which the largest banks in town are the hub. Try to imagine an economy in which there is no need to go to a bank to conduct business. Then there would be no need for huge bank buildings with large areas for customer service. Therefore, the traditional logic of a bank being an attraction of business and traffic to an area would become obsolete.

How would this affect business districts and downtown areas? Essentially it would imply that banking facilities could be fragmented into departmental entities, located all over town, in the suburbs where property is less expensive, and closer to the homes of employees. These entities would not be for the public, but rather buildings with tight security, storm proof and bomb proof, where hundreds of employees work before their electronic keyboards and video screens. Individuals and other businesses would have less motivation to work in downtown areas. The trend toward home offices and decentralized operations would increase, along with the use of fax, telephone, and computer communications. Some writers have called these offices in homes "telecommuting hubs." People would no longer need to commute to work, except by telephone. There would be less need for freeways for commuters, for there would be fewer commuters. There would be a hundred fewer reasons to work "downtown" in thousands of cities. Fewer people would need cars. Cities would turn into smaller, self-contained areas where people could live, shop, and work within walking distance of their homes.

What does this mean for you? The way you bank, the way you live, the way you borrow money, and what you borrow money for will be largely influenced by the changes in the banking industry. Whether or not you like the potential face of the future of banking (and I do not like many aspects of it), the new world of banking will be ever more challenging. As a result, the reasons are stronger than ever for businesspeople to become more sophisticated in their loan proposals. Borrowing money is a financial function, but it is also an art, an art of dealing with banks and bankers in ways that keep their interest and motivation high on matters relating to *your* business.

What You Can Still Bank On

Though many of the changes coming in banking seem to suggest a world devoid of stability and constancy, there are things in the world of banking that will never change. These enduring principles and practices will last far beyond political, cultural, or technological change. They must be observed and used by the person who relies on banks and bankers for credit. These are things *you can bank on:*

- The principle that banks need and want to lend money to make a profit.
- The principle that, regardless of technology, the most important business decisions will be made by human beings, one on one.
- The principle that documentation and verification will be ever more important to a good bank credit relationship.
- The power of integrity in banking matters—As society runs through this cycle that "bigger is better," the aspect of integrity will gain even more power in light of the cold, inhuman specter of giant corporate dominance.

- The "pendulum effect"—Cycles move, fads and trends change and often reverse. While the trend may now be of "consolidation" of the banking industry, as this trend reaches the outward limit, advantages of the opposite trend become more apparent, and the reverse tends to occur. This pattern may well occur in banking, with the current headlong rush into mergers and consolidation continuing until public opinion and political powers recognize the need for many banks offering a broader array of services so as to diversify risk. This goal is best presented in a unit bank system that serves communities, individual businesses, and consumers best of all.
- The principle that political and philosophical directions are often made obsolete by technological advances—For example, many states have had controversies over branch banking. A universal computerized banking system will render that controversy moot.
- The principle that there will always be some community bankers who have identified a specific niche of the marketplace and will survive the most aggressive of consolidation efforts—These survivors are heroes in a sense, fighting for values they cherish against increasing odds. They should be supported and treated with respect.
- The principle that some traditional institutions should survive for what they contribute to a society—On a television program about the global changes affecting the world, Britain's Prince Charles spent some time focusing on the traditional agricultural industries, including the wine growers of Europe, commenting that the rich cultural traditions that they contribute to society far outweigh

their economic contributions. Indeed, massive conglomerates make far more economic sense, but
massive conglomerates cannot make the cultural,
traditional, and ethical contributions that are so
important to a society. In the banking world, a
powerful tradition with invaluable cultural signifi-
cance is the small-town or suburban community
bank that is owned by people in the community
and invests its loans and services in the people it
knows best. If these institutions are forced into
insolvency, our culture will have lost much, as will
the loan customers who rely upon and are best
served by these institutions. For example, would a
rancher in Billings, Montana, receive the specialized ranch lending he needs from a clerk educated
in New York City? Or can a branch of "Metropolis
Megabank" ever have the knowledge, insight, and
passion to support a community infrastructure as
well as a locally owned community bank presided
over by a board of directors of leading citizens?
These are critical concerns for the loan customer of
the future.

- The five Cs of credit—Credit, collateral, cash flow,
  capital, and character are basic requirements of any
  credit decision, and no amount of "progress" will
  alter this.
- The need for "high touch"—This is a direct requirement and a response to "high tech." As society
  becomes ever more automated and business gravi-
  tates to large corporate systems, social trends prove
  that people require and demand greater personal
  service, recognition, and response to their needs.
  An excellent example is the new computerized telephone systems that route calls automatically by
  computer voice and key response to the appropri-

ate department or answering machine. The concept is to save money by eliminating operators. But business analysts report massive complaints and anger from customers. In many cases the businesses that adopt such systems show a higher rate of customer loss. People want human contact.

- The principle that people value human dignity and respect—Indeed, all people need to be treated with dignity and respect. Bankers for centuries have understood this principle of respect for the customer. The philosophy is easily seen in the great advertising campaigns banks initiate about service and the importance of the individual. Few things are more personal to human beings than their pocketbooks. Their bank accounts represent financial security. When the banking industry's manner of doing business becomes impersonal and people become objects, then people will demand a different system. For the loan customer, as well as the loan officer, this principle is paramount and has many far-reaching implications.

- The principle that figures don't lie, but people do— Numbers can be manipulated, but facts speak for themselves. There is no greater principle than the power of truth and the importance of clearly presenting the facts. Your ability as a customer to gather factual information and present it with clarity is a powerful tool.

- The principle that profitability will always be the moving force in business—Your business should be profitable to the banker. The banker's support should be profitable for you. If either party forgets or abuses this principle, problems will arise.

- The principle that while change is inevitable, the important values of serving people, communities, and business are enduring and lasting.

- The principle that hard work, discipline, persistence, and industry will ultimately be rewarded.
- The principle that confidence in a system, a business, an individual, or a bank is of bedrock importance to its survival.
- The fact that a good financial statement will make an impression on your banker. It is said that a good financial statement is like a good novel to a banker.

The Impact of Confidence and How It's Been Undermined

President Franklin Roosevelt presided over a nation in crisis, and he better than anyone communicated the importance of confidence: "The only thing we have to fear is fear itself."

After the instability of the Great Depression, the American dream of prosperity had turned into a nightmare. Business had lost confidence in its ability to survive, while banking simply became a matter of holding on to what little capital was left as long as possible. Roosevelt provided the leadership to bring confidence back to business. Much of that newfound confidence was because of specific steps that were implemented, such as deposit insurance and laws to prohibit monopolization of an industry.

The banking industry responded with confidence and stability for fifty years, until a few powerful men in Washington, D.C., and New York City started tinkering with the system. The system now has less confidence in itself than at any time since the early 1930s. Unfortunately, business leaders and the public have lost a part of their confidence in the system as well. The result is knee-jerk reactions that tighten credit and further hurt the economy. Banks are afraid to lend money because they fear a declining real estate market, a recession, regulatory criticism, and the rocky road ahead.

Economists such as Alan Greenspan (chairman of the Federal Reserve) spent nearly a year in 1991 repeatedly reporting, "This recession is over," trying to talk the American people out of a recession—a recession at least partially brought on by improper government policies. But a singular lack of confidence nationwide caused those words to ring hollow. In 1992 the economy was the most important crisis issue in Washington.

The problem America faces is not a cyclical recession. It is a financial structure whose fabric has been weakened by fundamental changes in the systems and in the way the industry is regulated, governed, and led by policymakers in Washington and by powerful "mega-interests," who by their grasping for power have undermined the very confidence upon which the system relies.

On December 9, 1941, Franklin Roosevelt spoke after the bombing of Pearl Harbor: "We will win the war and we will win the peace that follows." He was correct about the war but only half right about winning the peace. He was referring to winning the global economic war in which America, Japan, and Germany were engaged. To that end, the government operated under economic policies intent upon stability, growth, and protection. But about 1970 these policies began to be attacked by a new breed of thinkers. The whiz kids of the 1970s and 1980s have seen partial achievement of their theories, with the impact that the entire system is destabilized.

As an account executive with Merrill Lynch, Pierce, Fenner & Smith in the early 1970s, I had the pleasure to be sent to New York and to receive training at Merrill Lynch's school on Wall Street. At that time the president of Merrill Lynch was Donald Regan. According to Regan, the problem the securities industry faced at that time was that interest in stocks and bonds was lackluster because the big money—the smart money—went instead into real estate.

Why invest in 100 shares of LMP Corporation that paid a 5 percent stock dividend that was taxable, and only hope for appreciation, when one could invest in an apartment complex and get a 15 percent tax-free cash flow, as well as almost guaranteed appreciation because of an inflationary economy? Plus there were ways to exchange real estate and reinvest in it without paying any tax! Banks were booming then, taking low-cost deposits and lending to real estate investors.

During the 1970s, Regan advocated devising some means to change the flow of money out of real estate and into the securities industry. Somehow the securities industry must be allowed to enter the banking industry, to reap the profits therein. Regan found unlikely allies in some of the biggest banks of New York, who wanted to diversify into the securities industry. What both were aiming for was a deregulated system. Years later, in the Ronald Reagan administration, who was one of the biggest supporters of the Tax Reform Act? Donald Regan. Why? Because as the Tax Reform Act took away tax deductions from the interest paid on real estate investments, it chased money out of real estate . . . to where? You guessed it. The securities industry. Indeed, the biggest booms in volume and value in the stock markets occurred after the Tax Reform Act was passed (under the guise of being an act to cut taxes).

Regan, through his support of "deregulation," caused some unexpected things to happen. While the brokerage industry entered the "money market" business, draining stable low-cost deposits out of the banking industry, the banking industry found profit margins thinner. Banks had to seek other measures of profitability, other markets. They jumped into loans for Third World nations and increased their lobbying for full interstate banking. They claimed that they had to expand in powers to compete with the Japanese. In truth, deregulation was the real problem, for American banks were having to compete with every brokerage house and big department store chains such as Sears, not to mention thousands of savings and loan institutions and credit unions, which were being chartered in wholesale numbers. This, of course, made borrowing more liberal. In an attempt to drag in new customers, big banks and small were willing to lend money freely. But then, when the excesses of that rapid growth began to surface and the regulators started cracking down, credit became more difficult to arrange.

The problem seemed to come to a head in late 1990 and early 1991. The Bank of New England in Boston was facing major problems in its loan portfolio. As regulators came in, instead of creating an environment of cooperation, they charged off tens of thousands of loans that were paying as agreed. The Bank of New England failed under pressure. Influential people such as John Sununu (then chief of staff for George Bush) were critical of regulators, particularly the Office of the Comptroller of the Currency (OCC), and the policies of loan review pressed by the chief comptroller, Robert Clark, under whose leadership over a thousand banks were closed. In banking circles Clark was nicknamed The Regulator from Hell because of his seemingly unreasonable treatment of real estate loans through his field examiners.

When the Bank of New England failed, bankers all over the country became more conservative in their lending practices than they had been in a long time. Some banks put forth new policies that they would lend "only on CDs." It was almost as if bankers were thinking, "We thought what happened in Texas was only a regional fluke, but now it is happening all over. If the regulators are going to criticize us for making loans, then we simply won't take any risk."

The phenomenon was so widespread, and had such powerful economic implications, that before long Washington was taking notice. The National Association of Home Builders flew a contingent to Washington to see the President, where they reported that the nation was in a housing slump like none seen since the Great Depression, because there was no source of loans. Reports of uncompleted office buildings in Manhattan indicated that values had dropped as much as 40 percent in less than twelve months. The same preliminary red flags that had appeared in Texas and then New England started appearing in areas formerly considered untouchable by recession, such as California and Florida. At this point a combination of factors was creating a self-fulfilling prophecy of severe recession. Then an unheard-of thing happened. While one agency of federal regulators (the OCC) was sending a signal that banks should be more conservative in lending practices, prominent members of the Federal Reserve Board, such as James LaMont, began to make public statements that bankers were not fulfilling their legal obligation of serving the public and business community and that they should be more liberal in making loans. More regulators out of Washington, D.C., followed suit by releasing similar statements.

Bankers simply responded by deciding that if Washington was that worried about an impending recession, they would stay out of the lending game altogether. Their attitude was reflected by bank president L. J. Richards, who, when asked what his criteria for making loans were, replied, "I've looked around and the only banks that are making money are the ones who make no loans. The examiners criticize every loan we make. So our new loan criterion is not to make loans unless they are secured by CDs." It will be many years before America and the American banking system fully recover from the policies that have systematically and fundamentally altered the system since the early 1970s.

Many Americans, including many bankers, now agree that it is time to look to the past for answers. The most stable and profitable period of the American banking system was from 1940 to 1970, a time of conservative and strict regulation bent on protecting banks, not consolidating the system. All indicators are that as a result, underwriting will be tougher than ever for some time to come. And Americans will not only need to work harder than ever at producing quality loan applications; they will need to understand the implications of political policy on their ability to borrow money.

Cycles of economics, regulatory trends, and lending attitudes such as this do nothing to benefit anyone. But they do point out that confidence is critical. On a specific level, the confidence your banker has in you and your business may be the single factor that will induce a banker to support you through his or her lending practices, even in times of economic recession. If a banker believes that you have the character and reliability to keep your commitments even through the roughest of times, then that confidence you have established will be richly rewarded.

Some Things Will Endure

Yes, there are things that endure even during the rapid changes our society offers. We live in an age of computerized communications that constantly present each business and individual with massive amounts of information. Thanks to the fax, the telephone, and other gadgets, the ability to receive and transmit information is unsurpassed in the history of civilization. The nation swings into recessions and booms with instant awareness of any national disaster or international event.

We live under greater pressure to make more quick decisions than at any time chronicled. The banking industry will go through changes according to power, fad, and popularity. The basic laws of economics will reveal whether these changes are beneficial or not. But with all of the changes, there are some constants, most of which have to do with the innate character of humanity. Those things are basic to survival and basic to success in the world of finance and borrowing. Those enduring principles will go far in determining your success or failure in the borrowing game.

17

Conclusion

In a career of banking, I have reviewed thousands of loan applications, made thousands of loans, and turned thousands down. In that period of time, I have worked with banks having assets in the billions and been president of banks in towns as small as seven thousand people and as large as one million. Whether a college student needs $500 to buy books or a major company wants millions to expand, I have seen a broad range of approaches in loan applications. The benefit of that experience is within this book.

Obviously good judgment has to be a key to making a successful loan presentation. The complexity and detail of the loan application will relate directly to the complexity and detail of the loan.

Once the board of directors directed me to arrange the lead credit for a multimillion-dollar grain elevator and processing company. Our bank was too small to handle the credit alone, so to serve the customer, we traveled throughout Texas, Kansas, and Oklahoma to find banks that were willing to participate in the loan. We decided to keep the first $500,000 of the loan and "participate out" the balance of the credit to other banks. In that case the documentation had to be very detailed and complete, for every lender had complex questions that had to be answered before its loan committee. That application was as thick as a book.

The same week, I handled a $1,000 loan for a local dry-cleaning business that needed a small amount of operating capital. There was no need for a "book" of documents in this case. However, the five Cs of credit still applied.

Often a smaller loan request is more difficult for the banker to decide on than a large credit. The reason is that larger credit requests usually provide enough documentation and financial detail that the guesswork and judgment calls are easier. Smaller loan requests from unsophisticated borrowers often provide only limited information.

Therefore, this book is an effort to give you, the borrower, big or small, individual or corporation, the benefit of every possible advantage. In some cases the instructions may appear to be too detailed and the effort too much just to apply for a small loan. But most bankers will tell you that it is a "rare" occurrence for any person to provide too much information with a loan application. Far too often there is too little information. Too much is left to the banker with his or her limited time and energy to ferret out. Too often good loans, to good businesses or good people, are therefore denied. In the Introduction, I said that forty thousand loan applications are turned down every day in America. We have itemized some of the major reasons that loans are turned down; some of these may have surprised you. Of those turned down, every day, about half could have been approved had they been properly prepared with the tools outlined in this book. This book has shown you step by step how to prepare, what to include, and why. I have outlined trends in banking to provide a framework for better understanding. I have outlined what some believe could be the future of banking, and some of the enduring qualities that will prevail regardless of technological or industry changes.

Bankers I Have Known

It wouldn't be fair to conclude this book without a profile of the bankers I have known. In the past few years I have traveled nationwide and spoken to bankers' groups from Montana to Illinois, from Wisconsin to Florida. I have met and worked with bankers from metropolitan New York and Boston to rural and small community bankers in New Mexico and Iowa. I have met with bankers in Austria, Germany, Hungary, and even Romania.

Bankers are an interesting group. They are professional, but not really a profession. For the most part, they have had to work their way up the corporate ladder to the position of responsibility they now hold. In a class I taught at the Southwestern Graduate School of Banking (at Southern Methodist University's Edwin Cox School of Business), I gave a test to a group of seventy bank executives and two examiners. I asked several questions about their careers and how they perceived the industry. When asked what their motivation was for being a banker, 10 percent responded that they were bankers because of the salary and financial security of the job, 35 percent that they were bankers because they loved the industry, and 55 percent that they were bankers because of what they could do for their community and employees, and because of the rewards of being community leaders. Most of these bankers were from small to medium-sized banks, serving local communities. It would be interesting to do a similar survey of bank executives from banks with, say, over a billion dollars in assets.

The responses to another question in that survey are telling about the industry. Exactly 50 percent indicated that they perceive that there are great changes happening in the industry. The changes were of such importance to this group surveyed that 50 percent of them indicated they were making plans to enter a new industry. So it is obvious that the changes in process that are coming are taking away some of the things about banking that formerly made it such an appealing industry. Bankers in that test referred to fourteen-hour days, confusion over regulatory requirements, unreasonable regulatory demands, lack of capital, and massive changes in the competitive arena making it ever harder to serve their customers and generate a profit.

In light of these pressures, bankers are going to be ever more cautious in the new loans that are placed on the books of their banks. Customers who study, work hard, and treat the loan application as a careful strategy will become the preferred customers of banks. Those who walk into a bank with a haphazard approach, hoping that the banker will roll out the red carpet and kneel at their feet, may be in for a surprise.

Marvin Carlile was one of the outstanding bankers with whom I have worked. He was cut out of an independent, self-reliant fiber, and he never doubted that it was his customers who made his position as president possible. He was an enigma of sorts, as are many bank presidents. Quick to smile, he had a sharp wit and an even sharper mind. He did not need to have long and detailed written loan applications. He ran his bank with sort of a secret underground of information sources. He knew when people needed to borrow money before they ever walked through the door of his bank. He memorized financial statements and consumed budgets with the delight that a child finds in eating an ice-cream cone on a hot summer day.

Carlile had a philosophy that if he trusted you, if you had proved yourself worthy of his trust, half the battle was won. The second half of the battle was to weave your way through his brilliant mind as he thrust and parried with you to find weaknesses in your loan application. Many times his questions weren't as much to get the factual answer as to see how competent and how quick the applicant was. He loved mental calculations.

One day I went to him with a brilliant idea. I had written a computer program that would analyze the financial position of the bank, line item by line item, every day. "It will save us a great deal of time and will show you to within a few dollars what the bank is making every day!" I showed him the several pages of ledgers, proud of my time-consuming accomplishment. He leafed through them and grunted, "You are a little high here. A little low there." It was then with amazement that I realized that every day this man mentally calculated all of the functions I had spent weeks programming.

This breed of banker took his role as a trustee of the deposits of the bank as a sacred trust, with great seriousness. He worked hard, from 6:00 A.M. to 6:00 P.M. daily, not as a matter of drudgery, but because of his fascination with and enthusiasm for the welfare of the bank. That breed of banker made a good living, rarely became super wealthy, but always stood out as a person of integrity and leadership in the community.

There are still thousands of bankers like that. I have met them. They are anxious to meet you and to engage in the game that is more fun to them than a game of poker or canasta. It is the game of credit—a game filled with intrigue, suspense, surprises, risk, and great rewards. It is a game that can make you wealthy, or it can have great cost if you don't play it well. This borrowing game is played out not on a tennis court or a football field, but in a bank office and sometimes in a boardroom.

Some people think that banking must be a boring or dry business. But there is no higher drama and excitement that influences, makes, or destroys the lives of people more than the game of banking. That drama is a real drama, hidden behind mahogany walls and formal agendas. If you doubt that the emotions are there, ask any bank president how he or she feels immediately before and immediately after loan or board meetings. One recently told me, "Ben, the emotions run so high that it takes me a full day to recover my equilibrium after a board meeting." And that emotion is often presented in very dry, polite, sophisticated, businesslike terms while the implications of the results on the lives of people boil like lava just under the surface.

In Summary

I have given you the rules and some of the strategies to winning this game. The insights, stories, and perspectives all come from my experience behind the loan desk. It is a wonderful desk, really—a piece of furniture across which come people's dreams and hopes in achieving their destiny. A group once asked me to speak about the definition of a good banker. The perspective I offered was surprising to many of them. I said, "The definition of a good banker is not a person just to be the caretaker and guardian of someone else's money. A good banker is a student of people. He evaluates the integrity and the ability of individuals and business owners, and determines what potential they have. He then gives them the opportunity, if they merit, to fulfill their destiny."

The opportunity to fulfill your destiny. Every person has the right to achieve his or her fullest potential. Sometimes the opportunity to accomplish that is related to a friendly word of advice here or some insight and direction there.

If you were my son or daughter and asked me how to borrow money, the ideas in this book would be my reply. In general, understand the perspective and position of those able to provide credit. Position yourself in the community as a person of skill and integrity. Prepare your application with documentation and facts. Practice your presentation. Make a good impression, and be prepared for the questions and objections. Deal with objections in advance when possible, but always deal with them. Be persistent, persuasive, and professional. Don't allow defeat to deter you, but look for alternatives, and pursue them with vigor. Respect and treat your banker as a friend, for your banker will be just that when he or she approves your credit.

The ironic but marvelous thing about the game of credit is that when the borrower wins, so does the banker. And when the borrower loses, so does the banker. In essence, all of the participants ultimately want you to win. I wish you well in all of your endeavors.

Epilogue:
Philosophical Meanderings on
Why Some People Never Borrow

The reasons for not borrowing are endless. Some of them
are good, and some are bad. Many people who grew up
during the Great Depression witnessed the bank holidays
and the contraction in the economy. Many of those people
learned a valuable lesson: never to borrow money for
frivolous or speculative projects and to pay off their debts
as fast as they could. That generation learned a simple,
basic financial rule. In a contracting economy, debt can
be a monster that can eat your assets.

Those who were raised in the 1940s through the
1970s saw a different side of debt. During inflationary
times, it made good sense to borrow as much as possible
and pay it back with cheaper dollars.

There is another attitude that is different from either
of these. This is an age of transition in the financial world.

In this age, when so many things are changing, a good philosophy is summed up as the

YOU-CAN-BANK-ON-IT PRINCIPLE:
THOU SHALT BORROW MONEY ONLY WHEN THE USE
OF THE PROCEEDS WILL PAY THE LOAN BACK WITH
AMPLE MARGIN FOR SAFETY.

The You-Can-Bank-On-It-Principle will not solve all of your ills. But it will save a lot of grief and heartache.

Notice that this principle implies there are some times when you should *not* borrow. When you are considering reasons for not borrowing, learn to distinguish the good ones from the bad ones. The following examples should help.

Some Reasons for Not Borrowing

I don't believe in borrowing money.
That's your decision. No one can argue with a matter of principle or conscience.

I don't borrow because I don't know if I can pay it back.
That's a good reason not to borrow money. If you aren't sure that you can pay it back, don't borrow.

I don't borrow because I don't want to pay interest.
Bad reason. If you follow the You-Can-Bank-On-It-Principle, interest will be covered from the return on your investment and then a good equity return as well. Interest is just a cost of doing business. And if you are borrowing for business purposes, chances are you will be able to deduct the expense off of your income tax anyway.

I don't borrow because I am scared of banks.
Bad reason. Don't let fear stand in the way of your
opportunity to achieve your goals in life.

*I don't borrow because I have never done it
before, and I don't have any credit.*
Can you imagine a baby refusing to walk because
he or she had never done it before? If this is your
only reason, go ahead and start building your
credit now.

*I don't borrow because I had a bad experience
with a banker once.*
Bad reason. You have had bad experiences with
food before, but did you stop eating? No, you
went on to better food. Find yourself a better
bank and good banker.

*I don't borrow because I have had a bank-
ruptcy, and my credit is ruined.*
If you haven't changed your habits or business
practices since filing bankruptcy, that is a good
reason not to borrow money. If you have filed
bankruptcy because of something beyond your
control, if you have acted in good faith and taken
care of all obligations within your power, you
might be able to find a banker who will work with
you.

*I don't borrow because I am too old to be in
·debt.*
This may be an excellent reason, but consider
this: if you have ample life insurance and you wish
to borrow money, it might add new meaning,
challenge, and interest (no pun intended) to your
golden years. Remember, Armand Hammer

didn't buy Occidental Petroleum until he was well past his sixties. At eighty-eight he was still borrowing money!

I don't borrow because the debt service will hurt my lifestyle and cause undue stress.
Excellent reason not to borrow money.

I don't borrow because I hate to see lenders get rich off of me.
If a lender is willing to back you fairly, you should be glad if he or she makes a reasonable rate of interest on the loan. After all, the lender is making your dreams possible.

I don't borrow because I'm afraid the project has too much risk.
Excellent reason not to borrow money.

I don't borrow because I don't like the paperwork.
Remember the sign in the rest room: no job is done right until the paperwork is done. We live in an age of documentation. Lenders will usually help you with the paperwork; often they will do it for you. Do not let the work stand in the way of your goals.

I don't borrow because I can't find a good banker I like.
This is a good reason not to borrow money. Borrowing is not only financial statements, it is human relationships of trust, integrity, and honor. If you cannot find a banker you can trust or who trusts you, don't borrow.

I don't borrow because the economy looks too risky.
Good reason. Many people have borrowed money at the wrong time, and it has ruined them. Timing is very important for your project.

I don't borrow because I want to stay liquid. I pay for everything with cash.
If you are in a position to do this, it's an excellent reason not to borrow money. But if you are in a position where you can use that liquidity to generate more income by borrowing and taking the tax deduction, consider a loan.

Summary Story

A bank robber was finally released from prison and after a few years became wildly successful as a businessman. He was interviewed in the penthouse suite of one of his office buildings and asked to what he attributed his success. He replied, tongue in cheek, "If I had known it was this easy to borrow from a bank, I would never have gone to the trouble to rob one!"

Well, the days of easy money appear to be gone from the American banking scene, but there is a point. The credit markets are available to sophisticated borrowers. These are the ones who will benefit, the ones who will do well. You have, by reading this book, vastly increased your odds of winning. I wish you well!

Index